The Institutional Dimension of the European Union's Area of Freedom, Security and Justice

P.I.E. Peter Lang

Bruxelles · Bern · Berlin · Frankfurt am Main · New York · Oxford · Wien

Jörg Monar (ed.)

The Institutional Dimension of the European Union's Area of Freedom, Security and Justice

"College of Europe Studies"
No. 11

Éditions scientifiques internationales
Brussels, 2010
1 avenue Maurice, B-1050 Brussels, Belgium
www.peterlang.com; info@peterlang.com

ISSN 1780-9665
ISBN 978-90-5201-615-3
D/2010/5678/28

Printed in Germany

Library of Congress Cataloging-in-Publication Data
The institutional dimension of the European Union's area of freedom, security, and justice / Jörg Monar, editor.
p. cm. — (College of Europe studies ; no. 11) ISBN 978-90-5201-615-3
1. Internal security—European Union countries. 2. Law enforcement—European Union countries. 3. Criminal justice, Administration of—European Union countries. I. Monar, Joerg, 1960-
HV8194.A2I57 2010 364.94—dc22 2010013811

CIP also available from the British Library

Bibliographic information published by "Die Deutsche Bibliothek"
"Die Deutsche Bibliothek" lists this publication in the "Deutsche Nationalbibliografie"; detailed bibliographic data is available on the Internet at <http://dnb.ddb.de>.

Acknowledgements

The plan for this book originated in 2007 in the context of the SECURINT project on European Union internal security governance of the University of Strasbourg which was funded by the European Commission under its Marie Curie Chair of Excellence programme from 2005 to 2008. In 2008 the College of Europe agreed to give its full support to this initiative. Without the concurrent efforts of all three institutions the book would not have seen the light of the day. This can in itself be regarded as a successful example of interinstitutional synergy – for which I am most grateful.

A lot of thanks are also due to the authors who during the whole period of preparation had to cope with the uncertainties regarding the Lisbon Treaty and fastidious requests from the editor regarding changes and updates right up to the final deadline of the entry into force of the new Treaty on 1 December 2009.

Yet my biggest measure of gratitude is reserved for Rina Balbaert at the College of Europe who's most careful, attentive and thoughtful copy editing transformed a rather disparate set of manuscripts flooded with editorial annotations into the coherent book now before the eyes of the reader. Her work has been beyond praise – and also in the name of all the authors I wish to put this here on record.

Jörg Monar

Bruges, December 2009

Table of Contents

List of Abbreviations

AFCO	Committee on Constitutional Affairs
AFET	Committee on Foreign Affairs
AFSJ	Area of Freedom, Security and Justice
AWF	Analysis Work Files
CATS	Committee Article Thirty-Six / Comité de l'Article Trente-Six
CBRN	Chemical, Biological, Radiological and Nuclear
CELAD	Comité Européen de Lutte Anti Drogue
CEPOL	Collège européen de police / European Police College
CFI	Court of First Instance
CFSP	Common Foreign and Security Policy
CIA	Central Intelligence Agency
CIREFI	Centre d'Information de Réflexion et d'Echange sur les Frontières et l'Immigration
CISA	Convention implementing the Schengen Agreement
CJEU	Court of Justice of the European Union
COMIX	(Schengen) Mixed Committee
COREPER	Comité des représentants permanents / Committee of Permanent Representatives
COSI	Comité de sécurité intérieure / Committee on Internal Security
COSPOL	Comprehensive Operational Strategic Planning for the Police
COTER	Committee on Terrorism
CRATE	Centralised Records of Available Technical Equipment
CTC	Counter-Terrorism Coordinator
CTS	Counter-Terrorism Strategy
DG	Directorate-General
DNA	Deoxyribonucleic acid
DROI	Subcommittee on Human Rights
EAW	European Arrest Warrant

EC	European Community
ECHR	European Convention on Human Rights
ECtHR	European Court of Human Rights
ECJ	European Court of Justice
ECOFIN	Economic and Financial Affairs Council
ECSC	European Coal and Steel Community
EDA	European Defence Agency
EDU	Europol Drugs Unit
EEC	European Economic Community
EEW	European Evidence Warrant
EIS	European Information System
EJN	European Judicial Network
EP	European Parliament
EPC	European Political Cooperation
EPP	European Public Prosecutor
ESDP	European Security and Defence Policy
ESRIF	European Security Research and Innovation Forum
EU	European Union
Eurasil	European Union Network for asylum practitioners
Eurodac	European Dactyloscopie
Eurojust	European Union Judicial Cooperation Unit
Europol	European Police Office
EUROSUR	European Border Surveillance System
FATF	Financial Action Task Force
FBI	Federal Bureau of Investigation
FISO	Frontex Intelligence Support Officer
FJST	Frontex Joint Support Team
FRA	Fundamental Rights Agency
Frontex	Frontières extérieures for 'external borders', legally: European Agency for the Management of Operational Cooperation at the External Borders of the Member States of the European Union
FSC	Frontex Situation Centre
FYROM	Former Yugoslav Republic of Macedonia
G8	Group of Eight
GAERC	General Affairs and External Relations Council

HDG	Horizontal Working Party on Drugs
HENUs	Heads of Europol National Units
IT	Italy
JHA	Justice and Home Affairs
JHA-RELEX	Justice and Home Affairs External Relations
JLS	Justice, liberté, sécurité
JRO	Joint Return Operation
LIBE	Committee on Civil Liberties, Justice and Home Affairs
MEP	Member of European Parliament
MEURO	Million Euro
MP	Member of Parliament
NATO	North Atlantic Treaty Organisation
NGO	Non-Governmental Organisation
OECD	Organisation for Economic Cooperation and Development
O.J.	Official Journal of the European Union
OLAF	Office de Lutte Anti-Fraude / European Anti-Fraud Office
OPS	Operations Unit
OSCE	Organisation for Security and Cooperation in Europe
PCTF	Police Chiefs Task Force
PES	Party of European Socialists
PNR	Passenger Name Records
PROCIV	Council Working Party on Civil Protection
PSC	Political and Security Committee
QMV	Qualified Majority Voting
RABIT	Rapid Border Intervention Team
RAU	Risk Analysis Unit
SCIFA	Strategic Committee on Immigration, Frontiers and Asylum
SEA	Single European Act
SEDE	Subcommittee on Security and Defence
SIS	Schengen Information System
SitCen	Situation Centre
SNE	Seconded National Expert

SWIFT	Society for Worldwide Interbank Financial Tele-communication
TEC	Treaty establishing the European Community
TE-SAT	Terrorism Situation and Trend Report
TEU	Treaty on European Union
TFEU	Treaty on the Functioning of the European Union
TREVI	Terrorisme, radicalisme et violence internationale
UK	United Kingdom
UNHCR	United Nations High Commissioner for Refugees
US	United States
USA	United States of America
VIS	Visa Information System

Preface by Beatrice Ask

Swedish Minister of Justice and President-in-Office of the EU Justice and Home Affairs Council

The construction of the European Union's "Area of Freedom, Security and Justice" (AFSJ) is one of the great European political projects of our time. In its importance it can easily be compared to the completion of the Internal Market in the 1980s and 1990s and the ongoing development of the Common Foreign and Security Policy. It is a project which is aimed directly at the European citizens, seeking to guarantee them a better access to justice, more protection against crime and a better handling of the challenges and opportunities of migration. Both opinion polls and elections regularly show how much these issues matter to citizens, and this for good reason as justice, freedom and security belong to the most fundamental public goods they have a right to expect their governments to deliver. That is why the Swedish EU Presidency of 2009 has made the further development of the AFSJ one of its main priorities, with a focus on securing agreement on a new strategic programme for the AFSJ for the years 2010 to 2014, the "Stockholm Programme".

It is our responsibility as decision-makers at both the European and the national level to define and deliver policies which take up the challenges of the construction of the AFSJ with ambition and realism. We would not be able to fulfil this responsibility without an effective institutional framework:

It is within and among the EU institutions that we have to agree on the AFSJ policies. This is often a complex and protracted process, not only because so many different national policies and legal systems have to be brought together, but also because in the context of the AFSJ often very sensitive issues of rights and freedoms of citizens are at stake. It is therefore of crucial importance that the institutional framework facilitates the decision-making through effective structures and procedures which allow decision-makers to benefit to the greatest possible extent from the expertise of European and national administrations and all available margins for political and technical compromises. That is why already the previous Swedish Presidency of 2001 launched the "Haga Process" for improving the efficiency of Council working methods in the AFSJ and why we took further initiatives on that during our current Presidency to exploit the new opportunities provided in view of the upcoming entry into force of the Treaty of Lisbon.

It is also mainly through the institutional framework of the EU that we have to ensure that our objectives and policies regarding the AFSJ are implemented. The persisting major differences between the domestic political contexts, legal systems and administrative organisations of the Member States make this implementation a constant major challenge for the construction of the AFSJ. Over the last few years Council and Commission have put into place various mechanisms to monitor and – wherever necessary – improve the implementation of AFSJ policies. Europol, Eurojust and Frontex also play an increasingly important role in supporting or coordinating action of national authorities in line with AFSJ objectives. The current Swedish Presidency has put a major emphasis on the strengthening of institutional monitoring and implementation capabilities in its preparatory work for the new Stockholm Programme.

Yet the need for effectiveness and efficiency in both decision-making and implementation is not the only challenge the institutional framework of the AFSJ has to address. Another one is that of legitimacy and transparency. Democratic legitimacy is all the more important for EU AFSJ policies as EU measures can directly affect the rights and freedoms of its citizens. We welcome the institutional strengthening of the role of the European Parliament since the Treaty of Amsterdam, which is going to be further enhanced by the extension of co-decision after the entry into force of the Treaty of Lisbon. It is from our perspective complemented by the improved scrutiny possibilities national parliaments will have with regard to EU measures in this sensitive domain. The judicial control exercised by the Court of Justice and the Court of First Instance also makes a substantial contribution to the legitimacy of EU action on AFSJ issues.

Legitimacy depends crucially on transparency. This not only because transparency is a basic condition for effective parliamentary and public scrutiny of decisions prepared or taken by the institutions, but also because it is only through sufficient transparency that we can ensure that all available expertise on AFSJ issues and the interests of stakeholders can be adequately taken into account. This is why the Swedish Presidency has worked to enhance further the transparency of the decision-making process by widening the range of accessible documents and consultations. The preparations of the Stockholm Programme is a case in point as the Swedish government sought an early open dialogue on this major strategic document not only with other EU governments and the European Commission, but also with the European Parliament and major stakeholders at the European and the national level. The first draft by the Presidency was published on the Presidency homepage the same day as it was distributed to the governments of the Member States. The Presidency also co-initiated and funded a major conference at the College of Europe in March 2009 to allow for a broad public debate on key options for the new multi-annual AFSJ programme.

We regard the publication of this book as a valuable contribution to the transparency of the institutional dimension of the AFSJ. There is clearly a specific need to present and analyse the institutional structures which have been put into place for the construction of the AFSJ: these have emerged and changed rather rapidly since the mid-1990s, resulting in a system of relative complexity and considerable dynamic which does not always help the desirable transparency. This book has the merit to cover all major institutional structures, asking systematically how they have adapted and responded to the challenges of the construction of the AFSJ in the context of their specific roles, roles which also have evolved over time. It does so with a spirit of constructive criticism, highlighting both existing problems and potential future improvements. I welcome the efforts made by all the contributors as the AFSJ remains a huge construction site for which we are in constant need of such thorough analysis and thoughtful suggestions on how to proceed further.

Stockholm/Brussels

November 2009

Part One

The Context

CHAPTER 1

The Institutional Framework of the AFSJ

Specific Challenges and Dynamics of Change

Jörg MONAR

1. Introduction

At a time when political developments tend to be explained mainly through "factors", "systems", "constraints" and other forces often apparently well outside of the control of individual human beings it is always slightly reassuring to have another look at the memoirs of the most prominent architects of the European integration process. For Monnet, clearly, people were at the centre of this great political project, they had to be convinced about it, they had to take the decisions and they had to take the risks and deal with the consequences. That is why he focused in his activities so much on convincing people and pushing them towards what he perceived as the necessary decisions.

Yet Monnet was also aware of how short-lived even the best policies can be if they lack a framework which supports their further development and longer-term duration. For him, this framework could only be provided by adequate institutions and that is why he spent so much effort on European institution-building. This belief in the crucial importance of institutions for the European construction has been put into sharp relief in the famous phrase of his memoirs: "*Rien ne se crée sans les hommes, rien ne dure sans les institutions*".[1] It has been invoked countless times, one of the more memorable recent occasions being Commission President Manuel Barroso's speech on the occasion of the 50th anniversary of the European Parliamentary Assembly on 12 March 2008.[2] The institutional dimension of the European integration process

1 [Nothing is created without men; nothing is lasting without institutions]. As a further reflection of his view of the vital role of institutions, Monnet also cites in his memoirs the Swiss philosopher Henri-Frédéric Amiel (1821-1881): "L'expérience de chaque homme se recommence. Seules les institutions deviennent plus sages: elles accumulent l'expérience collective, et, de cette expérience et de cette sagesse, les hommes soumis aux mêmes règles verront non pas leur nature changer, mais leur comportement graduellement se changer", Jean Monnet, *Mémoires* (Paris: Fayard, 1976), p. 460.

2 European Commission, RAPID Press Communication, SPEECH/08/143, 12 March 2008.

has also had its more controversial sides, not only because of tendencies towards bureaucratic growth and complex structural proliferation, but also because so much debate and effort has often gone into further institutional developments that the EU has not without reason being accused of institutional navel-gazing[3] and prioritising institutional issues over policy issues. Yet it is undeniably through its institutional framework that the European construction has been able to transform – with more or less success – its political aspirations into policies which today shape the lives of nearly 500 million citizens. And whenever those citizens hear about the EU this is most likely in connection with an action taken by – or another crisis emerging from – "Brussels" which has become synonymous for the often poorly understood conglomerate of institutions having their seat in the European capital.

Monnet's *dictum* places a major emphasis on the stability and duration providing function of institutions, but at least as important in the case of the European Union, which continues to be marked by a high degree of diversity, is the capacity of institutions to provide a framework in which those who have to take and implement decisions can transform diversity into the formulation and implementation of common policies. These functions of institutions must be of particular importance if the Union moves into a new major policy field which before has been largely outside of the established framework and in which both the diversity of national policies, legislation and structures and national sovereignty reserves. In such cases the capacity of the institutional framework of the Union to evolve, adapt and cope with diversity and resistances at the level of the Member States is put to the test, and a lot of the progress EU decision-makers may be able to make will depend on the extent to which the institutional framework can respond to the challenges of opening up and exploiting the potential of the new policy field.

The emergence of the EU's "Area of Freedom, Security and Justice" (AFSJ) from of its Justice and Home Affairs (JHA) cooperation predecessor has been – and still is – such a test case for the evolutionary capabilities of the Union's institutional framework. And it is a test of some importance: since the entry into force of the Amsterdam Treaty in 1999 the AFSJ has not only become fundamental treaty objective but has also become one of the most rapidly developing domains of EU policy-making with more than 1,200 texts adopted by the JHA Council

3 So for instance by British Foreign Secretary David Milliband in a speech given in the House of Commons on 12 November 2007, Hansard House of Commons Debates, 12 November 2007, Vol. 467, part 4, column 410.

in just ten years.[4] Covering a rather wide range of fields from asylum, immigration and borders over civil and criminal justice cooperation to police cooperation the AFSJ is aimed at contributing to two of the most fundamental public goods public authorities can provide to European citizens: justice and security. In terms of ambition and relevance the AFSJ can easily be placed in the same category as political project as the Internal Market, Economic and Monetary Union and the Common Foreign and Security Policy. This is even explicitly recognised by the Treaty of Lisbon, whose amended Article 3 TEU places the AFSJ as a fundamental treaty objective before all three of the aforementioned ones.

It is the purpose of this book to provide a first more comprehensive assessment on how the EU institutional framework has adapted to and evolved because of the emergence of the AFSJ and to provide an analytical survey of the main institutional characteristics, problems and development trends of the construction of the AFSJ. This will be done through substantive chapters on both the long-established institutions of the EU (Council, Commission, Parliament and Court) – which had to adapt to the demands of the AFSJ project – and on new institutional structures (Europol, Eurojust, Frontex and the liaison magistrate system) which have been introduced to the EU institutional framework to fulfil certain AFSJ specific functions.

In order to prepare the ground for the subsequent detailed analysis of the individual institutions, this introductory chapter will first analyse the specific challenges and problems the EU institutional framework has had to cope with in the case of the AFSJ and then the main dynamics of institutional change which can be identified in the AFSJ. The chapter will finish with some conclusions on the specificity of the institutional framework of the AFSJ and its possible further development under the Treaty of Lisbon.

2. Specific Institutional Challenges of the AFSJ

2.1. The Particular Sensitivity of the AFSJ Domain from a Sovereignty, Territoriality and Political Point and the Preference given to Cooperation

EU action in the JHA domain touches upon core functions of the state: Providing citizens with internal security, controlling access to the national territory and administering justice have always belonged to basic justification and legitimacy of the existence of the state since the gradual emergence of the modern nation state in the $17^{th}/18^{th}$ century

4 Statistical information obtained from the Secretariat General of the Council of the EU.

and its theoretical underpinning in the writings of Thomas Hobbes, John Locke, Montesquieu and Rousseau. As a result, state functions regarding security, justice and borders belong to the core elements of the (formerly "regalian") powers of the state and are as such heavily protected by the principle of national sovereignty. This principle and its territorial emanation, the principle of territoriality according to which only national authorities and their agents can exercise law enforcement powers within the national territory, continue to be major issues and, often enough, obstacles in the construction of the AFSJ. In addition, some of the key issues of the JHA domain, especially internal security and the control of migration, are highly sensitive at the domestic level with a high potential of making national governments win or lose elections.

It is not that surprising, therefore, that EU governments – at least most of them – have been reluctant to relinquish control over national governance instruments in the JHA domain. This is strongly reflected in the Treaty framework. Before its reform by the Treaty of Amsterdam the "old" Maastricht Treaty "third pillar" was entitled "cooperation in the fields of Justice and Home Affairs", emphasising thereby the intergovernmental nature of this area of EU policy-making. Although the Treaty of Amsterdam has brought substantial reforms and the at least symbolically much more substantial objective of the AFSJ "cooperation" between the Member States remains the prevailing principle of the AFSJ. As a result of the sensitivity of this domain the development of the AFSJ has been marked by a strong political preference for focusing EU action on reinforcing cooperation between the national systems rather than subjecting Member States to any major effort to "integrate" them into a single system with a strong set of common rules and common institutions with cross-border operational powers. The emphasis on "cooperation" rather than "integration"[5] is particularly strong in the context of Title VI TEU:

Article 29 TEU defines "common action by the Member States" – i.e. not any "common policy" or action by the Union or its institutions – as the primary instrument to achieve a high level of safety within the AFSJ. The two main "third pillar" agencies – Europol and Eurojust – are identified as the means through which "closer cooperation" between the respective competent authorities of the Member States is to be achieved

[5] The term of "integration" is used here – along the lines of the definition of economic integration developed in Bela Balassa, "Towards a Theory of Economic Integration", in: *Kyklos*, 1961, pp. 1-17, at 1 – with the very basic meaning of a process leading to the creation of single new system through the merging of several separately existing ones as opposed to "cooperation" as a process where these systems interact but remain essentially separate.

(Article 29 TEU), with the Treaty not providing for any more distinct role or power of those agencies than that "to facilitate [...] coordination" between the national authorities through various activities (Articles 30(2)(a) and 31(2)(a) TEU). "Approximation" of rules on criminal matters is only to take place "where necessary" (Article 29 TEU) and limited to "minimum rules relating to the constituent elements of criminal acts and to penalties in the fields of organised crime, terrorism and illicit drug trafficking" (Article 31(1)(e) TEU). In order to exclude any potentially more invasive impact on the national systems there are the "constitutional safeguards" of Article 33 TEU, which provides that Title VI "shall not affect the exercise of the responsibilities incumbent upon Member States with regard to the maintenance of law and order and the safeguarding of internal security" and Article 35(5) TEU pursuant to which the ECJ "shall have no jurisdiction to review the validity or proportionality of operations carried out by the police or other law enforcement services of a Member State or the exercise of the responsibilities incumbent upon Member States with regard to the maintenance of law and order and the safeguarding of internal security". Within the category of the numerous provisions protecting national systems against "integrative" effects also falls Article 34(2)(b) and (c) TEU which explicitly exclude any direct effect of framework decisions and decisions under Title VI TEU. The armour of protection of the national systems is completed by a range of institutional provisions such as the unanimity requirement in the Council for "third pillar" matters and the limited role of the European Parliament.

Yet even in the "communitarised" fields of Title IV TEC the principle of cooperation has a firm foundation. Although this is a "Community" policy-making domain the Title does not provide for the establishment of any "common policy", and rather than defining a general competence for the EC to act in a field where a lot of common measures are envisaged the Treaty such as asylum (Article 63(1) TEC) is limited to the listing of the main types of measures. The potential impact on the national systems is, again, reined in by an emphasis on "minimum standards" in the fields of asylum and refugee policy (Article 63(1) and (2) TEC) and on cooperation, mutual recognition and the promotion of the "compatibility of rules" in the field of judicial cooperation in civil matters (Article 65 TEC). The unanimity requirement – arguably the most effective barrier to unwanted "integration" – has also been maintained for two particularly sensitive fields under Title IV TEC, legal immigration and family law.

The particular sensitivity of its policy fields from a sovereignty, territoriality and political point of view and the resulting preference for cooperation rather than integration have meant three main challenges for the development of its institutional setting:

Firstly, the institutional framework had to develop specific capabilities to facilitate and support cooperation and coordination between the Member States as "harder" and more hierarchical approaches to governance in this domain (central command and control functions, strong legislative harmonisation) were politically impossible or even not available under the Treaties. The establishment of the three major agencies – Europol, Eurojust and Frontex[6] – as well the extensive use of liaison magistrates[7] and the introduction of the Counter-Terrorism Coordinator[8] – which all have cooperation and coordination supporting functions without executive operational powers – has been one of the responses to this challenge, the introduction of a highly differentiated structure of Council committees and working parties[9] another.

Secondly, in terms of "output" the policy-making institutions, i.e. especially the Council and (more reluctantly because of its traditional focus on legislative action) the Commission, had to use a wider range of "soft governance" instruments to achieve progress in line with the AFSJ objectives as traditional EC legislative instruments were considered too invasive and politically difficult. The extensive use of multi-annual programming documents (by Council and Commission), mutual evaluation mechanisms (by the Council), scoreboards (by the Commission) and common threat assessments (by Europol and Frontex) indicates that this challenge has been met with a flexible, pragmatic response.[10]

Thirdly, finally, the institutional framework of the AFSJ had to integrate – and in a certain sense "absorb" – two major systems of intergovernmental cooperation with their structures and cultures of decision-making which strongly reflected the sovereignty protective and cooperation oriented preferences of the Member States: TREVI and Schengen. This can be regarded as a challenge of its own:

---

6 See the respective chapters in this volume.

7 See the chapter by Emmanuel Barbe in this volume.

8 See the chapter by Gilles de Kerchove and Serge de Biolley in this volume.

9 See the chapter by Hans G. Nilsson and Julian Siegl in this volume.

10 On the strong "soft governance" elements in the development of the AFSJ see Jörg Monar, "Specific factors, typology and development trends of modes of governance in the EU Justice and Home Affairs domain", *NEWGOV Working Paper*, No. 1/D17, European University Institute, Florence, 2006. (http://www. eu-newgov.org/database/ DELIV/D01D17_Emergence_NMG_in_JHA.pdf).

2.2. The Intergovernmental Origins of the AFSJ

Seen from the perspective of the Community institutional framework, on whose initial setting up Monnet had had so much influence, the AFSJ has come largely in from the "cold" of the intergovernmental cooperation of the TREVI framework in the 1970s and the Schengen framework of the 1980s. The cooperation on JHA issues in the EC context was – because of the lack of competences – rather limited prior to the establishment of the AFSJ so that TREVI and Schengen can with good reason be regarded as the primary origins from which the AFSJ emerged. This has resulted in both structural and "cultural" challenges for the later development of the AFSJ institutional setup.

The TREVI ("*Terrorisme, radicalisme et violence internationale*") cooperation framework was established by the EC Member States of the time in 1975 in response to the growing terrorist challenges several of them were facing in the 1970s. TREVI was an extremely lose form of intergovernmental cooperation. It was not based on any formal Treaty provisions, lacked any institutional basis, did not dispose of any legal or other instruments of its own, had a very narrow mandate (initially focussed on the fight against terrorism only) and operated outside of the EC framework as part of European Political Cooperation.[11] TREVI consisted mainly of meetings between national ministries and law enforcement authorities arranged by the country holding the EC Presidency at often irregular intervals. Regular meetings at the ministerial level were also foreseen, but at least until the second half of the 1980s these were less regular and also less substantial than originally envisaged. TREVI was not a propitious territory for the (EC) Commission which had initially to struggle to be accepted at all in this framework. It succeeded in doing so mainly on grounds of its expertise and action possibilities on the Internal Market related internal security issues, but never acquired the institutional influence it had in the EC context and later also developed in the AFSJ context.[12] Yet, in spite of its limitations, TREVI provided the EC Member States with a framework in which they could gradually develop their cooperation in other areas (such as the fight against drug trafficking and organised crime), set up a range of additional working parties and explore more intense mechanisms of information exchange and operational cooperation. As a result, TREVI was regarded as a success story, and although it was felt at the beginning of the 1990s that JHA cooperation needed to go further than TREVI, the Member States retained in the subsequent Maastricht Treaty

11 On the origins an characteristics of TREVI see Serge A. Bonnefoi, *Europe et sécurité intérieure: TREVI, Union européenne, Schengen* (Paris: Delmas, 1995).

12 See the chapter by Richard Lewis and David Spence in this volume.

reforms quite a few elements of the TREVI framework, such as a limited role for the Commission, no effective role at all for the Parliament and the Court and a special coordinating committee[13] which helped to continue TREVI decision-making practices. After TREVI was absorbed in 1993 into the institutional structures and procedures of the EU, quite a few senior officials of the Member States retained a certain nostalgia for the "good old times" of TREVI when cooperation appeared to have been more flexible and much less subject to procedural rules and bureaucratic embedding.[14] As a result, TREVI left a lot of intergovernmental heritage in the institutional setup of the AFSJ which have taken a long time to recede. Some of the persisting negotiation "culture" preference in Council for least common denominator consensus-finding – even in fields in which qualified majority voting is now possible – can continuously be traced back to the TREVI origins of the AFSJ. The retention of a right of initiative for the Member States – which in the fields of police and judicial cooperation criminal matters has "survived" even the Lisbon Treaty reforms[15] – can also be regarded as a resilient relic of this intergovernmental inheritance.

An additional dose of intergovernmentalism was injected into the emergence of the institutional setting of the AFSJ also by the Schengen system. During Schengen's period of forced exile from the Community from 1985 to 1999, the Schengen members never failed to emphasise that its role was to be that of a precursor of EC policy-making on the complete implementation of free movement and all related compensatory JHA measures. The Preamble of the 1990 "Convention implementing the Schengen Agreement" (CISA)[16] even explicitly referred to the EC Treaty objective of an Internal Market without internal frontiers and its Article 134 ruled out the adoption of any measures incompatible with Community law. The institutional setup of the Schengen system also mirrored to a considerable extent the EU Council hierarchy with its ministerial/official level distinction[17] and a supporting (small) secretariat. Yet in other respects it was institutionally more similar to the intergovernmental TREVI setting, in particular because it gave no role to the European Commission, Parliament or Court. Specific procedural

13 The Article K.4 Committee, now the Articles 36 Committee (CATS).

14 The "TREVI Blues" were much in evidence when the author carried out a couple of interviews with national officials about the impact of the Maastricht Treaty reforms in 1994/95.

15 Art. 76 TFEU provides that initiatives in these fields can – apart from the Commission – also be brought by a quarter of the Member States.

16 *O.J.*, No. L 239 of 22 September 2000.

17 The ministers met in the "Schengen Executive Committee" whose decisions were prepared by working parties consisting of national officials.

features of the Community system, such as majority voting, never found their way into Schengen. When Schengen was incorporated into the EU system in 1999, which considerably strengthened the Union's policy-making potential in the fields of asylum, migration and borders, another tradition of policy-making on the basis of intergovernmental consensus-finding entered the construction of the AFSJ. This did not help with institutional transparency – with Schengen came a "culture" of keeping institutional proceedings as far out of the public domain as possible[18] – and made it more of an uphill struggle for the Commission to develop its role in the newly communitarised JHA fields of Title IV TEC. It should also be recalled that it was Germany, one of the original founders of Schengen, which insisted during the Amsterdam Treaty negotiations on retaining unanimity for another five years even for the communitarised fields,[19] which also led to a limitation of the Parliament's role to consultation instead of co-decision until the beginning of 2005.

Taken together the particular sensitivity of the AFSJ domain from a sovereignty, territoriality and political point and its intergovernmental origins have meant a considerable risk of insubstantial decisions or even paralysis for the Council. While there are enough examples for such problems of effectiveness especially under unanimity conditions – the much delayed and thinned-out 2008 Framework Decision on the European Evidence Warrant (EEW) is one of the most recent ones[20] – the

18 See on this and the "contempt" with which the ministers continued to treat the principle of transparency after the incorporation of Schengen, Steve Peers, "Integrating the Schengen acquis into the EU legal order", *Cambridge Yearbook of European Legal Studies*, Vol. 2, 1999, pp. 100-101.

19 See Rita Beuter, "Germany: Safeguarding the EMU and the interests of the Länder", in: Finn Laursen (ed.), *The Amsterdam Treaty* (Odense: Odense University Press, 2002), pp. 110-111.

20 The unanimity rule showed in this case again its full impact: The scope of the EEW has been restricted to already available evidence in the form of documents, objects and data (not covering, for instance, DNA samples or the monitoring of bank accounts), and the condition for the abolition of the double criminality principle for 32 serious offences has been raised to the relatively high level of them being punishable in the issuing state by a custodial sentence of at least three years. The effectiveness of the EEW could also be reduced by a specific "territoriality clause", allowing a Member State to refuse a warrant for offences committed wholly or mainly within its territory. In addition Germany, which had not played the most constructive role during the negotiations, has reserved its right to issue a declaration making the execution of an EEA subject to verification of double criminality in cases relating to terrorism, computer-related crime, racism and xenophobia, sabotage, racketeering and extortion or swindling, if it is necessary to carry out a search or seizure for the execution of the warrant. (Council Framework Decision 2008/978/JHA of 18 December 2008 on the European evidence warrant for the purpose of obtaining objects, documents and data for use in proceedings in criminal matters, *O.J.*, No. L 350 of 30 December 2008).

Council has, over the years, nevertheless been able to adopt a constant stream of texts some of which, such as the 2002 Framework Decision on the European Arrest Warrant, have covered substantial new ground. Besides political factors favouring common action – such as the 9/11 attacks – a lot of credit for this is also due to the Directorate General H of the General Secretariat of the Council which has played an important role in securing continuity from one Presidency to the other and facilitating compromise building among the national delegations.[21]

2.3. The Diversity of the JHA Policy Fields

Also a specificity of the AFSJ domain is that it comprises a set of rather diverse policy fields: asylum, immigration, border controls, judicial cooperation in civil matters, judicial cooperation in criminal matters and police cooperation. Both the objectives pursued and the instruments used to achieve them are necessarily rather different if one compares, for instance, the fields of asylum policy, judicial cooperation in civil matters and police cooperation: in the first, the main focus is on the common definition of minimum guarantees and procedures regarding asylum seekers, in the second it is essentially the facilitation of the cross-border administration of civil justice and in the third enhanced information exchange and operational interaction between national law enforcement authorities.

This diversity also constitutes a challenge for the institutional framework: ever since the introduction of Justice and Home Affairs cooperation into the EU by the Treaty of Maastricht all these fields have been brought together under the responsibility of the JHA Council and one EU Commissioner, and have been administratively dealt with by one Directorate-General in the Council and (later) one in the Commission. Yet this has obviously not reduced in any way the diversity of the governance challenges and possible responses. The institutions had therefore to adapt their structures to the complexity and differentiation of this policy-making domain. This has been done through the already mentioned highly differentiated structure of Council committees and working parties, through the build-up by the Commission of a fully-fledged Directorate-General out of the initially rather small task force in the Secretariat General[22] and the delegation of certain analysis functions to Europol and Frontex within their respective spheres of competence. For the European Parliament the combination of these different fields in a single policy-making area means quite a heavy burden for its LIBE

---

21 See the chapter by Hans G. Nilsson and Julian Siegl in this volume.

22 See the chapter by Richard Lewis and David Spence in this volume.

Committee which has to maintain a coherent scrutiny of the entire domain through its legislative and own-initiative reports.[23]

2.4. The Strong Operational Dimension of the AFSJ Domain

The progress of EC/EU integration has traditionally been strongly linked with an extensive use of legislation for setting common rules. While there are some fields of the AFSJ, such as asylum and migration, where legislative instruments are central to progress, there are others, especially police cooperation and external border control and surveillance, where operational information exchange and coordination as well as the carrying out of joint operations are of more and often enough central importance. Legislative measures on the one hand and operational measures on the other have obviously substantially different rationales and requirements, the need for speed, trained personnel, special technical equipment and flexibility in deployment, for instance.[24]

As a result of the operational needs of the AFSJ rather different instruments of governance need to be used, and this often enough in one and the same field. The institutional framework of the AFSJ had to be enabled to cope with (more traditional) legislative tasks as well as those (new) operational needs. Judicial cooperation in the fight against cross-border crime needs, to give an example, both legislative action for minimum harmonisation of certain procedural and substantive provisions of criminal law – which can be taken through the legislative process involving Council, Commission and Parliament – and operational coordination and cooperation of prosecution services – in which Eurojust plays an important and steadily growing role.[25] The successful instrument of the liaison magistrates[26] also facilitates cross-border operational cooperation between judicial authorities.

The operational dimension of the AFSJ domain has contributed to the resilience of the intergovernmental element in the institutional framework of the AFSJ as the Member States want to retain full control of their operational means and therefore prefer institutional mechanisms which can give them a maximum of control. An example for this is the strategic role the Management Board – consisting of Member States' representatives – plays in the functioning of Europol.[27] Another, the fact that Frontex cannot deploy any operational means (CRATE equipment

23 See the chapter by Emilio De Capitani in this volume.

24 See RABIT and CRATE instruments at the disposal of Frontex are an example. See the chapter by Mintze Beuving in this volume.

25 See the chapter by Maylis Labayle and Hans G. Nilsson in this volume.

26 See the chapter by Emmanuel Barbe in this volume.

27 See the chapter by Michael Niemeier and Marc André Wiegand in this volume.

or RABIT teams) without the respective Member States' agreement.[28] The implementation of all operational measures by national authorities makes this dimension a difficult one to scrutinise by the European Parliament and to monitor and evaluate by the European Commission.

2.5. The Strong Degree of Differentiation within the AFSJ

Although the AFSJ is formally designed as a single "area" it is the most differentiated of all the constructions which the EU integration process has produced so far: currently only 21 of the 27 Member States fully participate in all the governance instruments and structures which have been developed within the AFSJ. The UK, Ireland and Denmark have all to various degrees "opt-out" arrangements, Cyprus remains excluded of the integrated Schengen border regime because of the partition of the island, and Bulgaria and Romania are not expected to be ready for assuming all the Schengen obligations before 2011. If this results already in a high degree of differentiation, this is taken even further by the "association" of Iceland, Norway and (operationally only since March 2009) Switzerland as non-EU Member States with the Schengen system.

This strong degree of differentiation has also necessitated an adaptation of the EU institutional framework: the Council had to adapt its procedures to the formula of "decision-shaping rather than decision-making" according to which – by virtue of the Association Agreements – the non-EU Schengen "associates" can participate in those parts of the JHA Council meetings which deal with Schengen items (so-called "mixed" agenda items) and express their views on proposed measures. This remains a peculiar arrangement as with regard to the formal adoption of these measures only the EU Schengen Member States have voting rights.[29]

The position of the "opt-outs" has also given rise to complex legal and even technical issues of participation, non-participation or partial participation – with regard, for instance, to the British partial participation in the Schengen Information System (SIS)[30] – have added to the complexity of Council decision-making on Schengen related AFSJ matters. Although the "opt-outs" participate in all AFSJ-related meetings – and even chair the Council working parties dealing with Schen-

[28] See the chapter by Mintze Beuving in this volume.

[29] See on this Peter Cullen, "The Schengen Agreement with Iceland and Norway: Its main features", *ERA-Forum: scripta iuris europaei*, Vol. 2, No. 4, December 2001, pp. 71-75.

[30] The UK has opted into the law enforcement related functionalities of the SIS but – because of its rejection of the abolition of controls at internal borders – not into the border control related ones.

gen issues when holding the Presidency – their position is often in need of clarification even if Ireland and the UK have already clarified their political stance. The Council Legal Service has in fact often to provide an in-depth analysis first before it can be decided whether or not a measure falls or does not fall within the remit of the British or Irish opt-out. When asked during a 2006-2007 British House of Lords inquiry about how this complex process works in practice the Parliamentary Under-Secretary of State for Nationality, Citizenship and Immigration, Joan Ryan, preferred to call in a senior official of the Home Office, Jonathan Sweet, to explain this to the Committee members:

> When it comes to discussing particular proposals which might be brought forward that relate to aspects of the Schengen Acquis, then those are discussed in the Schengen Acquis Working Group, for instance, which is within the Council structure. Clearly, in relation to each individual instrument, if it is an instrument which, if one accepts the Council Legal Service analysis for example, builds on a part of the underlying Schengen Acquis into which the UK had not opted, then we do not participate in that instrument. We can contribute to the discussions – we are still in the working group and we do contribute to the discussions – but we will not, at the end of the day, formally be a party to that instrument.[31]

Tensions within the Council over issues of differentiation had on one occasion even to be settled by the ECJ when in 2005 the UK brought two actions of annulment against the Council for not allowing it to participate in the adoption of two Schengen measures, Council Regulation (EC) No. 2007/2004 of 26 October 2004 establishing Frontex and Council Regulation (EC) No. 2252/2004 of 13 December 2004 on standards for security features and biometrics in passports and travel documents issued by Member States. On 18 December 2007, the Court, giving clear signs of disapproval of the British selective opt-in approach, ruled that the Council had been right in refusing British participation in these measures as these were building upon parts of the Schengen Acquis which the UK had clearly not yet accepted.[32]

The differentiation also adds an additional element of complication to the work of the Commission as – depending on the issues concerned – it has to take the position of the Schengen "associates" into account in

---

31 House of Lords (EU Committee), 9th Report of Session 2006-2007, Schengen Information System II (SIS II), *HL Paper* 49 (London: The Stationary Office, 2007), p. 122.

32 Case C-77/05, *United Kingdom v Council* [2007] ECR I-11459, and C-137/05, *United Kingdom v Council* [2007] ECR I-11593. For a critical review of these judgements see Maria Fletcher, "Schengen, the European Court of Justice and flexibility under the Lisbon Treaty: Balancing the United Kingdom's 'Ins' and 'Outs'", *European Constitutional Law Review*, Vol. 5, 2009, pp. 84-89.

its Schengen related proposals and will often not be sure initially whether Ireland and/or the UK will eventually decide to participate in a proposed measure or not. In the case of the 2007 "Rome I"-Regulation on contractual obligations,[33] for instance, the British government announced in 2005, when the Commission had made its initial proposal, that it would not opt into the proposed instrument. Yet later it had second thoughts, engaged in a public consultation exercise,[34] and then finally informed the Council in July 2008 that it would opt-in after all.[35]

For the European Parliament's LIBE Committee the differentiation is not helping with the transparency of scrutiny as MEPs should obviously know to which countries a measure under scrutiny will eventually apply. From a democratic legitimacy point of view it also makes the position of British and Irish MEPs slightly awkward when they have to vote on Schengen measures which will apply to other EU citizens – but not to their own.[36]

2.6. The Divide between the "First" and the "Third" Pillar Fields

The (in)famous "pillar divide" is the last, but certainly not the least, of the specific challenges to which the institutional framework of the AFSJ had to adapt. Although linked together by the common objective of the AFSJ and the common institutional framework (in particular the JHA Council) the "first pillar" fields (asylum, immigration, border controls, judicial cooperation in civil matters) are separated from the "third pillar" fields (police and judicial cooperation in criminal matters) not only by a different legal basis[37] but also by different decision-making procedures,[38] separate decision-making structures in the Council below the level of the COREPER[39] and different legal instruments. This

---

33 It converted into an EC Regulation and revised the 1980 Rome Convention on the law applicable to contractual obligations (consumer contracts, property purchase contracts, etc.). Regulation (EC) 593/2008 of 17 June 2008 on the law applicable to contractual obligations (Rome I), *O.J.*, No. L 177 of 4 July 2008.

34 See UK Ministry of Justice, "Rome I – Should the UK opt in?", *Consultation Paper* CP05/08, London, 2 April 2008.

35 Letter of notification: Council Document 12143/08 of 24 July 2008.

36 Within the UK a slightly similar situation, the right of Scottish MPs to vote on "English" legislation in the House of Commons, is quite controversial. See Steve Peers, "UK and Irish opt-outs from EU Justice and Home Affairs (JHA) law", *Statewatch EU Lisbon Treaty Analysis*, No. 4, June 2009, p. 8 (http://www.statewatch.org/news/2009/jun/uk-ireland-analysis-no-4-lisbon-opt-outs.pdf); and "Devolution: Conservatives plan to limit Scottish MPs' voting rights", *The Guardian*, 2 July 2009.

37 The respective provisions of Title IV TEC and Title VI TEU.

38 Mainly qualified majority under Title IV TEC and unanimity under Title VI TEU.

39 See the chapter by Hans G. Nilsson and Julian Siegl in this volume.

divide, which cuts through the entire domain, means the current Treaty framework – as a result of a political decision of the Member States as "Masters of the Treaties" – imposes a distinct cleavage on the whole institutional setup of the AFSJ which can in this form not be found in any other EU policy field.

In the case of legislative measures the pillar divide means that depending on whether a Title IV TEC or Title VI TEU measure is aimed at the Commission has to propose different legal instruments, take into account in its proposal the differences in terms of legal effects of these instruments,[40] and deal with a different decision-making context in the Council.[41] It also has to content itself with its rather different possibilities to ensure the full and timely implementation of the acts adopted.[42]

For the Council the pillar divide means not only a sharp division between "first" and "third" pillar committees and working parties[43] – which is at least in part artificial[44] and counterproductive – but also that for the achievement of certain "cross-pillar" objectives parallel legal instruments have to be adopted both under Title IV TEC and Title VI TEU – with a corresponding loss of time and effort. In the case of criminal sanctions against the facilitators of illegal immigration, for instance, the Council had because of the Title IV EC competences in the fields of immigration and border controls had on 28 November 2002 to adopt both a "first pillar" Directive on defining the facilitation of unauthorised entry, transit and residence and a "third pillar" Framework Decision on the strengthening of the penal framework for the same types of offences.[45]

40 Art. 34(2) TEU provides that "third pillar" decisions and framework decisions shall not have direct effect.

41 In contrast with the "first pillar" are generally applying unanimity requirement as well as a shared right of initiative of the Member States which can be used to preempt Commission initiatives (as in the case of the July 2000 "four presidencies" initiative by Portugal, France, Sweden and Belgium on the establishment of Eurojust).

42 Under Title VI TEU the Commission cannot bring Treaty infringement proceedings against a Member State failing to implement a decision or framework decision. The Commission has on various occasions pointed to the related serious implementation deficits of the "third pillar" (see, for instance, COM(2006) 333 final, Brussels, 28 June 2006, p. 16).

43 See the chapter by Hans G. Nilsson and Julian Siegl in this volume.

44 It separates, for instance, the Council bodies in charge of migration policy aspects under the direction of the Strategic Committee for Immigration, Frontiers and Asylum (SCIFA) from those dealing with the law enforcement aspect of the fight against illegal immigration under the direction of the Article 36 Committee (CATS).

45 Council Directive 2002/90/EC of 28 November 2002 defining the facilitation of unauthorised entry, transit and residence, *O.J.*, No. L 328 of 5 December 2002; and Council Framework Decision of 28 November 2002 on the strengthening of the penal

For the European Parliament the divide means that its legislative powers are divided between the two extremes of full co-decision on most Title IV TEC matters[46] on the one hand and its mere consultation by the Council on Title VI TEU matters on the other. Unsurprisingly the Parliament has on several occasions contested "third pillar" legal bases for AFSJ measures with the hope of the Court declaring a "first pillar" basis applicable instead. Yet apart from delaying the entry into force of certain AFSJ measures this has occasionally also had other undesired effects. An example for the costs of such interinstitutional conflicts arising from the pillar divide is the annulment the European Parliament sought in May 2004 of the Council decision to conclude the agreement with the United States on the anti-terrorism related processing and transfer of Passenger Name Records (PNR) data because of both its concerns about adequate protection of personal data and the aim to assert its co-decision rights. Yet in its judgement of 30 May 2006 the Court did not enter into the substance of the data protection arguments put forward by the Parliament and annulled both the Commission's data protection "adequacy" decision and the Council's decision to conclude the agreement only on grounds of the chosen "first pillar" legal base not being adequate.[47] As a result, the Parliament's successful application for annulment turned into somewhat Pyrrhic victory as the Court's ruling not only made Council and Commission move to a "third pillar" legal base for the renegotiation of the agreement – which excluded the Parliament even further – but also provided the US government with an opportunity to force the EU to accept that the operation of the agreement would be automatically subject to subsequent changes in US legislation.

For the Court of Justice, finally, the divide pillar has meant the need to rule on various occasions on the borderlines between first and third pillar AFSJ legal bases and institutional competences. The above mentioned PNR-case is one example, the annulment by the ECJ – upon application by the Commission – on 13 September 2005 of Council Framework Decision 2003/80/JHA on the protection of the environment through criminal law ECJ on grounds of an inappropriate "third pillar" legal basis another.[48] With Article 36 TEU imposing a number of restrictions on the Court's role in the "third pillar",[49] the Court has in a number

framework to prevent the facilitation of authorised entry, transit and residence (2002/946/JHA), *O.J.*, No. L 328 of 5 December 2002.

46 With the exception of legal immigration and family law.

47 Joined Cases C-317/04 and C-318/04, European Parliament v Council of the European Union and Commission of the European Communities [2006] ECR 1-4721.

48 Case C-176/03, *Commission v Council* [2005] ECR I-7879.

49 The most notable being that according to Article 35(1) and (2) TEU the Court can only accept preliminary ruling requests from the jurisdictions of member states who

of cases systematically reasserted its right to guard the EC domain against possible infringements from "third pillar" measures and to upheld general principles of EC/EU law across the pillar divide most notably as regards the protection of fundamental rights, thereby preparing the ground for the abolition of the limitations of its role under the Lisbon Treaty.[50]

3. Dynamics of Change within the AFSJ Institutional Framework

3.1. The Widening Agenda

The institutional framework of the AFSJ – as that of the EU as a whole – is constantly evolving, at certain periods more rapidly and fundamentally, at others less. Amongst the factors accounting for this dynamic the significant widening of the political agenda of the AFSJ must be ranked high. It is sufficient to compare the total of 144 texts adopted by the JHA Council during 2008 and the enormous range of activities of the institutions across the different policy fields[51] with any of the years of JHA cooperation during the 1990s to realise how dramatic this widening of the agenda has been. The widening of the agenda has driven – and provided justification – for institutional growth and innovation. In the mid-1990s the European Commission could hardly have found work for – let alone justified – to have an entire Directorate-General dealing with JHA matters (the current DG JLS), and this with a sizeable total staff of currently 591.[52] The innovative step taken with the establishment of Frontex in 2005 – and its subsequent rapid growth[53] – would also not have been possible without the massive widening of the external border policy agenda since the Seville European Council meeting in June 2002 and the launching of the integrated border management concept.

This is not the place to embark upon an analysis of all the European, international and domestic political reasons why this massive widening

have submitted a declaration to that effect, and this only in relation to framework decisions, decisions and conventions, not as regards common positions or primary law.

50 See the chapter by Vassilis Hatzopoulos in this volume.

51 See Jörg Monar, "Justice and home affairs", *Journal of Common Market Studies*, Annual Review, Vol. 47, 2009, pp. 151-190.

52 European Commission, Distribution of Staff by Statutory links and DGs, 2 August 2009 (http://ec.europa.eu/civil_service/docs/bs_fonct_ext_dg_en.pdf).

53 See the chapter by Mintze Beuving in this volume.

has taken place.[54] The enabling provisions of the Amsterdam Treaty reforms, the political leadership (occasionally) exercised by the European Council – such as on the occasion of the 1999 Tampere European Council meeting – or certain leading political figures (such as EU Commissioner Antonio Vitorino when holding the JHA portfolio 1999-2004), certain external pressures or events (like the 9/11 attacks) and the "spill-over effects" generated by progress in other EU policy areas (such as the abolition of controls at internal borders and economic and monetary integration) must surely count amongst the key factors.

Yet one should also not underestimate the impact which the institutional development of the AFSJ itself has had on the widening of the AFSJ agenda: from 1999 onwards the European Commission, enabled to play a more prominent role by the Amsterdam reforms and strengthened by a very active Commissioner in charge as well a rapid growth of the newly established Directorate-General had not only the potential but also all imaginable political interest to becoming a driving force in the AFSJ domain. In that it succeeded through a massive increase of policy and legislative initiatives[55] – which has certainly contributed significantly to the widening of the AFSJ agenda. The special agencies certainly also favoured rather than hindered the widening of the AFSJ agenda. It is quite unlikely, for instance, that without the previous establishment of Frontex, its risk assessments and its evaluation of operational needs the innovative instrument of the Rapid Border Intervention Teams (RABITs) would have seen the light of the day in 2007.[56] While the widening of the AFSJ agenda therefore generated institutional growth within the AFSJ, this institutional growth in turn contributed to the widening of the agenda, leading to a dynamic circle.

3.2. The Changing Institutional Balance of Power

In its 1990 judgement on the Chernobyl Regulation Case the ECJ reaffirmed the existence of an "institutional balance", set up by the Treaties, meaning

> a system for distributing powers among the different Community institutions, assigning to each institution its own role in the institutional structure

---

[54] A fairly comprehensive analysis is provided by Wenceslas de Lobkowicz, *L'Europe de la sécurité intérieure. Une élaboration par étapes* (Paris: La Documentation Française, 2002); and Thorsten Müller, *Die Innen- und Justizpolitik der Europäischen Union. Eine Analyse der Integrationsentwicklung* (Opladen: Leske+Budrich, 2003).

[55] See the chapter by Richard Lewis and David Spence in this volume.

[56] See the chapter by Mintze Beuving in this volume.

of the Community and the accomplishment of the tasks entrusted to the Community.[57]

Far from being only a formal constitutional principle, the institutional balance can be regarded as essential for guaranteeing a smooth and effective interaction between the different interests represented by the EU institutions.[58]

In the case of the AFSJ the institutional balance has changed – and keeps changing. The former absolute predominance of the Council – which throughout the 1990s had largely initiated, decided upon and implemented JHA policies all on its own[59] – started to be mitigated during the 1999-2004 "transitional period" by the increasingly proactive role assumed by the European Commission.[60] Then from 2005 onwards under the double impact of the Commission obtaining an exclusive right of initiative in the "first pillar" fields and the European Parliament gaining co-decision on most of those fields as well the Council has become much more dependent on interinstitutional compromise-building, at least in the co-decision fields.

However, the shift in the institutional balance between the Council and the Commission has been only gradual, and it has been neither continuous nor smooth. The Commission's major 2001 proposal for a Directive on economic migration aimed at regulating the entry and residence conditions for all third-country nationals exercising paid and self-employed activities, for instance, completely failed in the Council and forced the Commission to come back with a substantially revised policy plan in 2005.[61] And in the case of the recent adoption of the EU Blue Card Directive the Commission still had to accept a substantial watering down of its original proposal.[62] Yet in this and other cases of major legislation, at least in the "first pillar" fields, the Commission has clearly become the main agenda-setter with major influence on policy orientation.

---

57 Case C-70/88, *European Parliament v Council* [1990] ECR 1-02041, para. 21-22.

58 Koen Lenaerts and Amaryllis Verhoeven, "Institutional balance as a guarantee for democracy in EU governance", in: Christian Joerges and Renaud Dehousse (eds.), *Good Governance in Europe's Integrated Market* (Oxford: Oxford University Press, 2002), p. 43.

59 See the chapter by Charles Elsen in this volume.

60 See the chapter by Richard Lewis and David Spence in this volume.

61 COM(2005) 699 final of 21 December 2005.

62 Council Directive 2009/50/EC of 25 May 2009 on the conditions of entry and residence of third-country nationals for the purposes of highly qualified employment, *O.J.*, No. L 155 of 18 June 2009. The Commission had to accept, in particular, that the EU Blue Card scheme will not replace schemes put into place by the Member States but only come in addition to those.

The shift in the institutional balance between the Council and the European Parliament has been very important from a constitutional point of view because of the introduction of co-decision in the respective Title IV TEC fields – with all it entails in terms of enhanced democratic scrutiny and impact possibilities on legislation. The introduction of co-decision in 2005 meant for the Parliament a first passage to full legislative co-responsibility in the AFSJ domain which led to a modification of its until then almost consistently critical and conflictual approach towards the Council.[63] The Parliament's The Parliament's LIBE Committee has risen to the challenge of not only coping with the massive expansion of the AFSJ agenda but also to become an effective counterpart of the Council in the changed interinstitutional context. The impressive number of agreements reached between Parliament and Council already during the first reading of AFSJ legislative acts subject to co-decision – 84% during the 2004-2009 legislative term – shows not only that the Parliament can build up effective majorities quickly but also that it can obtain concessions from the Council at an early stage as Presidencies might wish to avoid the procedural complications and consensus-building strains within the Council and complexity of protracted co-decision procedures.[64]

In terms of the impact of the shift in the institutional balance on policy substance the evidence so far is more mixed. On the one hand the Council negotiations are now "overshadowed" right from the start by the need to come to an agreement with the Parliament – which has led to the Council seeking earlier and better contacts to the EP, and the Council cannot any longer largely ignore strongly held EP positions, such as those of the defence and promotion of fundamental rights,[65] as this was still possible in the 1990s. On the other hand, however, the Parliament seems in some cases willing to go quite far with its concessions to the Council in order to reach an agreement already during the first reading of the co-decision procedure. A key example is the 2008 Returns Directive,[66] branded as a "directive of shame" by some NGOs because of the lower standards of protection for those which are subject to expulsion orders on which a majority of the Member States in the Council successfully insisted. It seems that in that case the Parliament accepted the highly controversial compromise with the Council because of pragmatic

63 On the tensions between Council and Parliament see the chapter by Charles Elsen in this volume.

64 See the chapter by Emilio De Capitani in this volume.

65 *Ibid.*

66 Directive 2008/115/EC of the European Parliament and of the Council of 16 December 2008 on common standards and procedures in Member States for returning illegally staying third-country nationals, *O.J.*, No. L 348 of 24 December 2008.

reasons – low standard minimum rules being considered better than none –, pressure on MEPs by their respective national governments and procedural constraints – compromises within the are more difficult to achieve during the second reading because then an absolute rather than simple majority is required.[67] With the Parliament apparently eager to avoid both internal and interinstitutional deadlocks which could impair its capacity to effectively exercise its newly gained co-decision powers these very powers seem to have – at least in certain cases – a limiting impact on its capacity to formulate and sustain policy alternatives to the Council's predominantly security oriented approach on a number of AFSJ issues.[68]

Not as a part of the emerging political compromise-building triangle – but with a significant impact on it in terms of affirming general principles of EC/EU law and defining the borderlines between the "pillars" – the Court of Justice has also increasingly emerged as a factor in the institutional balance of the AFSJ which it had not been under the Maastricht JHA cooperation. An early starting shot for the affirmation of the Court's role was its 1998 ruling in Case C-170/96 in which the Commission sought the annulment of a Joint Action of the Council on airport transit visas which the Commission felt should have been adopted on a "first" rather than "third" pillar basis. The Court did not annul the Joint Action but also rejected the Council's argument that the Court was lacking jurisdiction, affirming its right to guard the EC domain against possible infringements caused by "third pillar" acts.[69] But it was only from 2003 onwards with the ECJ's strengthening of the mutual recognition principle in the *Gözütok and Brügge* Case on the application of the *ne bis in idem* principle,[70] the ruling in the famous *Pupino* Case[71] concerning the legal effects of a Title VI TEU Framework Decision, the aforementioned 2005 Decision on the protection of the environment through criminal law ECJ on grounds of an inappropriate "third pillar" legal basis another[72] and the – ongoing – series of decisions regarding fundamental rights protection in the context of the financial and other

67 See the comprehensive analysis in Diego Acosta, "The good, the bad and the ugly in EU migration law: is the European Parliament becoming bad and ugly?", *European Journal of Migration and Law*, Vol. 11, 2009, pp. 19-39.

68 See on that Ariadna Ripoll Servent, "Setting priorities: functional and substantive dimensions of irregular immigration and data protection under co-decision", *Journal of Contemporary European Research*, Vol. 5, No. 2, pp. 225-242, who also analyses the example of the 2006 Date Retention Directive.

69 Case C-170/96, *Commission v Council* [1998] ECR I-2763.

70 Joined Cases C-187/01 and C-385/01, *Gözütok and Brügge* [2003] ECR I-1345.

71 Case C-105/03, *Pupino* [2005] ECR I-5285.

72 Case C-176/03, *Commission v Council* [2005] ECR I-7879.

property sanctions imposed on alleged terrorists and terrorist groupings included in the so-called "terrorist lists" – which reached a first peak in terms of impact with the 2006 ruling of the CFI in the *Modjahedines* Case –[73] that the Court really fully entered into the interinstitutional equation.[74] How much of an immediate political impact decisions of the Court can have on the interinstitutional dynamics within the AFSJ was shown when the Commission followed up its September 2005 victory before the Court regarding the annulment of Council Framework Decision 2003/80/JHA on the protection of the environment through criminal law (see above) already two months later with a by normal interinstitutional almost aggressive proposal to amend no less than eight previously adopted "third pillar" legislative acts in line with the Court's affirmation of Community competence.[75]

The clearly identifiable shifts in the institutional balance have brought the institutional framework of the AFSJ surely closer to what Pierre Pescatore has called the institutional "quadripartisme" of the Community system.[76] As far as this classic model can be taken as the point of reference the "abnormal" relative weakness of the Commission has been remedied, the quasi-exclusion of the Court ended and the Parliament's quest for a legislative role commensurate with the importance and sensitivity of this domain for the individual citizen at least partially been satisfied.

With the ascent of the Commission and the Parliament the range of other actors which can potentially influence policy-making within the institutional framework has also increased: The Commission normally consults a wide range of European "stakeholders" beyond governments and ministries before making a legislative proposal – which national governments using their right of initiative in the Council often do not. With the new powers of the European Parliament party political and lobby group interests have also been opened up new pathways of influence. Although this may occasionally add to the complexity of compromise finding it should surely be welcomed from a democratic participation and transparency perspective, especially as the JHA domain was for such a long time a near exclusive preserve of inter-ministerial cooperation veiled in secrecy.

---

73 Case T-228/02, *Modjahedines* [2006] ECR II-4665.

74 A critical survey of the relevant AFSJ case-law is provided in Vassilis Hatzopoulos, "With or without you… Judging politically in the field of area of freedom, security and justice", *European Law Review*, Vol. 33, No. 1, 2008, pp. 44-65.

75 COM(2005) 583 final of 23 November 2005.

76 Pierre Pescatore, "L'Exécutif communautaire: justification du quadripartisme institué par les Traités de Paris et de Rome", *Cahiers de Droit Européen*, Vol. 11, No. 2, 1978, pp. 378-406.

However, in at least two respects these changes in the institutional balance are at variance with the "normal" trends of change in the institutional history of the Community. It has rightly been underlined that the latter has always been marked by the progressive growth of the powers of the Parliament.[77] Yet in the case of the AFSJ the growth of the role of the Commission has at least been as important as that of the Parliament. The second point of difference is the emergence and quite significant roles of the special agencies Europol, Eurojust and Frontex. While it would certainly go too far to regard this as part of a defensive strategy of the Council it cannot be denied that the introduction of those agencies and the relatively high extent to which they are – at least as far as their operation functions are concerned – exempt from effective control by the Commission and the Parliament are a relatively innovative way of shielding the Member States competences against shifts in the institutional balance.

3.3. The Blurring of the "Pillar Divide"

Our survey of the dynamics of change in the institutional dimension of the AFSJ would not be complete without a brief look at what could be described as the gradual blurring of the "pillar divide". The drafters of the Amsterdam Treaty surely intended to keep the "intergovernmental" Title VI TEU fields of police and judicial cooperation in criminal matters as carefully separated from the "communitarised" Title IV TEC fields of asylum, migration, border controls and civil justice as possible. Yet institutional developments have increasingly blurred this fundamental treaty imposed divide:

The Court of Justice has probably played the most important role in this respect. This is not the place to provide a full review of the relevant case-law, but the already briefly mentioned *Pupino* ruling is surely an outstanding example. It concerned the legal effects of a Title VI TEU Framework Decision during the time frame foreseen for its transposition by Member States. The framework decision contained provisions for the protection of particularly vulnerable victims – in this case young children – in criminal proceedings. The Italian Code of Criminal Procedure contained some provisions to such effect, but these were more restrictive and did not cover the situation in question. The question was therefore whether the rules of the Italian Code should be interpreted extensively in order to make them compatible with the framework decision. Notwithstanding Article 34(2)(b) TEU, which excludes any "direct effect" of framework decisions, the Court held that that "the principle of conforming interpretation is binding in relation to framework decisions adopted

---

77 Jean-Paul Jacqué, "The principle of institutional balance", *Common Market Law Review*, Vol. 41, No. 2, 2004, pp. 383-391.

in the context of Title VI TEU" and that "when applying national law, the national court that is called upon to interpret it must do so as far as possible in the light of the wording and purpose of the framework decision in order to attain the result which it pursues".[78] While falling short of a full direct effect under EC law – which would give rise to a *contra legem* conclusion and force the substitution of the incompatible national legislation – the Court went a long way with this decision to align the legal effects of "third pillar" framework legislation with "first pillar" Community law principles, reducing to a considerable extent the legal "pillar divide".

Institutional practice has also contributed to the blurring of the pillar divide. The analysis of the texts adopted by the Council in the AFSJ domain contradicts to some extent the traditional assumption that "communitarisation" tends to lead to a greater use of binding instruments than this is normally the case in "intergovernmental" areas of cooperation. Yet the annual statistics of the Council show in fact that in one of the "communitarised" fields of Title IV TEC – immigration – more non-binding than binding instruments have been used for much of the last decade whereas in one of the "intergovernmental fields" of Title VI TEU – judicial cooperation in criminal matters – more binding than non-binding instruments have been adopted. Furthermore the "communitarised" field of external border controls has seen a nearly equal use of both binding and non-binding measures.[79] This points towards a rather pragmatic attitude of national delegations in the Council: rather than having a systematic preference in the context of the "third pillar" for "intergovernmental" non-binding measures they are prepared to make an extensive use of binding instruments if they are dealing with a field which is more appropriate for legislative action – which is certainly the case for judicial cooperation in criminal matters.

Other examples for cross-pillar institutional dynamics can be found with regard to the special agencies. With the establishment of Frontex in 2005 the original "third pillar" model of an operational agency tightly under the control of the Member States – which was first implemented in the case of Europol and Eurojust – was transposed to the "first pillar" field of border controls. In the "reverse" direction certain "first pillar" features – such as qualified majority voting in the Management Board and funding out of the EU budget – have been transposed to Europol on

---

78 Case C-105/03, *Pupino* [2005] ECR I-5285, para. 43.

79 See Jörg Monar, "Specific factors, typology and development trends of modes of governance in the EU Justice and Home Affairs domain", *NEWGOV Working Paper*, No. 1/D17, European University Institute, Florence, 2006. (http://www. eu-newgov.org/database/DELIV/D01D17_Emergence_NMG_in_JHA.pdf), pp. 17-18.

the occasion of the replacement of the Europol Convention by the new Europol Decision of April 2009.[80]

4. Conclusions and Prospects

4.1. The Question of the Specificity of the Institutional Dimension of the AFSJ

The institutional framework of the AFSJ has some features which can surely be regarded as quite specific: the particular sensitivity from the national sovereignty and political point of view – which has oriented the framework towards cooperation and coordination rather than integration; the strong intergovernmental origins – which have left their traces to the present day; the diversity of the policy fields to be dealt with – which have encouraged both diversification and growth; the important operational dimension – which has led to the establishment of the special agencies; the high degree of differentiation – which adds complexity to institutional procedures; and the "pillar divide" – which has required some peculiar arrangements not helping with effectiveness. The institutional growth both in terms of new institutional structures created and staff numbers has been very significant, exceeding most probably by far that of any other single policy-making domain of the EU since the entry into force of the Treaty of Amsterdam.

Yet the specificity of the AFSJ institutional context should also not be overstated. Considerable national sensitivity on the competence and control side as well as major operational needs, for instance, are challenges with the CFSP/ESDP domain had had to struggle with as well – with different institutional solutions as a result. And institutional proliferation and shifts in the institutional balance have been a recurrent feature of the European construction since its inception.

It would therefore be fair to say that the institutional development of the AFSJ has added some new features – such as the special operational agencies – to the institutional phenomena of the European Union and that its evolution has been different because of its intergovernmental origins, but that there has also been a growing convergence with the mainstream EU institutional framework mainly as a result of Commission, Parliament and Court acquiring and developing roles more and more similar to the Community model.

---

80 Council Decision of 6 April 2009 establishing the European Police Office (Europol) (2009/371/JHA), *O.J.*, No. L 121 of 15 May 2009.

4.2. Prospects under the Treaty of Lisbon

The Treaty of Lisbon is likely to have a significant impact on the institutional framework of the AFSJ firstly because of the formal abolition of the "pillar divide" and secondly because of new shifts in the institutional balance:

Under the revised Treaty architecture all AFSJ fields will be governed by Title V TFEU which constitutes a "merger" of current Title IV TEC and Title VI TEU. As a result, the current pillar division will be removed, and with it the current legal divide cutting through the AFSJ. The current EC legal instruments will take the place of the current Title VI TEU instruments in the fields of police and judicial cooperation in criminal matters. This will put an end to the need to adopt "parallel" legislative acts under the different "pillars" in certain domains of "cross-pillar" implications (such as money laundering) and reduce the potential for controversies over the appropriate legal basis, and should thus contribute to more efficiency and transparency in the decision-making process.

Some elements of the "pillar divide" will survive however, and this mainly in the field of decision-making rules. This brings us already to the shifts in the institutional balance. The Treaty of Lisbon will make the current "co-decision" procedure – under the new name of the "ordinary legislative procedure" (Article 294 TFEU) – with an exclusive right of initiative of the European Commission, co-decision by the European Parliament and qualified majority (QMV) voting in the Council – the standard decision-making procedure under new Title V TFEU. This will result in a corresponding other major shift of the institutional balance in favour of the Parliament. The corresponding gain of democratic accountability and participation for the AFSJ could be reinforced by a closer cooperation between the European Parliament and the national parliaments whose position with regard to AFSJ matters will be strengthened by the Treaty.[81] The reform of the decision-making procedures should also to some extent work in favour of the Commission, whose negotiation position will be strengthened by the extension of QMV in the Council. Needless to say that the extension of QMV is also likely to enhance the decision-making capacity of the Council. In addition to the codification of the strategic planning and "emergency brake" functions of the European Council with regard to the AFSJ,[82] the introduction of a non-rotating President could strengthen the supreme political leadership function of the European Council in this domain. The introduction of the new *Comité de sécurité intérieure* (COSI), finally,

81 See the chapter by Emilio De Capitani in this volume.

82 See the chapter by Hans G. Nilsson and Julian Siegl in this volume.

could increase operational planning and coordination capabilities and provide an opportunity for the streamlining of part of the Council working structures.[83]

Yet there will be a range of exceptions, and it is in this respect that the shadow of the "third pillar" looms large: as currently under Title VI TEU the Commission will have no exclusive right of initiative in the fields of police and judicial cooperation in criminal matters. Article 76 TFEU provides that initiatives can also be brought by a quarter of the Member States. A unanimity requirement will still apply to certain issues of particular sensitivity to Member States, creating important "islands" of unanimity in the general passage to QMV.[84] Similar exceptions can also be found with regard to the role of the European Parliament which will be given co-decision powers on most of the AFSJ issues, but will be limited to assent or consultation procedures on the subject matters requiring unanimity in the Council. All this means that from an institutional and procedural point of view the old "pillar" division will continue to exist at least to some extent. This "hidden" continuation of the pillar separation could lead to a continuation of some of the existing problems with the adoption of cross-cutting packages of measures on certain JHA issues because of different procedures, majority requirements and forms of involvement of the Parliament.[85]

The Treaty of Lisbon will remove most of the current restrictions on the role of the Court and thus strengthen its position.[86] Yet with regard to the Court the "third pillar" will also have an afterlife, although it will be a temporary one: by virtue of Article 9 of the Lisbon Treaty "Protocol on Transitional Provisions" the legal effects of EU acts adopted on the basis of the "third pillar" prior to the entry into force of the Treaty of Lisbon will be preserved until those acts are repealed, annulled or

83 See the chapter by Michael Niemeier and Marc André Wiegand in this volume.

84 Unanimity will continue to apply to measures concerning family law with cross-border implications (Art. 81(3) TFEU), the establishment of minimum rules concerning "other" (i.e. not explicitly mentioned) aspects of criminal procedure (Art. 82(2)(d) TFEU), the identification of "other" (i.e. not already explicitly mentioned) areas of serious crime for which minimum rules concerning the definition of criminal offences may be introduced (Art. 83(1) TFEU), the establishment of the European Public Prosecutor's Office (Art. 86(1) TFEU) and the possible extension of its mandate (Art. 86(4) TFEU), legislative measures regarding operational cooperation between national law enforcement authorities (Art. 87(3) TFEU) and the laying down of the conditions and limitations under which national law enforcement authorities may operate in the territory of another Member State (Art. 89 TFEU).

85 This is largely in line with the compromises already arrived at in the context of the Constitutional Treaty. See Jörg Monar, "Justice and Home Affairs in the EU Constitutional Treaty. What added value for the 'Area of Freedom, Security and Justice'?", *European Constitutional Law Review*, Vol. 1, 2005, pp. 226-246.

86 See the chapter by Vassilis Hatzopoulos in this volume.

amended. While this seems at least technically a necessity Article 10 of the same protocol has clearly been inspired by a political desire not to give up too quickly on some of the intergovernmental elements of the "third pillar". According to this article – for a period of five years – the powers of the Commission to launch infringement proceedings (Article 258 TFEU) will not be applicable to legal acts adopted on the basis of Title VI TEU and the restricted powers of the Court of Justice of the European Union with regard to these acts under Title VI TEU of the Treaty on European Union will remain unchanged.

In spite of the formal abolition of the "pillar divide" part of the old institutional regime is therefore going to survive well into the second decade of the century. To that one has to add the fact that the new Treaty reconfirms with only minor changes all of the existing "opt-out/opt-in" arrangements in favour of the UK, Ireland and Denmark to the fields of police and judicial cooperation. This concession, which is likely to increase differentiation within the AFSJ with all the "costs" it entails for the institutional framework, had to be made to the three "opt-outs" in order to make them accept the "communitarisation" (in all but name) of the Title VI EU fields within the framework of new Title V TFEU with the introduction of qualified majority voting and co-decision by the European Parliament.

Overall the reforms of the Treaty of Lisbon, while likely to have a significant positive impact on decision-making and democratic control, are therefore not without some more shadowy sides. Much will depend on whether the new multi-annual "Stockholm Programme" to be adopted by the European Council in December 2009 and the subsequent Action Plan to be drawn up by the Commission for its implementation from 2010 onwards will use the new action possibilities offered by the Treaty – why minimising as far as possible the effects of its more questionable compromises. The splitting of the AFSJ portfolio between two Members of the European Commission announced by President Barroso in November 2009, with Cecila Malmström (Sweden) going to be responsible for home affairs (i.e. internal security, migration and borders) and Viviane Reding (Luxembourg) for justice, fundamental rights and citizenship,[87] can be taken as an indication that the Commission considers the post-Lisbon and post-Stockholm AFSJ as an area of considerable further growth and hence worthy of further institutional investment.

---

87 European Commission Press Release, IP/09/1837, 27 November 2009. Interestingly, a corresponding splitting up of the DG JLS (see the contribution of Richard Lewis and David Spence in this volume) into two separate Directorate-Generals seems to have been ruled out for the time being. This could help with maintaining policy coherence across the different AFSJ fields.

4.3. Final Remark

After this introductory voyage through the intricacies of the challenges and dynamics of the institutional framework of the AFSJ one final consideration of the *dictum* of Jean Monnet mentioned at the beginning might set a useful reminder. And this time it is the first part of it, that which says "*rien ne se crée sans les hommes*".[88] The creation of institutions does not stop with their formal establishment but is a process of constant creation and development taken forward on a daily basis by those who are part of those institutions and try to ensure that they deliver on their objectives. As analysts of these institutional developments we should therefore always keep in mind that real people are behind each of those institutions and consider how much human effort (and surely often enough also frustration) is involved in the daily functioning and development of what in the case of the AFSJ has become a big and complex institutional framework. The importance of people is all the greater if new structures have to be created in response to new political demands – and most of the relevant AFSJ structures are such a recent creation. We should appreciate what has been achieved and – in the interest of the European citizens who depend on "freedom, security and justice" – wish those who give life to those institutions the best possible success for the future.

---

88 [Nothing is created without men].

PART TWO

THE EU INSTITUTIONS

CHAPTER 2

The Council in the Area of Freedom, Security and Justice

Hans G. NILSSON & Julian SIEGL

1. Introduction

The Council of the European Union (EU) is a key institution for policy-making in the Area of Freedom, Security and Justice (AFSJ). In the Justice and Home Affairs (JHA) Council formation, it brings together the ministers of justice and of the interior from the Member States, including in some Member States ministers with special responsibility for immigration and asylum issues.[1] The Council of Ministers, as it is also called, thus constitutes the main channel for national interests in the creation of an AFSJ, while at the same time being a central factor for progress in this dynamic process.

As main decision-making authority in the AFSJ, the JHA Council has adopted more than 1,200 texts since 1999, making the area one of the most active and fast developing EU policy domains.[2] The JHA Council provides a common institutional framework for the AFSJ, which unites diverse policy fields with different legal bases under one common objective. The communitarised first pillar contains migration and asylum policy, border control, and judicial cooperation in civil matters in Title IV TEC. In most of its parts, the Council acts by qualified majority voting and shares the legislative power with the European Parliament (EP) in the co-decision procedure. As an important exception, legal migration and family law with cross-border implications are subject to the consultation procedure which requires unanimity in the Council. In the first pillar domain of the AFSJ, the normal legal instruments of Community law are used. The intergovernmental third pillar combines police cooperation and judicial cooperation in criminal matters in Title VI TEU. Here, the Council mainly acts by unanimity and only consults the EP in the consultation procedure. Furthermore, the third pillar domain has distinct legal instruments, namely framework

1 Formally, the Council constitutes one single body which meets in nine different formations.

2 See the research conducted by Jörg Monar on the number of texts adopted in the JHA Council; e.g. Council of the European Union, *Preparing the Stockholm Programme – Conference in Bruges on 4-5 March 2009*, 10576/09, Brussels, 2 June 2009, p. 2.

decisions, decisions, common positions and conventions (Article 34 TEU), although it may be noted that conventions are no longer used in practice. The divide in the Treaty basis is reflected in the Council's complex working structure in the AFSJ, with different strings and procedures of decision-making in the two pillars. Along with differentiated integration as another central feature of the AFSJ, the pillar divide has significant impact on the JHA Council and its policy-making.

The JHA Council represents the ambivalence which characterises EU policy-making in the AFSJ. On the one hand, its actions are driven by the need for closer cooperation and integration in the JHA domain, and by the understanding of mutual benefits arising from this. Moreover, the JHA ministers are well aware of the demands and expectations of citizens in this field. On the other hand, it is in the Council where Member States try to defend their competencies regarding core elements of national sovereignty in this sensitive area. This inherent tension between innovation and reluctance turns the JHA Council into the decisive venue for negotiations on the emerging AFSJ. This chapter analyses the institutional features of the JHA Council, and the interplay of the main actors within this framework. It will start with an overview of the working structure of the Council in the AFSJ, before the main bodies and actors involved in policy-making in the JHA Council will be examined. As will be shown, efficient and coherent policy-making in the JHA Council is subject to several institutional challenges, and the changes brought about by the Treaty of Lisbon only partly overcome these challenges.

2. The Working Structure of the Council in the AFSJ

The institutional framework for decision-making in the JHA Council is marked by distinct structural features. These features reflect both the origins of policy-making in the JHA field outside the Community structure and the successive development of the Treaty basis with the Treaties of Maastricht (1993) and Amsterdam (1999). Council decision-making in the AFSJ takes place in a four-tier system, as opposed to the classical three-tier Council hierarchy with working groups of experts from national ministries, the Committee of Permanent Representatives (COREPER) and the Council meetings at ministerial level. The Council's working structure in the JHA field features an additional level, situated between the working groups and COREPER. It is composed of two coordination committees bringing together senior officials from the national ministries. This fourth layer is a relict of the TREVI group, an intergovernmental framework for JHA cooperation outside the Community Treaty basis in the pre-Maastricht period. As one central predecessor of the Union's activities in the JHA field, the TREVI working groups were incorporated in the Council's decision-making structure with the creation of the third pillar by the 1993 Treaty of Maastricht. The group of coordinators of the TREVI cooperation became the Article K.4 Committee, a senior coordination committee named after the respective article in the Maastricht version of the TEU. The TREVI steering groups system equally found way into the Council's institutional framework after the Treaty of Maastricht. This initially led to a five-tier decision-making system in the JHA field in the post-Maastricht period, with three steering groups on immigration and asylum, on police cooperation, and on judicial cooperation. Due to coordination problems and limited effectiveness, however, the three steering groups disappeared on occasion of the institutional changes with the Treaty of Amsterdam (1999), establishing the current four-tier system in the Council's working structure in the AFSJ.[3]

The Treaty of Amsterdam has had a significant impact on the Council's decision-making structure in the JHA field. On the one hand, with the incorporation of the Schengen Acquis into the Treaty framework, differentiated integration has become a central feature of the AFSJ. Considerable institutional adaptation has been required to manage the national opt-outs of Denmark, Ireland, and the United Kingdom, as well as the participation of non-Member States in the Schengen cooperation.[4] On the other hand, as a result of the partial communitarisation of the third pillar, the pillar divide in the Treaty basis of the AFSJ has had a significant effect on the working structure of the JHA Council. It gave rise to the creation of two senior coordination committees by splitting up the former K.4 Committee. The Article 36 Committee is the direct descendant of the K.4 Committee, named after the new article number in the TEU and often referred to as CATS, after its French abbreviation (*Comité de l'Article Trente-Six*/Committee Article Thirty-Six). Its counterpart in the first pillar is the Strategic Committee on Immigration, Frontiers and Asylum (SCIFA), which was not established by the Treaties, but on the basis of a mandate of COREPER. Judicial cooperation in civil matters is negotiated in the normal three-tier structure. The two senior coordination committees CATS and SCIFA supervise the working parties involved in legislative work in their respective field. As an unusual fourth layer in the JHA Council's working structure, the two coordination committees reflect the sensitive nature of many aspects in the AFSJ, on which in particular the ministries of the interior seek to keep control through an additional supervisory level. The political

[3] The Council's working structure in the AFSJ will be reformed if the Treaty of Lisbon enters into Force. See section below on "The Lisbon Treaty: overcoming the challenges? in this chapter.

[4] See section below on "Differentiated integration" in this chapter.

importance attributed to the JHA field at national level has thus been translated into a complex decision-making structure in the Council.

As a key institutional feature of the AFSJ, the pillar divide is also reflected in the working group structure of the JHA Council (see Chart in annex 1). The working parties with legislative functions are separated according to the Treaty basis of their respective area of responsibility.[5] The working groups generally consist of national experts with instructions from their ministries, and of representatives of the Presidency, the Council Secretariat and the Commission. In the first pillar, five working parties are subordinate to SCIFA, including the working party on migration and expulsion which meets in the two formations migration admission and migration expulsion. As mentioned above, there is no senior coordination committee in judicial cooperation in civil matters. The Committee on Civil Law Matters directly reports to COREPER. Formally one preparatory body, the committee meets in different formations depending on the agenda – e.g. general questions, contract law or Rome III. In the third pillar, CATS coordinates the work of nine working parties, six of them dealing with police and customs cooperation and two with criminal judicial cooperation. The ninth working party, the multidisciplinary working group on organised crime, consists of national experts from both the ministries of interior and the ministries of justice to ensure evaluation and cooperation between police, customs and judicial authorities in the fight against organised crime. The working parties in the two pillars thus operate under different senior coordination committees with separate strings of decision-making, although third pillar working parties may also deal with certain files under qualified majority voting and co-decision having a first pillar (EC) legal base.

In addition to the working parties preparing the legislative work of the JHA Council, there are also horizontal working groups with evaluation and coordination functions in the JHA field. All horizontal working groups report directly to COREPER. The working party on collective evaluation and the working party on Schengen evaluation perform evaluation tasks regarding both the first and third pillar domain of the AFSJ. Furthermore, focusing on specific aspects, four horizontal working groups seek to ensure coordination within the Council between the AFSJ and other policy fields. With a cross-pillar perspective, the High Level Working Group on Asylum and Migration deals with countries of origin and transit in the framework of the Union's global approach on migration. It reports to the General Affairs and External Relations Council formation. The Horizontal Working Party on Drugs (HDG) brings together high level experts in law enforcement, external relations

---

5 See the diagram on the working structure of the Council in the AFSJ in annex 1.

and health in order to coordinate all relevant EU policies, programmes, and initiatives in the field of drugs. The working party on civil protection serves as a venue to discuss any matter related to civil protection, such as the management of consequences of disasters. Finally, the working party on legal data processing plays a coordinating role in the creation of the European e-Justice system, with a horizontal relevance concerning many areas of civil, criminal and administrative law. Besides the standing Council working groups, there are *ad hoc* working parties on JHA matters which cease to exist once their specific mandate has been fulfilled. These *ad hoc* working parties are either linked to one pillar, as the Ad Hoc Group on Information Exchange dealing with information exchange relating to the third pillar. Or they are of a horizontal nature, as the JHA-RELEX Ad Hoc Support Group established to increase coherence within the external dimension of the AFSJ. Additionally, the Council Presidency can initiate the temporary formation of Friends of the Presidency Groups to support the preparatory bodies in dealing with specific policy issues. These groups owe their name to the fact that the Presidency determines the participating Member States, even though practice is that all Member States participate. For instance, the French Presidency in 2008 took the initiative of convening a JHA-RELEX Friends of the Presidency Group, with the task to consider possible working methods to better manage JHA external relations. The outcome of this group led to the creation of the JHA-RELEX Ad Hoc Support Group. Likewise, the Czech Presidency set up a Friends of the Presidency Group in January 2009 to develop a practical guide for facilitating the Schengen evaluation process, and the Swedish Presidency in the second half of 2009 initiated a Friends of the Presidency Group to negotiate the issue of individual rights in criminal proceedings. Temporary and *ad hoc* groups thus contribute to the preparatory work for the JHA Council.

The various policies constituting the AFSJ are brought together at COREPER level, where the Member States' Permanent Representatives deal with all JHA issues in COREPER II. The fact that the Permanent Representatives – and not the deputy Permanent Representatives in COREPER I – are in charge of JHA matters indicates the political importance attributed to the AFSJ. COREPER II is assisted by the JHA Counsellors, who meet as an informal group and report directly to COREPER II, CATS and SCIFA. The JHA Counsellors are officials from the national ministries of the interior and of justice who are delegated to the Permanent Representations. Permanently based in Brussels and in close contact with each other, the JHA Counsellors build a sort of "mini-COREPER", and their meetings can contribute considerably to the efficiency of the decision-making process. COREPER II prepares the meetings of the JHA Council, which is at the top of the Council's working structure in the AFSJ.

3. Institutional Features of Policy-Making in the JHA Council

Within the Council's working structure in the AFSJ, the Council Presidency, the General Secretariat, the preparatory bodies including the meetings of the JHA Counsellors, and the JHA Council constitute the central bodies and actors. After examining these institutional factors and their contribution to the dynamic progress in the AFSJ, the role of the European Council and the European Commission as additional factors of influence on policy-making in the JHA Council will be analysed.

3.1. The Council Presidency

In the AFSJ, as in other EU policy fields, the rotating Presidency fulfils essential functions in the Council by taking charge of agenda-management, brokerage and representation.[6] In this area, however, holding the Presidency is a significant task for the Member State in office. Yet, the Presidency's privileged access to information and resources has also proven to be an opportunity for setting legislative priorities and shaping the decision-making process.

The features of EU policy-making in the AFSJ – characterised by dynamic progress and high output within a complex institutional structure – implies a heavy workload for the Member State holding the Presidency. The Council Presidency sets the agenda, and arranges and chairs the large number of meetings on all levels of the JHA Council's working structure. During the Swedish Presidency in 2009, the Swedish ministry of justice – as there is no ministry of the interior in Sweden – was responsible for 51 working parties of the Council. This accounts for about 25% of the entire Council agenda. At the same time, the Presidency acts as a broker within the Council, often together with the Commission especially in negotiations on co-decision files. This brokerage function requires additional informal meetings for searching compromises, particularly with regard to sensitive and sovereignty-related policy issues negotiated in the AFSJ, and it is further hindered by the unanimity requirement in third pillar. As in other policy fields, the General Secretariat provides assistance to the Presidency in order to fulfil these tasks. With regard to agenda-setting, the Presidency's poten-

[6] Jonas Talberg, "The power of the Chair: formal leadership by the Council Presidency", in: Daniel Naurin and Helen Wallace (eds.), *Unveiling the Council of the European Union. Games Governments Play in Brussels* (Basingstoke: Palgrave Macmillan, 2008), p. 187.

tial to actually influence the Council's agenda in the AFSJ is limited not only by the proposals brought up by the Commission, but also by the multi-annual working programmes.[7] In the third pillar, however, the Member States' right of initiative provides a facility for agenda-setting, which is used by the Presidency or groups of Member States holding successive Presidencies. Furthermore, the trio Presidencies, introduced to increase continuity in the work in the Council, enable the Member States involved to prioritise certain issues for a longer period. The further completion of the AFSJ was one of the three main themes of the team programme of Germany, Portugal and Slovenia for the period from January 2007 to June 2008.[8] This policy field was also covered at length in the subsequent 18-month programme prepared by France, the Czech Republic and Sweden.[9]

In several cases, Member States were able to use their Council Presidency to provide input and leadership towards the creation of an AFSJ. During its Presidency in 2007, Germany successfully pursued its objective of transposing main provisions of the Prüm Treaty into EU law.[10] The Treaty, signed by seven Member States in the German town of Prüm in 2005 and thus not part of the *acquis communnautaire*, was aimed at establishing a network for data exchange to enhance cross-border police and judicial cooperation. At an informal meeting of JHA ministers in January 2007, the German Presidency tabled a first proposal to integrate the Prüm Treaty into the Union's legal framework.

Informal JHA Council meetings, held once per term in the country of the Presidency, generally enable the Presidency to present its priorities, as it can deliberately set the agenda of these meetings. Without the constraints of formal procedures, the working atmosphere at these meetings might sometimes lead to substantial results, although the meetings nowadays tend to be more and more formalised due to the participation of 400 to 500 persons. After the informal meeting in Dresden in January 2007 and based on a legislative initiative made in February 2007, the German Presidency pushed the negotiations on the transposition of the Prüm Treaty through the different Council working

7 For the role of the multi-annual programmes in policy-making in the JHA Council, see section below on "The European Council" in this chapter.

8 Council of the European Union, *18-month Programme of the German, Portuguese and Slovenian Presidencies*, 17079/06, Brussels, 21 December 2006.

9 Council of the European Union, *18-month Programme of the Council*, 11249/08, Brussels, 30 June 2008, pp. 65-77.

10 Rocco Bellanova, "The 'Prüm process': the way forward for EU police cooperation and data exchange?", in: Elspeth Guild and Florian Geyer (eds.), *Security versus Justice. Police and Judicial Cooperation in the European Union* (Aldershot: Ashgate, 2008), pp. 203-224.

levels, leading to political agreement at the JHA Council in June 2007. Consequently, strategic planning by the Council Presidency can bring forward legislative action in the AFSJ. The possible impact of the Council Presidency is also illustrated by the European Pact on Immigration and Asylum, which contains common political objectives and strategic guidelines in migration and asylums policy. Prepared to make migration one of the priorities of its Presidency in the second half of 2008, France circulated a first draft of the Pact already in January 2008.[11] It then started bilateral negotiations with other Member States already during the Slovenian Presidency in the first half of 2008. These extensive negotiations resulted in a broad agreement at the informal meeting of JHA ministers in Cannes in July and the adoption of the Pact at the European Council in October 2008. However, the example of the Pact also reveals the limits of a Presidency to impose its interests. As the original version of the Pact drew criticism from some Member States, it was considerably watered-down to a compromise text. In order to shape the agenda and to foster its own priorities, the Presidency depends heavily on the consent of the other Member States in the Council.

The Presidency is also in charge of the relations with other EU institutions. In this respect, the contact between the Council and the European Parliament (EP) is of growing importance in the AFSJ. The co-decision procedure in the first pillar – where the Council legislates together with the EP – has a significant effect on policy-making in the JHA Council. In order to avoid lengthy negotiations in the conciliation committee, both institutions generally seek to reach an agreement in the first or second reading of the co-decision procedure by cooperation and exchange on all stages of the decision-making process.[12] In fact, in the period from 2004 to 2008, more than half of the regulations and directives adopted by the Council and the EP in the AFSJ were agreed in first reading.[13] In this period, the Regulation on the law applicable to non-contractual obligations (Rome II) was the only legal act to be agreed on in the conciliation committee. The increasing number of co-decision files in the AFSJ amounts to a considerable workload for the Presidency and the assisting Council Secretariat, which includes monitoring of legislative progress in the EP, practical coordination of work schedules with the Parliament, and searching for compromises.

---

[11] Jörg Monar, "Justice and Home Affairs", *Journal of Common Market Studies*, Vol. 47, No. s1, Annual Review, 2009, p. 154.

[12] Fiona Hayes-Renshaw and Helen Wallace, *The Council of Ministers* (Basingstoke: Palgrave Macmillan, 2006, 2nd ed.), pp. 207-227.

[13] See the table in the annex 2. The figure is currently around 65%. See also the chapter by Emilio De Capitani in this volume.

3.2. The Council Secretariat

The General Secretariat of the Council plays an important role in policy-making in the JHA Council. In the first decade of JHA cooperation after the Treaty of Maastricht, the Secretariat even acted as an initiative-taker and motor. The JHA field is covered by the Directorate-General H of the Council Secretariat, one of the largest DGs in the Council. It consists of a coordination team, a secretariat for data protection, and four directorates. These are the directorates 1) asylum, visa, immigration, frontiers; 2) judicial cooperation in civil and criminal matters; 3) police and customs cooperation, Schengen; and 4) civil protection. Moreover, the position of a special Counter-Terrorism Coordinator (CTC) was established after the March 2004 Madrid train bombings, with the task to align the Council's work in combating terrorism and to overview all instruments available for this purpose in the EU.[14] This position further highlights the importance attributed to the AFSJ in the Council Secretariat.

As in other policy fields, the Council Secretariat organises and coordinates the policy-making of the JHA Council and its working parties, and ensures their coherence. Furthermore, and arguably of particular importance in the AFSJ, the Council Secretariat provides substantial support for the Council Presidency. It thus reduces the heavy workload for the Presidency in the JHA field. On the one hand, the experience of the Council Secretariat as "institutional memory" can be helpful for the Presidency when dealing with the at times very technical dossiers in the complex working structure of the JHA Council. On the other hand, because of the trust Member States grant to it as "honest broker", the Secretariat adds to the searching for compromises in the JHA Council. The actual role of the Council Secretariat in this respect varies between Presidencies. The Council Secretariat's role depends on the general attitude of the Member State holding the Presidency, on the experiences and resources of this Member State, and on the working relationship between officials from the Presidency and the Council Secretariat.

A particular feature of the AFSJ is the Council Secretariat's role in mutual evaluations. Based on a Joint Action of 1997, the Council Secretariat assists the Presidency in preparing peer evaluations of the application and implementation of measures in the fight against organised crime in the Member States. As the rounds of mutual evaluation proceed during the term of several successive Council Presidencies, it is in fact the Council Secretariat which carries them out. Four rounds of mutual evaluation were conducted until 2009. The fifth round on financial crime and financial investigation is scheduled for the period from 2009

---

14 See the chapter by Gilles de Kerchove and Serge de Biolley in this volume.

to 2011. With its leading role in mutual evaluations, the Council Secretariat contributes to an important element of building trust in the AFSJ, which also helps to identify needs and possibilities for future forms of operational coordination in the fight against organised crime.

In the first years of JHA cooperation after the Treaty of Maastricht (1993), the Secretariat played a considerable role as initiative-taker and legal drafter.[15] While the Commission was restricted by curtailed competencies and limited resources in the third pillar, the Council Secretariat could draw on the Council of Europe expertise of some of its senior staff to take the role of a motor for policy progress in the JHA field. The impact of Secretariat leadership can be illustrated by the creation of Eurojust, the EU body for judicial cooperation established in 2002. The Council Secretariat lobbied for the inclusion of Eurojust in the Tampere Programme, ensured cooperation between the successive Presidencies involved in the negotiations that followed, and provided the formula for an institutional setting of Eurojust acceptable for all Member States.[16] The Council Secretariat still plays an important role in Council decision-making in the AFSJ, though its impact on the outcome depends on the cooperation with the Council Presidency.[17]

3.3. The Preparatory Bodies

The work of the preparatory bodies constitutes a central element of policy-making in the JHA Council. The various groups and committees not only prepare the work for the JHA Council. In general, a large number of decisions in the Council are settled at working party level and in COREPER. For the AFSJ, estimations assume a share of 80%. Corresponding to the dynamic progress and high output produced in the AFSJ, the Council working groups in the JHA field meet on a regular basis. For instance, the Visa Working Party held meetings on 23 days in 2008, and the Working Party on Cooperation in Criminal Matters convened on 25 days during the same year. These regular sessions contribute to an increasing socialisation of the national experts involved in preparatory work for the JHA Council, and help building networks with a European perspective. Together with the common professional background of the national delegates and their shared technical expertise, this socialisation can facilitate the negotiations in the AFSJ at working group level.

---

15 Hans G. Nilsson, "The Justice and Home Affairs Council", in: Martin Westlake and David Galloway (eds.), *The Council of the European Union* (London: John Harper, 2004, 3rd ed.), pp. 137-138.

16 Derek Beach, "The facilitator of efficient negotiations in the Council: the impact of the Council Secretariat", in: Naurin and Wallace (eds.), *op. cit.*, pp. 219-237.

17 Talberg, *op. cit.*, p. 201.

When a new legislative proposal is on the table, negotiations in the Council usually start with the reading of the text in the working party in charge of the dossier. On important legislative proposals, the JHA ministers might first hold a general debate at a Council meeting. During the readings in the working group, the legislative proposal is examined in detail, and the national experts – with instructions from their ministries – ask for clarifications and express their reservations. The readings at working group level aim at a common understanding of the dossier among the Member States. For this purpose, the Commission explains certain aspects of its proposal in more detail and seeks to respond to questions and concerns. If an initiative has been taken by a Member State, or by a group of Member States, it is for the lead Member State to explain the initiative. At the same time, the working parties try to identify the uncontroversial provisions of the dossier as well as its main points of disagreement. Furthermore, compromise proposals are tabled by the Presidency, the Commission or other Member States to reduce the number of reservations. As master of the agenda, the Presidency decides on the number of readings in the working group and on the timing for referring the complete dossier to the higher levels of the Council's working structure. Already during the readings in the working group, the Presidency can refer the most controversial aspects of a legislative proposal to the JHA Council to receive political direction for the negotiations. Agreement on ostensibly political matters might therefore be found already at working group level, while very technical provisions might cause disagreement and are referred to more senior levels of the decision-making structure. In general, however, the four-tier system in the JHA Council's working structure makes it relatively difficult to take decisions on controversial aspects at working group level. There is a tendency in decision-making in the AFSJ to refer the negotiations on controversial points from the working parties to the senior coordination committees or higher up in the Council's working structure.

Following the four-tier system in the JHA field, all legislative proposals in the AFSJ – except for those on judicial cooperation in civil matters – are examined by the senior coordination committees before they are discussed by COREPER II. CATS and SCIFA, consisting of senior officials from the national ministries at the level of Directors or Director Generals, usually meet once per month. They have the task to ensure horizontal coordination of policy-making in their area of responsibility and to provide strategic guidelines. Set up by a decision of COREPER II, SCIFA is mandated to give substantive input to the Permanent Representatives and to quickly forward the issues agreed at working party level. By contrast, the Treaty basis of CATS (Article 36 TEU) provides for a direct contribution of the Committee to the preparation of the JHA Council with regard to third pillar matters. In practice, however, CATS is subordinate to COREPER II. The Permanent Representatives thus fulfil their central role in the Council's working structure also in the AFSJ. Due to the working groups' tendency to refer controversial aspects to higher levels, CATS and SCIFA are often confronted with tasks of problem-solving and searching for compromises. However, the two committees sometimes neither have the technical expertise of the working groups nor the political position of COREPER to resolve these problems. This often results in a repetition of arguments already known from the working groups. Therefore, controversial points of decision-making in the AFSJ might be referred to COREPER II even if they are not essentially political in nature.

As the most senior preparatory body in the Council, COREPER is of central importance for policy-making in the JHA Council. According to the Treaty and the Council's rules of procedure, COREPER is responsible for preparing the work of the Council, and it examines the items on the agenda of the Council meetings in advance. At COREPER level, the two strings of the JHA Council's working structure – at working group level and between CATS and SCIFA – are brought together. COREPER II seeks to ensure not only coherence between first and third pillar policy-making in the AFSJ, but also consistency of JHA matters with policies and actions in other EU policy fields. At the same time, COREPER II serves as a filter to reduce the workload of the Council meetings, as the Permanent Representatives try to find agreement on outstanding points and finalise decisions in place of the JHA ministers. In general, the AFSJ carries considerable weight on the agenda of COREPER II. This is because of the dynamic legislative progress in the AFSJ, the political importance of many issues under negotiation, and the tendency in the JHA Council's preparatory bodies to refer controversial points to higher levels of the working structure. However, partly due to the level of technical detail of some issues referred to it, COREPER II does not always fulfil its filter function in the AFSJ.[18]

The JHA Counsellors meetings can play a decisive role for finding compromise at different levels of the Council's working structure. The informal group meets frequently, often several times a week. For 2008, Council documents give evidence of 57 meetings of the JHA Counsellors. However, as Member States have several JHA Counsellors based at their Permanent Representations for the different policy fields of the AFSJ, the actual composition of the group depends on the agenda.[19] Several aspects turn the meetings of the JHA Counsellors into a favour-

[18] See section below on "The JHA Council" in this chapter.

[19] Most Member States have about five JHA Counsellors, though some have up to ten. The Presidency usually has twelve to fourteen Counsellors for the AFSJ.

able venue for reaching a compromise. On the one hand, the JHA Counsellors have close links to the national ministries which delegate them to Brussels. They regularly meet their national colleagues who attend session in CATS, SCIFA or at working group level, and might travel to their capital from time to time. Furthermore, due to their professional background, their personal contacts and their career perspectives after returning to the national level, the JHA Counsellors usually maintain a feeling of belonging to "their" national ministry. At the same time, the professional experience in the national ministries provides them with a general knowledge of their area of responsibility. The JHA Counsellors also gain technical expertise on the files under negotiations, as they generally follow the discussions in the working groups. On the other hand, based at the Permanent Representations, the JHA Counsellors have close links to the Permanent Representatives as key actors in Council decision-making. The distance to their capital might also give the JHA Counsellors a certain room for manoeuvre, which helps to reach compromises. The permanent presence in Brussels and the high number of meetings foster the socialisation of the JHA Counsellors at EU level, and the personal contacts might increase the level of trust between them. Negotiations in the JHA Counsellors meetings are generally more personal, conducted only in English or French without translation. Taken together, these features lead to a particular problem-solving capacity of the JHA Counsellors meetings, which can have a significant impact on the decision-making process in the JHA Council.

Due to the informal status of the JHA Counsellors meetings, neither the precise function of this group nor its position in the Council's working structure is explicitly defined. COREPER II, the senior coordination committees, and sometimes also the working parties refer files to the JHA Counsellors in order to examine outstanding issues, to discuss changes or new compromise proposals, and to finalise drafts. It is the Presidency which decides to hold a meeting of the JHA Counsellors. They also join other committees to participate in their negotiations. At the same time, the JHA Counsellors often examine the position of the European Parliament in the legislative procedure, and they might prepare the Council's position in the co-decision procedure. The JHA Counsellors meetings thus provide an additional and important venue for decision-making, which contributes to the legislative process but also adds to the complexity of the Council's working structure in the AFSJ.

3.4. The JHA Council

The JHA Council is the central venue for decision-making in the AFSJ. Here, Member States' ministers of the interior and of justice meet every other month to discuss, negotiate and legislate on JHA matters. As each Member State is represented by one minister at the Council table, the JHA Council is *de facto* divided into two configurations. The ministers of the interior and the ministers of justice meet separately to deal with those issues on the agenda which concern their respective field of competence. Some Member States, such as France and Finland with special ministries for immigration, even send three ministers to the JHA Council meetings. The exact portfolio of the ministers can also vary, depending on the division of portfolios in national governments. The Council's Treaty basis only requires the presence of a representative of each Member State at ministerial level (Article 203 TEC). Therefore, Member States might also be represented at the Council table by State Secretaries who must, however, be authorised to commit their government. The Council meetings are chaired by the Presidency, and the Commission is represented at the table by the Commissioner for Justice, Liberty and Security. Each national minister is accompanied by a delegation, consisting of the Permanent Representative and at least three advisers. Together with the delegations from the Presidency, the Council Secretariat and the Commission, around 150 persons are present in the conference room at a Council meeting, not counting the translators or the persons sitting in the listening room. Furthermore, JHA ministers often meet their colleagues from Iceland, Lichtenstein, Norway, and Switzerland in the margins of the Council to discuss Schengen-related issues in the Mixed Committee (COMIX).[20] JHA Council meetings usually take place six times per year. Their venue is the Council's Justus Lipsius building in Brussels, except for sessions in April, June, and October, when Council meetings are held in Luxembourg. Additionally, once during each Presidency, the JHA ministers convene for an informal meeting in the country of the Presidency. All these regular meetings increase personal contacts between the ministers in the JHA Council, and this facilitate decision-making in the AFSJ.

Policy-making in the JHA Council makes a major contribution to the dynamic progress in the AFSJ. The JHA ministers adopted 164 texts in 2007 and 144 texts in 2008.[21] According to the general mode of Council decision-making, and based on the work of its preparatory bodies, the JHA Council adopts texts in two ways. At each Council meeting, a list of "A" items is usually approved without further discussion by the ministers, as these texts were already approved by COREPER II. Either, the so-called "A points" were already discussed by the ministers at a previous meeting and sent back to COREPER for finalisation. Or,

---

20 See section below on "Differentiated Integration" in this chapter.

21 Jörg Monar, "Justice and Home Affairs", *Journal of Common Market Studies*, Vol. 46, No. s1, Annual Review, 2008, p. 109; Monar, "Justice and Home Affairs", *op. cit.*, Annual Review, 2009, p. 151.

similar to administrative acts and statutory instruments at national level, agreement on these texts was already reached by COREPER and requires formal adoption by the ministers. As the Council of Ministers constitutes one single institution, JHA texts might also be adopted as "A points" by other Council formations, and JHA ministers approve texts from other policy fields as part of their "A" items list. A second group of texts – so-called "B points" – are subject to discussion in the Council meeting, and might be adopted by the ministers afterwards. As regards legislative voting, the voting behaviour in the JHA Council is characterised by a preference for consensus. Even in procedures which only require a qualified majority, the JHA ministers often adopt legislative texts by consensus or unanimity. Regarding the 28 regulations and directives adopted in the AFSJ between 2004 and 2008 in co-decision and with qualified majority voting in the Council, only four legal proposals were rejected by one or more Member States. In addition to the general preference for consensus in the Council, the often politically sensitive nature of dossiers in the AFSJ might prevent JHA ministers from voting against their colleagues.

Besides the formal adoption of texts, JHA ministers actively engage in negotiations during the legislative process. JHA Council meetings are used for exchanges of views and general debates on legislative proposals. Moreover, JHA ministers debate key aspects of important dossiers, either to give political direction on controversial aspects while the text is still under negotiation at working group level, or to resolve outstanding points of disagreement. These policy debates are sometimes held on the basis of a questionnaire by the Presidency focussed on central provisions of a proposal. Due to the political status of the ministers and their room for manoeuvre, and facilitated by the negotiation experience of most of them, negotiations in the JHA Council meetings can result in outcomes which might not be achievable at other levels of the Council's working structure. In order to reach an agreement, the Presidency can also start bilateral contacts during the Council session with those delegations which keep a reservation on a dossier. However, reaching an agreement sometimes turns out to be a difficult task in the JHA Council.

Even at ministerial level, legislative decision-making in the AFSJ might be hindered by the political importance and sensitive nature of the issues under negotiation, especially when unanimity is required in the Council. Difficult negotiations often lead to lengthy decision-making processes in the AFSJ. The legislative process of the 15 framework decisions – the legal instrument in the third pillar to approximate laws and regulations of the Member States – adopted between 2004 and 2008 took 38 months on average.[22] The unanimity requirement as the main

[22] See the table in annex 2.

obstacle to rapid policy-making might even impede an agreement altogether. This can be exemplified by the negotiations on a proposal for a Council Framework Decision on certain procedural rights in criminal proceedings. Regardless of the debates on the proposal in four JHA Council meetings, various compromise proposals made by the Presidency, and a call from the European Council to finalise the negotiations, the JHA Council was unable to reach an agreement on this file.[23] However, non-decisions clearly constitute an exception in policy-making in the AFSJ. In general, the JHA Council is able to reach an agreement on the files under negotiation, even if only after a lengthy decision-making procedure and at the price of a substantially watered-down outcome. Here, the output of the JHA Council reflects the general tendency of negotiations under the unanimity requirement towards lowest common denominator outcomes.

Even if the JHA ministers reach a political agreement on a legislative proposal, the formal adoption of the text might be delayed by parliamentary scrutiny reservations. In these cases, the JHA ministers only reach a general approach on the legislative proposal subject to parliamentary scrutiny reservations. In the intergovernmental third pillar, the degree of national parliamentary scrutiny is arranged by the Member States individually.[24] The various procedures of parliamentary involvement to control executive decision-making sometimes result in extensive delays before the formal adoption of an act in the JHA Council. This is often due to constitutional requirements in some Member States, where the national parliament has to adopt the national law implementing a framework decision before a parliamentary scrutiny reservation can be lifted. For instance, the JHA Council reached a consensus on a Framework Decision on the fight against organised crime in April 2006, but outstanding parliamentary reservations in six Member States delayed the formal adoption of the text for more than two years until October 2008. In this respect, the 2008 Council Framework Decision on combating racism and xenophobia constitutes an extreme case. More than six years of negotiations on the proposal, which resulted in a general approach at the JHA Council in April 2007, were followed by another period of 19 months until the formal adoption of the text in November 2008. Consequently, even after lengthy negotiations in the JHA Council, the formal adoption might be further delayed by scrutiny reservations of national parliaments.

---

23 Council of the European Union, *2807th Meeting of the Council of the European Union (Justice and Home Affairs)*, 10699/07, Brussels, 13 September 2007, p. 12.

24 Steve Peers (ed.), *EU Justice and Home Affairs Law* (Oxford: Oxford University Press, 2006, 2nd ed.), p. 52.

Despite the dynamic progress in the AFSJ, the meetings of the JHA Council have been subject to criticism regarding their efficiency. Due to the tendency in the AFSJ to refer controversial points to higher levels of the Council's working structure, parts of the JHA Council meetings might be devoted to detailed negotiations on issues which are not essentially political in nature. This has attracted criticism from the JHA ministers, as it is expressed in the reports of the Future Group on Police and Immigration and the Future Group on Justice. These informal advisory groups brought together the ministers of the interior and the ministers of justice of the six Member States holding the Council Presidency in the period from 2007 to 2009. The groups were established in order to identify new challenges and define possible solutions for future action in the AFSJ. The report of the Future Group on Police and Immigration criticises the lengthy discussion-making procedures and the lack of time for substantial discussion in the JHA Council.[25] Likewise, the report of the Future Group on Justice complains about the fact that technical aspects and drafting issues of less political interest appeared on the JHA Council's agenda.[26] According to the Future Group on Justice, this reduces the opportunities to discuss real political issues, which sometimes leads to inefficient JHA Council meetings and discourages ministers to attend. There is in fact a tendency in some Member States to send a State Secretary instead of JHA ministers to the Council sessions. At each of the seven JHA Council meetings in 2008, at least three Member States were not represented by a minister, while other Member States usually send both their minister of the interior and their minister of justice. At three of these meetings in 2008, even more than a quarter of all national delegations did not include a minister. However, irrespective of this tendency and the criticism mentioned above, the JHA Council has proven to be a very active decision-making body.

3.5. The European Council

The AFSJ regularly appears on the agenda of the European Council, and this makes the summits of the Heads of State or Government an additional factor of influence on the JHA Council and on policy-making in this area in general. The European Council sets strategic guidelines for the future development of the ASFJ, and it provides impetus for the decision-making process in the JHA Council. The space regularly

25 Council of the European Union, Freedom, Security, Privacy – European Home Affairs in an open world – Report of the Informal High-Level Advisory Group on the Future of European Home Affairs Policy ("The Future Group"), 11657/08, Brussels, 9 July 2008, p. 19.

26 Council of the European Union, High-Level Advisory Group on the Future of European Justice Policy – Proposed Solutions for the Future EU Justice Programme, 11549/08, Brussels, 7 July 2008, pp. 9 & 11.

devoted to JHA issues in the European Council Presidency Conclusions further demonstrates the political importance of the AFSJ.

By adopting multi-annual programmes, the European Council sets policy orientations and priorities for the further development of the AFSJ. With the Tampere Programme (1999-2004), the Hague Programme (2005-2009), and the future Stockholm Programme (2010-2014), strategic planning is a distinctive feature of the AFSJ and affects policy-making in the JHA Council. The Tampere European Council in October 1999 marked a key event in the participation of Heads of State or Government in JHA policy-making. At this meeting, the European Council placed the creation of the AFSJ at the top of the Union's political agenda and developed an ambitious working programme for this purpose. It was only the second time in the history of the Union that an entire European Council was devoted to a single policy issue.[27] This step was motivated by the rather unsatisfactory Vienna Action Plan of 1998, which was worked out as a framework to implement the provisions on the AFSJ in the Treaty of Amsterdam. Based on a Commission Communication, mainly drafted in CATS and SCIFA and adopted by the JHA Council in December 1998, the measures provided for in the Vienna Action Plan displayed a relatively low level of ambition. Therefore, the Heads of State or Government took the lead at the Tampere European Council, supported by a meticulous planning by the Finnish Presidency and assisted by the Council Secretariat. In Tampere, the Heads of State or Government set a number of ambitious policy orientations and priorities, which resulted in the first multi-annual working programme for the AFSJ. The JHA ministers, however, were not deeply involved in the preparation of the Tampere Programme, although an informal meeting was held in Turku in September 1999. This has been seen as a reason for certain non-cooperation of the JHA Council in the aftermath, leading to mixed results regarding the implementation of the programme.[28] The probable reason for this, however, might be the sensitive nature of the ambitious objectives set at the Tampere European Council. In any case, the JHA ministers took a much more active part in the preparations of the subsequent Hague Programme. The draft of the Hague Programme was developed in the JHA Council and mainly "rubber-stamped" by the European Council.[29] Regarding the preparation of the next multi-annual programme for the period from 2010 to 2014, the Swedish Presidency in 2009 went a step further. The process of developing the future Stockholm Programme involves not only the JHA

27 The first one was the extraordinary European Council meeting on employment in November 1997.

28 Jan Werts, *The European Council* (London: John Harper, 2008), p. 134.

29 Peers, *op. cit.*, p. 22.

ministers – the informal meeting of JHA ministers in Stockholm in July 2009 was entirely devoted to the programme – but also to a great extent the Council's senior level committees in the AFSJ. Even though the Heads of State or Government thus no longer play the same leading role in drawing up the agenda in the AFSJ, the formal adoption by the European Council still gives considerable political weight to the multi-annual programmes. It generally makes the JHA Council subject to political pressure from the European Council, as the Heads of State or Government can call on the Council to implement the programmes. This is further enhanced by an evaluation system ("scoreboard"), under which the Commission reports on the implementation of the multi-annual programme to the European Council each year.

Similar to the multi-annual programmes, the European Council also sets guidelines for integration in the AFSJ by adopting sectoral action plans and strategic programmes, and by monitoring their implementation. Examples for this are the repeatedly amended EU Action Plan on Combating Terrorism or the Global Approach to Migration.[30] In order to increase the political weight of the 2008 European Pact on Immigration and Asylum, the French Presidency successfully promoted its adoption by the European Council. As the Pact also exemplifies, the priority of the AFSJ on the European Council's agenda increases when a Head of State or Government shows a strong interest in the AFSJ. The French President Nicolas Sarkozy advocated the idea of a European Pact already during the national election campaign in 2007, and made it a priority of the French Presidency in 2008.[31] Similar to other action plans and strategic programmes adopted by the Heads of State or Government in the AFSJ, the Pact also includes a report and review mechanism. With the regular monitoring of the implementation and the impact of texts adopted at previous summits, JHA issues have a considerable share in the European Council's "rolling programme".[32]

In addition to its role as agenda-setter, the European Council monitors the policy developments in the AFSJ and seeks to take the decision-making process forward. On a regular basis, the Heads of State or Government take stock of policy-making in the AFSJ, sometimes in a comprehensive and detailed way. In the Presidency Conclusions, the European Council regularly welcomes progress achieved on key dossiers in the AFSJ, or it calls on the Council to intensify work on files

---

30 Council of the European Union, *Brussels European Council 15/16 December 2005 – Presidency Conclusions*, 15914/1/05, Brussels, 30 January 2006, pp. 9-14; Council of the European Union, *EU Action Plan on Combating Terrorism*, 7233/1/07, Brussels, 29 March 2007.

31 Monar, "Justice and Home Affairs", *op. cit.*, Annual Review, 2009, p. 154.

32 Westlake and Galloway (eds.), *op. cit.*, p. 187.

under negotiation in this domain. This might include precise deadlines for the JHA Council – sometimes also for the European Parliament – to reach political agreement on a pending dossier. The provisions in the Presidency Conclusions on the AFSJ are mainly drafted by COREPER II. In 2007 and 2008, JHA matters were on the European Council's agenda at two meetings each year, which resulted in a total of 18 pages of Presidency Conclusions dealing with the AFSJ. On these 18 pages, only 15 sentences were different from the draft conclusions agreed by the Permanent Representatives. Although some of the sentences were politically sensitive, many of these changes were minor or purely editorial. This again demonstrates the important role of COREPER in the AFSJ.

In exceptional cases, the European Council even directly engages in decision-making in the AFSJ. At the extraordinary European Council meeting in September 2001 after the 9/11 terrorist attacks, the Heads of State or Government agreed on the introduction of a European Arrest Warrant, whereas the JHA Council had a more modest approach on this issue. The European Council directed the JHA ministers to finalise this agreement at the JHA Council in December 2001 at the latest. At their informal meeting in Ghent in October 2001, the Heads of State or Government stepped in again when the JHA Council could not agree on the abolition of double criminality, and they instructed the Council to abolish this principle for a wide-ranging set of offences. In this particular case, with the issue of extradition belonging to the core of national sovereignty, the European Council acted as ultimate decision-making authority in the AFSJ. This resulted in an agreement on the European Arrest Warrant at the JHA Council meeting in December 2001, the final confirmation at COREPER in the following week, and the formal adoption of a framework decision by the JHA Council in June 2002. The European Arrest Warrant has arguably become the biggest success in EU criminal judicial cooperation.[33] While such direct decision-making in the AFSJ by the Heads of State or Government is rather exceptional, their regular political interventions carry considerable political weight and serve as an impetus for further development. The European Council thus complies with its intention declared at Tampere to maintain the AFSJ at the very top of the political agenda, often with explicit reference in the Presidency Conclusions to the demands and expectations of citizens in this field.

---

33 Isabelle Pérignon and Constance Daucé, "The European Arrest Warrant: A growing success story", *ERA-Forum*, Vol. 8, No. 2, 2007, pp. 203-214.

3.6. The European Commission

The Commission constitutes an additional factor of influence on policy-making in the JHA Council, with particular importance in the first pillar domain of the AFSJ. Initially, the Commission's role in the JHA field was limited in the Treaty of Maastricht, and it was only with the Treaty of Amsterdam that it gained full right of initiative in all areas of the field. At the beginning, the Commission service was only a task force, and it only became a full-fledged Directorate-General in October 1999. The number of staff has increased steadily to some 700 persons. Representatives of the Commission are generally present in the Council working groups, and the Commissioner for Justice, Liberty and Security takes part in the JHA Council meetings.

The Commission initially played a rather modest role in policy-making in the JHA Council. At the beginning of JHA cooperation in the EU, national ministries of the interior and of justice regarded the Commission with suspicion, as they were only used to work in a purely intergovernmental setting in the Council of Europe and in the United Nations. With the Treaty of Amsterdam, however, and the advent of the dynamic Commissioner Antonio Vitorino, the Commission started to gain in influence and to obtain Member States' confidence. As agenda-setter, honest broker, and manager of ever increasing financing programmes, the Commission now plays a considerable part in policy-making in the JHA Council. Strengthened by its exclusive right of initiative and qualified majority voting in the Council, the Commission exerts influence especially in the first pillar, where it serves as a motor of integration. In certain other areas, however, Member States are still cautious about the role of the Commission in policy-making in the JHA Council, notably in areas such as police cooperation and counter-terrorism which touch upon the provision of security as core function of the state.

4. Institutional Challenges to Policy-Making in the JHA Council

Irrespective of high output produced in the JHA Council, there are several institutional challenges to efficient and coherent policy-making in the AFSJ. These challenges arise from differentiated integration in the AFSJ, from the pillar divide, and, to a lesser extent, from the interrelation and overlapping of JHA policies with other policy fields. The Council has reacted to these challenges with a number of institutional arrangements and pragmatic solutions.

4.1. Differentiated Integration

As a central feature of the AFSJ, differentiated integration poses a challenge for coherent policy-making in the JHA Council. The opt-outs of Denmark, Ireland, and the United Kingdom on the one hand, and the participation of the non-Member States Iceland, Liechtenstein, Norway, and Switzerland in the Schengen cooperation on the other hand, result in a varying territorial scope of the AFSJ and increase the complexity of the Council's working structure in this area. In practice, the national opt-outs in the AFSJ are often circumvented in the Council by pragmatic, consensus-orientated norms.[34] The opt-out protocols of Denmark, Ireland and the United Kingdom – relating to migration and asylum policy, judicial cooperation in civil matters, and the Schengen cooperation – differ in their legal design and in their implications for the policy fields they cover. Consequently, it is not always evident whether a proposal is subject to an opt-out or not. This sometimes leads to different interpretations of the opt-out protocols. Regarding two Regulations on passports and on the border agency Frontex, disagreement about the scope of the British and Irish Schengen opt-out resulted in a judgement of the European Court of Justice.[35] In general, even if a proposal is covered by an opt-out, the delegation affected remains at the negotiation table at all levels of the Council's working structure. The delegation participates in shaping the decision, although the relevant minister is not allowed to vote on the legal act. This is in line with the general preference for consensus in decision-making in the JHA Council, and also due to the fact that measures subject to opt-outs are often linked to areas where all Member States fully participate. This pragmatic "participatory" solution facilitates decision-making in the JHA Council in practice, though it does not reduce the legal complexity arising from the various national opt-outs.

The participation of the non-Member States Iceland, Liechtenstein, Norway, and Switzerland in the Schengen cooperation is ensured by institutional arrangements at all levels of the Council's working structure in the AFSJ. In the institutional arrangement of the Mixed Committee (COMIX) procedure, the relevant working groups and the senior coordination committees meet with delegations of the four non-Member States to discuss all aspects relating to the Schengen Acquis. The COMIX procedure is also applied at COREPER II and ministerial level. In the margins of COREPER II and the JHA Council, the Permanent

---

34 Rebecca Adler-Nissen, "Behind the scenes of differentiated integration: circumventing national opt-outs in Justice and Home Affairs", *Journal of European Public Policy*, Vol. 16, No. 1, 2009, pp. 62-80.

35 *O.J.*, No. C 51, 23 February 2008, p. 5.

Representatives and the JHA ministers of all EU Member States meet their colleagues from the four countries associated with Schengen. The need to integrate all States participating in the Schengen cooperation into the decision-making process thus adds to the complexity of the Council working-structure in the AFSJ.

4.2. The Pillar Divide

The pillar divide arguably poses the biggest challenge to efficient and coherent policy-making in the AFSJ. The JHA Council is confronted with differences in the legal basis, the legal instruments, and the legal procedures of the first and the third pillar. This artificial divide between closely interrelated policy fields makes coherent policy action across the pillars a difficult task. Such cross-pillar action is necessary, for instance, in the fight against illegal immigration in the first pillar, which also requires third pillar measures to combat trafficking in human beings. As another example, counter-terrorism even requires measures to be taken in all three pillars. Separate policy processes might lead to an imbalance in policy outcomes, as the co-decision procedure and qualified majority voting in the Council have an impact on both pace and substance of legislative action. E.g. in the data protection regime, there are significant differences in the protection of personal data between the first and the third pillar.[36] Furthermore, as a consequence of legal complexity arising from the divide in the Treaties, policy-makers might be facing uncertainty regarding the correct legal basis and instrument for intended legal action. Concerning the question of Community competencies in criminal matters, different interpretations of the Treaty basis resulted in judgements of the European Court of Justice on a Framework Decision on environmental crime and on a Framework Decision on ship-source pollution.[37] With regard to the Directive on data retention, Ireland unsuccessfully challenged the legal basis of the instrument.[38] The pillar divide can thus be a heavy burden on policy-making in the JHA Council.

The reproduction of the pillar divide in the Council's working structure further impedes comprehensive cross-pillar action in the AFSJ. The split of the JHA Council's working structure – at working group level and between the senior coordination committees – leads to two separate strings of decision-making, which give rise to coordination problems. The two working parties with functions in both the first and third pillar domain of the AFSJ – the Working Party on Collective Evaluation and

36 Monar, "Justice and Home Affairs", *op. cit.*, Annual Review, 2009, p. 166.

37 Valsamis Mitsilegas, "The competence question: the European Community and criminal law", in: Guild and Geyer (eds.), *op. cit.*, pp. 153-170.

38 *O.J.*, No. C 82, 4 April 2009, pp. 2-3.

the Working Party on Schengen Evaluation – only perform evaluation tasks. With a view to cooperation in civil and criminal law, the report of the Future Group on Justice criticises the artificial divide in JHA Council's work.[39] The report emphasises the need for restructuring the working groups and proposes to "arrange them by general topics irrespective of the different legal basis".[40] In exactly the same wording, that recommendation had already been a result of the Haga Process. This process was launched by the Swedish Presidency in 2001 to improve efficiency of the working methods and the working structure of the JHA Council.[41] However, the alternative structure of the JHA working parties developed in the Haga Process was not implemented afterwards, as this reform process generally did not result in real changes in the working of the JHA Council.[42] Restructuring the JHA Council's working groups thus remains a field of action for future attempts to enhance efficiency and coherence in policy-making in the AFSJ, and the Swedish Presidency in 2009 again initiated a process in this direction.

4.3. Overlapping Policy Areas and the External Dimension of the AFSJ

The various policy fields combined in the AFSJ are linked with and affected by other policy areas, and this requires coordination in the Council for coherent and efficient policy-making. Ensuring coordination between the AFSJ and other policy fields is – apart from COREPER and the senior committees – the task of four horizontal working parties mentioned above. These are the High Level Working Group on Asylum and Migration, the Horizontal Working Party on Drugs, the Working Party on Civil Protection, and the Working Party on Legal Data Processing. Furthermore, if the scope of a legislative proposal in the AFSJ extends beyond the field of responsibility of the JHA ministers, policy-making in the Council may include *ad hoc* arrangements across different policy areas. Legislative measures on labour migration, as for example, do not only deal with the admission to the territory, but also with access to the labour market and social security rights granted to third-country labour migrants. Therefore, the JHA ministers held a joint meeting – also referred to as "Jumbo Council" – with the ministers for employment and social policy in December 2007, where they discussed two legislative proposals for Council Directives on labour migration. During

---

39 Council of the European Union, 11549/08, *op. cit.*, p. 9.

40 *Ibid.*, p. 10.

41 Council of the European Union, *Working Methods in the JHA Area*, 10336/01, Brussels, 26 June 2001, p. 5.

42 Council of the European Union, *Alternative Structure of the Working Parties in the JHA Area*, 5549/02, Brussels, 22 January 2002; Nilsson, *op. cit.*, p. 136.

the negotiations on these two proposals in the Working Party on Migration and Expulsion, most national delegations also included employment experts. Moreover, the Slovenian Presidency in 2008 organised a joint meeting of migration and social security experts to discuss in every detail one provision on access to social protection. As an alternative model of cooperation, the Czech Presidency in 2009 referred the negotiations on provisions related to social security schemes from the Working Party on Migration and Expulsion to the Social Questions Working Party, together with a precise mandate and a number of questions to focus on. Working groups sometimes also hold joint meetings, for instance between the second and third pillar Working Parties on Terrorism. However, by cooperating across different policy fields, policy-making in the Council might be complicated by different views of sectoral experts and inconsistencies in the position of a Member State.

Due to the blurring divide between internal and external security, the external dimension of the AFSJ is of growing importance and poses a particular challenge to coherent policy-making in the Council.[43] For instance, efficient counter-terrorism measures or efforts to manage migration flows require cooperation with third-countries. The Council has reacted to this demand with several programmes and institutional arrangements, seeking to increase coherence within the external dimension of the AFSJ and with the Union's external policy in general. In December 2005, the Council adopted a JHA-RELEX Strategy for the external dimension of the AFSJ.[44] This strategy sets thematic priorities, defines underlying principles, and presents delivery mechanisms and tools, all with a view to enhance consistency in all external aspects of policy-making in the AFSJ. It also includes a monitoring mechanism with progress reports by the Council Secretariat and the Commission. With the aim to further ensuring continuity in the JHA-RELEX policy, the French, Czech and Swedish Presidencies presented the first JHA External Relations Multi-Presidency Work Programme in July 2008.[45] Furthermore, the JHA-RELEX Ad Hoc Support Group mentioned above was created in October 2008. It was established with a mandate to facilitate the exchange of information and to support the committees and working parties involved in the JHA-RELEX area. A proposal to create a full-fledged JHA-RELEX working party found no majority in the Council, as many national delegations preferred maintaining the in-

43 Wyn Rees, "Inside out: the external face of EU internal security solicy", *Journal of European Integration*, Vol. 30, No. 1, 2008, pp. 97-111.

44 Council of the European Union, *A Strategy for the External Dimension of JHA: Global Freedom, Security and Justice*, 15446/05, Brussels, 6 December 2005.

45 Council of the European Union, *JHA External Relations Multi-Presidency Work Programme*, 10546/08, Brussels, 1 July 2008.

volvement of existing committees and working groups in the external dimension of the AFSJ. The mandate of the JHA-RELEX Ad Hoc Support Group originally provides for a restricted period until the end of 2009, though the Swedish Presidency in 2009 proposed to transform it into a permanent group. For the moment, however, the definite institutional arrangements in the Council's working structure to coordinate the external dimension of the AFSJ remain open.

5. The Lisbon Treaty: Overcoming the Challenges?

The Treaty of Lisbon provides for fundamental changes in the Treaty basis of the AFSJ, with significant impact on the JHA Council if the Treaty enters into force. The Treaty of Lisbon reunites the Treaty basis of the AFSJ in the new Title V of the Treaty on the Functioning of the European Union (TFEU). The ordinary legislative procedure of the TFEU – with the Commission's exclusive right of initiative, co-decision with the European Parliament and qualified majority voting in the Council – is, in general and with some exceptions, applicable to all aspects of the AFSJ. The Treaty of Lisbon thus formally brings the pillar division in the AFSJ to an end, with a considerable impact on the procedures and decision-making processes in the JHA Council. Moreover, the Treaty of Lisbon provides for the creation of a Council committee – already named COSI (*Comité de Sécurité Intérieure*/Committee on Internal Security) – with the task of ensuring that operational cooperation on internal security is promoted and strengthened (Article 71 TFEU). Therefore, if it enters into force, the Treaty of Lisbon will lead to a restructuring of the Council's working parties in the AFSJ. The Swedish Presidency in 2009 opened the discussion on this reform, including the proposition that the senior committees should only take on a strategic role and no longer be involved in legislation under the Treaty of Lisbon. This proposition, however, was met with resistance by some delegations. In general, the agreement of the Member States on the Treaty of Lisbon was only achieved by introducing a range of exceptions in the new Title V of the TFEU. Because of various specific procedural provisions in the Treaty of Lisbon, police and criminal judicial cooperation in fact remain separated from other policy fields in the AFSJ. Consequently, the changes provided for in the Treaty of Lisbon only partly reduce the legal complexity and procedural inconsistency which the JHA Council is currently confronted with.

The new Treaty codifies the European Council's task to define the strategic guidelines for legislative and operational planning in the AFSJ (Article 68 TFEU). As this corresponds to the agenda-setting by the Heads of State or Government carried out via the Tampere Programme and the Hague Programme, the Treaty of Lisbon provides a legal basis for an already existing feature of policy-making in the AFSJ. The European Council is also assigned an important role in the so-called "emergency brake" mechanism introduced by the new Treaty. If a Member State considers that a draft Directive or Regulation on criminal procedure law or on minimum rules concerning the definition of criminal offences and sanctions affects fundamental aspects of its criminal justice system, it may request that the proposal be referred to the European Council. In this case, the "emergency brake" mechanism leads to a suspension of the ordinary legislative procedure, and the European Council has four months time to find a consensus and to refer the draft back to the Council. If applied, this mechanism thus provides a framework for the European Council to act as ultimate decision-making authority in the AFSJ. The "emergency brake" mechanism also includes that, if no agreement can be found in the European Council, a group of at least nine Member States may establish an enhanced cooperation by a simplified procedure (Article 82(2)(2) and Article 83(3)(2) TFEU). Enhanced cooperation might lead to further differentiation in the AFSJ. Furthermore, the opt-outs of Denmark, Ireland, and the United Kingdom are extended by the Treaty of Lisbon to police and criminal judicial cooperation. Consequently, the Treaty might even increase differentiated integration in the AFSJ and the inconsistency of its territorial scope, which might further add to the complexity in the institutional structure of the JHA Council.

6. Conclusions

As main decision-making authority, the Council makes a major contribution to the dynamic development of the AFSJ. Policy-making in the JHA Council has produced high output, despite the complexity in the Treaty basis and other institutional challenges. With institutional arrangements and pragmatic solutions, the JHA Council has demonstrated its capacity for institutional adaptation. This includes the important role of the informal JHA Counsellors meetings, the pragmatic handling of Member States' opt-outs in the decision-making process, the mixed committee procedure for non-Member States participating in the Schengen cooperation, and more specific arrangements such as the establishment of a JHA-RELEX Ad Hoc Support Group.

However, the institutional framework of JHA Council has also attracted criticism, mainly concerning the reproduction of the pillar divide in the working group structure and the four-tier system's tendency to refer controversial but not essentially political matters to higher levels. Furthermore, even if institutional arrangements and pragmatic solutions add to the efficiency of policy-making in the JHA Council, they also increase the complexity of the Council's working structure in the AFSJ. This might raise concerns on transparency and democratic control.

If it enters into force, the Treaty of Lisbon partly reduces the complexity in the Treaty basis in the AFSJ. Several changes and innovations laid down in the Treaty of Lisbon affect policy-making in the JHA Council and its working structure. This applies to the reuniting of the Treaty provisions on the AFSJ as a result of the formal abolition of the third pillar, additional opt-outs, and the possibility for direct interventions of the European Council and enhanced cooperation in the "emergency break" mechanism. However, the actual impact of the Treaty of Lisbon will depend on the institutional adaptation of the JHA Council to a new Treaty basis, and its practical application by the actors involved in policy-making in the AFSJ.

Annex 1:

The Working Structure of the Council in the AFSJ[1]

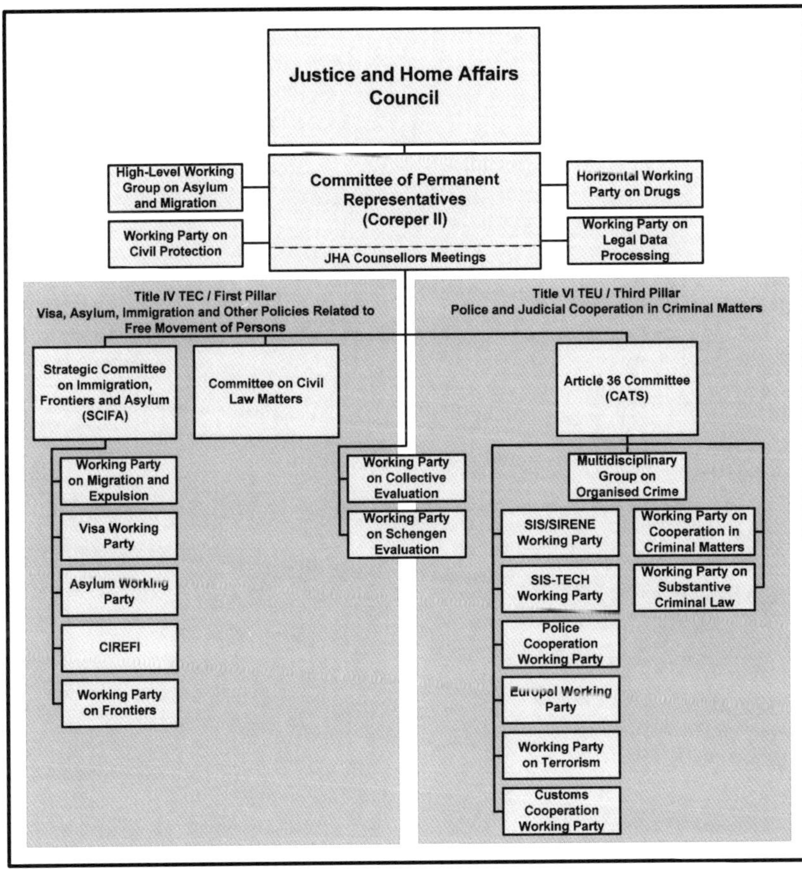

1 Without temporary and *ad hoc* groups; Council of the European Union, *List of Council Preparatory Bodies*, 11602/09, Brussels, 9 June 2009.

Annex 2:

Main Legal Acts Adopted by the Council in the AFSJ (2004-2008)[1]

1st pillar legal instruments Total	2004	2005	2006	2007	2008
Regulations of the EP and the Council	**3**	**3**	**8**	**5**	**3**	**22**
Ø decision-making process (months)	17	22	21	28	29	23
1st reading agreement EP and Council (number out of total of instruments)	1/3	1/3	6/8	3/5	3/3	14/22
Directives of the EP and the Council	**1**	**1**	**1**	**-**	**3**	**6**
Ø decision-making process (months)	35	16	6	-	36	28
1st reading agreement EP and Council (number out of total of instruments)	0/1	1/1	1/1	-	2/3	4/6
Council Regulations	**8**	**2**	**3**	**2**	**8**	**23**
Ø decision-making process (months)	11	8	4	12	17	12
Council Directives	**5**	**2**	**-**	**-**	**1**	**8**
Ø decision-making process (months)	23	41	-	-	24	28
3rd pillar legal instruments Total	**2004**	**2005**	**2006**	**2007**	**2008**
Council Framework Decisions	**1**	**4**	**2**	**-**	**8**	**15**
Ø decision-making process (months)	41	33	41	-	40	38
based on Member State(s) initiative (number out of total of initiatives)	0/1	2/4	2/2	-	2/8	6/15
Council Decisions (Art. 34 TEU)	**2**	**6**	**2**	**5**	**7**	**22**
Ø decision-making process (months)	9	17	9	20	15	16
based on Member State(s) initiative (number out of total of initiatives)	2/2	2/6	0/2	2/5	5/7	11/22

1 Including Regulations and Directives as part of the AFSJ *acquis* but adopted outside Title IV TEC; see European Commission, *JAI-Acquis*, October 2008.

CHAPTER 3

The Commission's Role in Freedom, Security and Justice[1]

Richard LEWIS & David SPENCE

1. Introduction: The Policy Context

This chapter discusses the evolution of the Commission's role in the so-called "third pillar" policy area, formerly known as Justice and Home Affairs and since the Treaty of Amsterdam "an Area of Freedom, Security and Justice" (hereafter "JLS", its French acronym).[2] The term "third pillar" is still often used, but this is now inaccurate, since the Treaty of Lisbon abolishes the "three pillar" concept. As with the Common Foreign and Security Policy, the EU's "second pillar", JLS began life as a purely intergovernmental policy area (Title VI TEU). It is not only the subject of political controversy over "competence" between the Commission and the Council, but it also receives a great deal of media attention since it covers issues high on the public agenda, ranging from policing and criminal justice through to drugs policy, immigration, asylum and counter-terrorism. JLS policy developed during the 1970s on an *ad hoc* basis in response to increased cross-border terrorism, drug smuggling and international crime. It evolved rapidly after the signature of the Schengen Convention in 1985 and reached undisputed relevance after the terrorist attacks in New York and Washington on 11 September 2001. The subsequent attacks in Madrid in 2003 and in London in 2005 ensured that European policy-making in the JLS field became a vital part of the EU policy landscape, epitomising how near to the citizen EU policy can be.

The Commission began as an observer of this originally intergovernmental process. Gradually, the Commission's expertise and its related first pillar competence, made it the policy-making focus of JLS, and embedded its responsibilities firmly in European Community legal

[1] This text is an updated and amended version of Chapter 11 of *The European Commission* (London: John Harper, 2006, 3rd ed.), edited by David Spence.

[2] In November 2004 the Commission's Directorate-General for Justice and Home Affairs was renamed 'Justice, Freedom and Security', and given the acronym based on the French Justice, Liberté et Sécurité, or JLS.

provisions. This chapter examines how JLS evolved to achieve almost full "communitarisation" in the Treaty of Lisbon and how the Commission's role became more central. While the Commission's efforts at policy-making within JLS were long constrained, it must be recalled that the seeds of Community competence in this policy area were present in the original Treaty of Rome's concern with free movement of goods (Article 3a), services, capital and people (Article 3c). "Communitarising" JLS, that is moving it from the third, intergovernmental pillar to the first, supranational, pillar was thus a logical consequence of integrated policy areas enshrined in the Treaty of Rome and managed by the Commission. Importantly, however, the process was slow, continually disputed and the subject of interinstitutional turf battles.

2. The Origins of Justice Freedom and Security Policies

The philosophy underlying an Area of Freedom, Security and Justice had its origins in the minds of the founders of the European Coal and Steel Community, itself part of the wider context of the European desire to prevent war and the totalitarian abuses that led to it in 1939. The challenge of European JLS policies over time has been to translate these concerns and ideals into an acceptable corpus of European law and practice, whilst respecting Member State prerogatives – the principles of subsidiarity and proportionality. The genesis of JLS policy lay in the Treaty of Rome's commitment to freedom of movement for goods, persons, services and capital. The free movement of "persons" was a cornerstone of the creation of the original common market. Underlying the concept was the assumption that common economic goals required labour mobility, and that this mobility would in turn bring about a host of other requirements relating to the transfer of social security rights and the protection of those who took the then relatively courageous step of working abroad in another Member State. Labour mobility became even more important with the advent of a common currency. The idea that this would bring in its wake issues of cross-border crime control and common frontier control lay far in the future. Indeed, the political implications of freedom of movement did not become apparent until the passage of the Treaty of Maastricht, signed at the end of 1992. Until then, only the economic consequences of free movement of persons were deemed pertinent.

Although the Single European Act of 1986 reiterated the ideals of its treaty predecessor with regard to the four freedoms, the Commission was mainly pre-occupied at the time with the freedom of movement for goods and capital on which Commission presidents and officials, particularly Jacques Delors, concentrated. This left the free movement of services and persons for later. Delors' and Internal Market Commissioner Lord Cockfield's contribution was the completion of the Single Market for goods and the laying of the foundations of the single currency. Very little intellectual capital was expended on the future policy area of JLS, despite budding interest in bringing the content of the Schengen Treaty into the Community sphere. The Schengen system was built on a loose system of border control cooperation agreed in the Luxembourg town of Schengen in May 1985 by France, Germany and the Benelux countries, the latter already enjoying an advanced open frontier system. The objective became free movement of persons within the internal borders of the EU. This implied an implementing convention designed to ensure that the security of the Schengen Member States would not be compromised as a result of lack of border controls. Implemented in 1990, this principally concerned asylum, visas and immigration. Significantly, each of these policy areas lay at the heart of national sovereignty.

Lord Cockfield's White Paper on completion of the Single Market in May 1985 (Commission 1985) did indicate that a Europe without frontiers could not be constructed without affecting a number of areas with which the Commission had never previously dealt. Cockfield articulated the general concern that opening frontiers and allowing goods to pass freely without customs or tax checks at national borders opened the way to potential abuse that would need to be controlled. At the same time, Commission officials concluded that the free movement within the EU had given birth to the notion of external as opposed to internal frontiers and that this had implications for people moving across internal frontiers. By logical extension, if free movement of lorry drivers, holiday makers, and business people were to be allowed within the Union, then admitting an individual and his or her chattels from outside the EU to one Member State meant admitting them to all. The European policy framework came later, despite the fact that the activities of terrorist groups in the 1970s and 1980s, notably the Provisional IRA, the Red Brigade and others, had already begun to set the agenda.

The Schengen agreements were the first solid Commission inroad into immigration and frontier controls, both of which long remained essentially intergovernmental. The Commission was a very present observer of the Schengen process until, in 1989, Adrian Fortescue, later to be the first Director General for JLS, was asked to reflect on the consequences for the EC of removing frontier controls.[3] The Community then began to move towards the incorporation of the Schengen arrangements into the EU Treaties, though it was only in 1999 with the Treaty of Amsterdam that this formally took place. Until then, they had

---

3 Adrian Fortescue, Justice and Home Affairs DG Moving into the Mainstream of European Commission, interview given for the European Commission Website 2002.

their own separate institutions deliberately mirroring those of the Council, since the Schengen agreements were envisaged as EU compatible and eventually absorbable.

There was, and still is, reluctance on the part of Member States to loosen their grip on a policy area which goes to the heart of sovereignty, namely with regard to who should be allowed on their territory. Some states, Denmark, the United Kingdom and – largely because of historical ties to the UK – Ireland, were indeed so reticent that they opted out of some or all of the arrangements that ensued – including Schengen. Even under the Lisbon Treaty the UK and Ireland would have the right to opt out of "Schengen building measures". According to the version of the relevant protocol, they might then have to withdraw from some of their existing opt-ins because the old and new provisions would cease to be compatible.

In terms of taking a political lead the Commission was thus demonstrably on sensitive ground. This reluctance of Member States led to the first tentative steps being taken on an intergovernmental basis, on the model of European Political Cooperation (EPC), which later became the second pillar. Indeed, although EPC largely dealt with foreign policy issues, its early committees also touched on issues relating to future JLS questions, such as consular cooperation and terrorism.

As a first step in concrete cooperation in this policy area, in 1975 the so-called TREVI group had been created by the European Council in Rome. It consisted of senior officials meeting in the margins of the EPC framework in three working groups: anti-terrorism, information and security; police cooperation (partly in response to cross-border football hooliganism); and organised crime and drugs. All these fora, including the EPC consular and terrorism working groups, included Commission participation. However, as in the early pre-Maastricht days of all EPC groups, the Commission was an observer and provider of information or occasional practical solutions based on the budgetary weight of the Community institutions. As for terrorism, participants had the impression that the importance or relevance of the information imparted by Member States' representatives was minimal. The detail necessary for meaningful coordination of policy or cross-border cooperation was left unspoken. Even in the consular affairs working group, it was difficult to make progress on substantial issues, such as the issuing of visas. Cooperation was confined to relatively trivial matters such as sharing car pools or printshop facilities. The essential feature of these tentative steps was the rigorously intergovernmental process. The European Parliament was absent from this process, as indeed was any reporting in the media. Importantly, however, the view was fast gaining ground that these issues were impossible to contain within the nation state framework and that EU action was therefore needed.

3. The Single European Act 1986 and the Treaty on European Union 1993

The Single European Act (SEA) was the result of the TREVI group's first hesitant attempts at cooperation in the field of JLS. De Lobkowicz describes the idea of free movement coming "out of hiding" as the completion of the Internal Market – the so-called 1992 programme – was announced.[4] The Single European Act (SEA) of 1986 reiterated the goal of free circulation of persons in a space without internal frontiers. Whereas the Treaty of Rome did not indicate a date by which free movement should be achieved, the SEA had set the time limit of 31 December 1992. The main problem of the SEA text was that legal responsibility for acting on this provision was left unstated. In addition, in a declaration attached to the Treaty, the Member States indicated that their power to act to protect their ultimate control of frontiers to prevent the ills of terrorism and crime, etc., remained. Admittedly, this did not prevent the creation in October 1986 of an Ad Hoc Group on Immigration (significantly by the UK Presidency). The Commission and the Council Secretariat were "associated" with the process as they were in EPC, albeit as in EPC, the Commission had no right of initiative.

The real breakthrough in JLS cooperation came with the Treaty on European Union (TEU) signed in Maastricht in 1992. The Treaty made formal mention of nine areas of interest: asylum, the crossing of external borders, immigration, combating drug addiction, combating international fraud, judicial cooperation in civil matters, judicial cooperation in criminal matters, customs cooperation and police cooperation. As Jörg Monar has pointed out, the issues were hardly new.[5] They had long been under discussion in various groups, so the "new" third pillar was in fact only new in that the issues now had a formal place in the Treaty. Adrian Fortescue argued that momentum had been built up over time for a radical new approach to be incorporated into treaty form: "for the first time the subjects had been identified as being necessary flanking measures for getting rid of frontier control [...]",[6] thus relating them to core

---

4 Wenceslas de Lobkwicz, *L'Europe de la sécurité intérieure. Une élaboration par étapes* (Paris: La Documentation Française, 2002).

5 Jörg Monar, "European Union – Justice and Home Affairs: A balance sheet and agenda for reform", in: Geoffrey Edwards and Alfred Pijpers (eds.), *The Politics of European Treaty Reform: The 1996 Intergovernmental Conference and Beyond* (London: Pinter, 1997) pp. 326-339.

6 Adrian Fortescue, unpublished internal speech to the legal service of the European Commission in 2002.

Community competence. This was given form in Title VI of Maastricht: "Cooperation in the fields of Justice and Home Affairs" – colloquially, but never officially known as "the third pillar".

Yet, the real achievements under Maastricht were actually few. Weak instruments, lack of clarity in the objectives, virtual exclusion of the European Parliament and the European Court of Justice from the process, lack of budgetary resources and what he called "the ubiquitous dead hand of unanimity" were all to blame, so that Desmond Dinan could comment:

> Given […] the cloak of […] confidentiality that shrouded the new Council formation and preparatory committee, the imprecision of JLS instruments and the ability of Member States to veto decisions, there was little or no headway on issues covered by the Third Pillar. Yet public support for EU-wide measures to combat illegal immigration and organised crime was remarkably high, despite widespread hostility to the EU and its institutions both during and after the Maastricht ratification crisis.[7]

This contradiction between public support and government reticence is a theme to which we return below. Importantly, however, despite this reticence many of the principles enunciated in soft law or in Commission position papers subsequently found their way into binding acts. In fact, "soft law" measures, consisting of non-binding declarations or recommendations of the Council that might be quietly ignored by the Member States, were in fact precursors of legal change. It was a slow process, but the Commission's expertise was growingly recognised. In 1994, the Member States were somewhat taken by surprise when the Commission produced a policy document on immigration and asylum,[8] a subject they had always deemed their sole preserve. Yet, the surprise was actually unfounded, for the Commission had invariably been associated with the various pre-Maastricht working groups and its Communication to the Council and Parliament on Immigration and Asylum Policies was a logical extension of the removal of frontiers. It was cited in discussions on immigration for many years thereafter.

Despite a seeming lack of progress, there were some advances in JLS policies. In May 1995, a uniform format for visas was agreed and in September, a binding list of countries requiring visas. Another advance of the post-Maastricht period was the passage of the Convention establishing Europol. Europol's main objective consisted of collating and disseminating information and facilitating the investigation of crime, whether international or domestic. Yet, political sensitivities cost Euro-

7 Desmond Dinan, *Ever Closer Union. An Introduction to European Integration* (Houndmills: Palgrave Macmillan, 2005), p. 568.

8 COM(94) 23 final of 23 February 1994.

pol three years after its convention was ratified (in July 1995) for it to enter into force, and even then its work was initially confined to anti-drug activities.

Although governmental hostility was certainly a reality, the contradictory phenomenon of the popular media calling for action in JLS was clearly a harbinger of further EU efforts, even if Commission initiatives were resisted or downplayed when they were made. In fact, as a concession to the Commission, amongst others, who wished to see greater "communitarisation" of the field, the Maastricht Treaty designated some subjects, notably asylum, immigration, drugs and civil judicial cooperation, as suitable to pass in due course into the first pillar. This was the so-called *passerelle* (bridge or gateway) mechanism, which was instrumental in levering certain aspects of JLS into a supranational framework and thus creating some unfinished business to be settled by the next Treaty, signed at Amsterdam in October 1997 and which entered into force on 1 May 1999.

4. The Treaty of Amsterdam

Adrian Fortescue argued that, after Amsterdam:

> Every chapter was ratcheted up: where Maastricht had given the Commission a right of initiative in the Third Pillar context, Amsterdam "communitarised". Where Maastricht had excluded any Commission right to take initiatives, Amsterdam gave it. The European Parliament's role was enhanced; money became available. The European Court of Justice entered the frame; the subject matter was listed by objective rather than just by catalogue.[9]

Although the section of the Amsterdam Treaty on police and judicial cooperation in criminal matters still spoke the intergovernmental language of "closer cooperation" and "joint actions", in sharp contrast, Article 63 TEC, relating to immigration and asylum, set a five-year timetable within which measures would have to be taken. And there were clear distinctions of procedure and objectives and a strengthening of the role of the Commission in policy formulation, despite its resource constraints, which hampered faster expansion and deepening of JLS. But, Amsterdam underlined three important issues affecting the role and powers of the Commission. First, it failed to gain "sole" right of initiative, despite the Treaty's explicit reference to the key area of immigration and asylum after 1 May 2004, when the Commission would gain that right. Second, unanimity remained the rule until 1 January 2005,[10]

---

9 Adrian Fortescue, unpublished internal speech to the legal service of the European Commission in 2002.

10 Since 1 January 2005, QMV and co-decision have been applied except for economic migration. Council Decision 2004/927/EC of 22 December 2004 (*O.J.*, No. L 396 of 31 December 2004).

and third, sensitive issues relating to cooperation in police matters and criminal justice remained in the restrictive intergovernmental "third pillar" (Maastricht) format. However, this was the principle. In practice, policy-making was somewhat different.

Although the Commission failed to gain sole right of initiative, the Member States in fact used their right of initiative on a limited scale, thereby leaving the field open for Commission initiatives, first through policy papers in the form of Communications or Green Paper consultative documents and then following these up with legislative proposals. Indeed, if the Commission considered that a Member State's informal ideas were sound, it worked with that state or took over the proposal itself. True, Member States frequently pre-empted the Commission (e.g. on the establishment of Eurojust), making the Commission tag along, and accommodating national positions as if they had been policy all along. If the Commission were not always successful in convincing some Member States of the added value of collective as opposed to national efforts,[11] its aspiration to play its classic policy motor role was clear. And it was in fact rare that the Member States did not look to the Commission to provide the background information and follow-up even when they themselves made the proposals. All this dovetailed well with Article 67 TEC, which laid down the procedure to be followed relating to Title IV TEC (free movement of persons) during the transitional period of five years. This specified that "the Commission shall [also] examine any request made by a Member State that it submit a proposal to the Council". It thus left a welcome loophole to the Member States and laid the main legal responsibility on the Commission. In sum, the overarching objectives in Article 61 TEC remained what they always were from the time of the Treaty of Rome, namely "measures aimed at ensuring the free movement of persons", though there was an important rider to the effect that this should be in conjunction with "flanking measures with respect to external border controls, asylum and immigration".

5. The Tampere European Council of October 1999

The key turning point in the process of translating the words of the Treaty of Amsterdam into concrete results was the special European Council held under the Finnish Presidency in Tampere on 15-16 October 1999. It was a strange meeting in that, as is usual with meetings of Heads of State and Government, the only official invitees, apart from the presidents and prime ministers, were foreign ministers. Ministers of

11 Virginie Guiraudon, "Immigration and asylum: A high politics agenda", in: Maria Green Cowles and Desmond Dinan (eds.), *Developments in the European Union 2* (Houndmills: Palgrave Macmillan, 2004), pp. 160-180.

justice or interior ministers were there only as "guests", akin to the presence of defence ministers in General Affairs Councils. Accounts of the meeting relate that, although consulted, JLS ministers had no access to the meeting itself. In addition, there was an unofficial meeting spear-headed by leading non-governmental organisations (NGOs), especially those concerned with refugee protection and human rights. A number of delegations, including the Commission, submitted contributions in writing prior to Tampere. The Commission took great care in its own preparations. Commissioner Antonio Vitorino visited national capitals to discuss Commission and national viewpoints. In his speech to the European Council, Romano Prodi referred to two guiding documents in the process, namely the Amsterdam Treaty itself and the JLS Action Plan adopted in Vienna a year earlier, characterising the EU's cooperation in JLS matters as equivalent in importance and scope to Economic and Monetary Union and CFSP and arguing that "national administrations should put aside any residual nostalgia for the days of pure intergovernmentalism which Amsterdam finally laid to rest".[12]

Prodi also laid out what he considered the essence of the coming five years, stressing the inclusion of non-EU nationals living in the Member States in the benefits of an Area of Freedom, Security and Justice stemming from free movement, and advocating the use of a so-called "scoreboard", consisting of a six-monthly report by the Commission. Prodi referred to a list of obligations arising from the Treaty, the proposals already made (whether from the Commission or the Member States) and progress or lack of it in the legislative process.

Tampere achieved more than the Vienna Action Plan of December 1998, itself the forerunner to the Amsterdam provisions. It was a political statement of intent that covered all fields of the Treaty. Again, asylum and immigration, subjects constantly in the headlines, were singled out. In addition, section D of the conclusions of the European Council was devoted to the need to use all the resources of the Union on external issues. The Commission had a distinct advantage. Not only did its aid budget exceed that of individual Member States, but the Commission Delegations also enhance the Union's international role in promoting JLS ideas and policies. Moreover, it is the Commission, which leads the negotiations with applicant states on their ability to implement the *acquis communautaire*, and the Commission, which manages practical projects for political and administrative adaptation designed to pave the administrative and political way for their entry into the EU. Thus, in asylum and immigration matters, attention was diverted away from purely domestic concerns to issues affecting third-countries from which

---

12 Romano Prodi, speech given at the Special European Council of Tampere, October 1999.

migrants were arriving. The issue was covered separately in the 1990 and 2002 Dublin Convention Regulation, which focussed on the Member State where asylum seekers were obliged to first lodge their application.

The Commission now began to devote far more intellectual and human resources to coordinating development policies and external relations aspects of migration policy (brain drain, remittances etc.) than in the past.

6. 9/11 as a Catalyst for the Commission's Role in JLS

The fight against international crime, terrorism and money laundering was already well underway before the attacks on the Twin Towers in New York on 11 September 2001. Intergovernmental, Europe-wide cooperation had started as early as 1975 on issues of terrorism and internal security in the framework of the TREVI group alluded to earlier. Twenty years later, the Madrid European Council in 1995 established that terrorism should be formally regarded as a threat to democracy, to the free exercise of human rights and to economic and social development. Since terrorism was increasingly seen to be operating on a transnational scale, it was recognised that it could not be dealt with effectively by means of isolated action and national resources alone. The Treaty of Amsterdam itself referred to the fight against terrorism, and terrorism was addressed both in 1998 in the Vienna Action Plan and in the conclusions of the Tampere Council of 1999.

This attention already paid to terrorism explains why the European legal and institutional structures in the area of Justice and Home Affairs were able to adapt rapidly to the increased demands they faced in the wake of 11 September 2001. On 20 September 2001, a range of JLS measures to fight terrorism was adopted by a special JLS Council meeting, followed by the adoption of a comprehensive EU Action Plan to Fight Terrorism at the extraordinary European Council on 21 September 2001. A detailed "Road Map" to implement the Action Plan was drawn up in October 2001; it is regularly updated. The Commission subsequently spearheaded counter-terrorism measures within the JLS sphere in five areas: (1) judicial cooperation, (2) counter-terrorism services cooperation (police and intelligence services), (3) financing of terrorism, (4) border controls and (5) external JLS measures. The establishment of a European police college (CEPOL) and Eurojust to coordinate national prosecuting authorities were immediate outcomes of a new conducive atmosphere in JLS. The fight against organised crime had already been boosted by the terrorist threat, and the Commission's role in both the external relations aspects (Roma Group) and the internal aspects, including organised crime (Lyon Group) of the G8 grew apace.

Adrian Fortescue, still Director General for DG JLS, was the well respected Commission representative in both groups. Following 9/11, the most significant developments included:

– agreement and legislation on a European Arrest Warrant, dispensing with traditional extradition procedures and expediting the arrest and transfer of suspects;

– agreement on a common definition of terrorist offences for criminal law purposes;

– provision for improved joint investigation between national police forces, the creation of an anti-terrorism unit within Europol and strengthened cooperation between anti-terrorist units;

– improved cooperation between the judiciary and prosecutors' offices;

– measures to give the intelligence services access to parts of the data of the Schengen Information System (SIS), and simplification of procedures to improve use of the SIS in the fight against terrorism;

– enhanced cooperation between Member States on a common list of terrorist organisations, on strengthening external border checks, on exchange of information on visas and on strengthening internal security;

– closer cooperation with Canada and the United States, including the appointment of liaison officers to the EU from both countries and mutual visits between Eurojust and Canada and the USA. Europol signed a Strategic Cooperation Agreement with the United States on 4 December 2001 and negotiated a second agreement with the USA on 20 December 2002, allowing for the transfer of personal data.

Many of these measures required Commission action. The proposals for a European Arrest Warrant and a definition of terrorist acts, which the Commission tabled immediately and steered through the Council in record time, paved the way for extending penalties for offences involving terrorism and were adopted more rapidly than might otherwise have been the case. The Commission had in any event already done preparatory work prior to 9/11. It had been drafting the texts over the summer and was awaiting a sensible political moment to communicate its legislative intentions. The work was accelerated and repackaged in the weeks following the attacks. Similarly, work by the Commission on the future requirements of the next generation of the Schengen Information System (SIS II) included the design of a new, simpler consultation procedure in the context of combating terrorism for alerts issued pursuant to Article 99 of the 1990 Schengen Convention; the possibility of running searches on the basis of incomplete data; access for public authorities responsible for vehicle registration; extended access for authorities which issue residence permits; and access for Eurojust, Europol and security services to the SIS.

In spite of these efforts progress in JLS as an EU policy sector still remained intergovernmental in inspiration. The Commission was powerless to stop Member States introducing national legislation on issues with high political profile, such as asylum and immigration, where it had hoped that future action would be coordinated within the EU framework. The establishment of a coherent EU strategy to address these issues, in the Commission's view, could only be effectively tackled through transnational cooperation. National efforts were not helpful. While the Commission attempted to steer EU measures on asylum and immigration through the Council, the UK and Germany continued to enact national legislation in these fields in 2003, 2004 and 2005. Controversial German legislation on immigration in response to its declining population and need for skilled immigrants obtained political agreement on 17 June 2004. Yet, significantly, many of the concepts in the German legislation, notably the need for better integration of immigrants and the requirements of the labour market, had already been present in Commission documents since 2000.

7. The Pressure of Events: The Hague Programme and Beyond

JLS issues frequently hit the headlines. The deaths of the smuggled Chinese in Dover in 2000, the ill-fated French Red Cross camp at Sangatte near Calais and cases where illegal immigrants are regularly sent back to Africa by the Italian coastguard, have made the public aware throughout Europe of JLS issues. The Commission often triggered European action after such cross-border crises, though it was sometimes criticised for doing so. In June 2004, a Commission Communication[13] assessed achievements and problems in JLS in the run up to the fifth anniversary of the Tampere European Council. The Commission's assessment was that, with the support of the public demonstrated in opinion polls, JLS was now firmly established as one of the Union's priority policy areas. Insecurity, crime and drugs headed the list of public concerns, behind only the issue of living standards.[14] Naturally, there was concern that combating terrorism, racism, illegal immigration,

[13] European Commission, Communication from the Commission to the Council and the European Parliament, *Area of Freedom, Security and Justice: Assessment of the Tampere programme and future orientations*, COM(2004) 401 final, Brussels, 2 June 2004. The Commission Staff Working Document SEC(2004) 680 contains a list of the most important instruments adopted in the Tampere framework.

[14] See Eurobarometer 63: Public Opinion in the European Union (First Results), DG PRESS, European Commission, July 2005.

people trafficking and other forms of exploitation might imply a measure of curtailment of freedom. Balance between freedom, security and justice and protection of fundamental rights has long been a major concern of the EU institutions. While much of the focus of JLS has been on increased coordination on asylum and immigration issues and on criminal matters, the Commission's emerging role in human rights is thus apposite. All Member States and potential Member States of the European Union must belong to the Council of Europe and are *ipso facto* signatories to the European Convention on Human Rights and Fundamental Freedoms which entered into force on 3 September 1953, giving effect to the Declaration of the Congress of Europe in The Hague in May 1948. The European Convention is also mentioned in the Single European Act of 1986 and in subsequent Treaties. The Council of Europe also passed a Social Charter[15] that came into force in 1961, guaranteeing social rights. Both instruments were reflected in the European Union's own Charter of Fundamental Rights.[16]

In terms of the number of instruments and policy papers, the Commission clearly made a considerable effort to push through measures in accordance with the Tampere mandate, though it was undoubtedly hampered by the absence of qualified majority voting and by national politics. A "scoreboard" demonstrates how active the Commission has been in making proposals to the Council. Yet, if rigorous efforts were made by the Commission, the Council demonstrated somewhat less vigour. Where agreements were reached, it was often at the cost of a watered down version of a Commission proposal. The Directive on family reunification is a prime example. It went into three proposals by the Commission before being accepted by the Council on 22 September 2003 (Directive 2003/86/EC). The Directive on long-term residence of third-country nationals (Directive 2003/109/EC) was a success for the Commission, however. As the usually diplomatic Adrian Fortescue contended,

> JLS is increasingly hostage to outside events and national election campaigns [...] In each case immigration and terrorism considerations were close to the surface. The subjects have to be kept out of the newspapers; meaning that the Member State concerned can make no concession in the Council because of the risk of attention being drawn to it [...] Our whole

15 The Social Charter is an instrument of the Council of Europe dating from 1961. Revised in 1996, the new version entered into force in 1999.

16 See *O.J.*, No. C 363 of 18 December 2000. The Charter has now been incorporated into the Treaty of Lisbon and as from 1 December 2009 will have the force of law.

immigration debate was virtually on hold for much of 2002 for electoral reasons.[17]

There was thus perhaps a degree of scepticism present when the Commission's Communication of June 2004 listed policy areas requiring attention. These were:

– A genuine common policy of management of migratory flows, including the facilitation of legal immigrants.

– A common European asylum system and a common status. The Commission laid out its ideas for the second stage of its asylum policy in a Communication in 2004.[18]

– Establishment of a judicial area in civil and commercial matters, especially the continuation of work on mutual recognition.

– Promotion of a coherent criminal justice policy also based on the principle of mutual recognition. This would include "putting Eurojust at the centre of European criminal justice policy to support and strengthen coordination and cooperation [...] relating to serious crime affecting several Member States". This would involve the creation of a European Public Prosecutor's Office.

– Stronger action to prevent crime and strengthening the fight against terrorism.

– Resolute external action in relation to third-countries.

The Dutch Presidency responded with a paper of its own, which was reviewed briefly at the JLS Council of 19 July 2004.[19] It highlighted five similar areas needing attention, echoing the Commission's priority list: adequate access to justice and protection of rights; a coordinated cohesive judicial system for civil and commercial matters that ensures effective jurisdiction and execution of judgements; effective capacity to regulate cross-border movement of persons; the power to protect against external and internal threats; and an integrated capacity to fight organised crime. Subsequently, the European Council of 4-5 November 2004 approved a new blueprint for the future: the Hague Programme.[20] As the Tampere Programme before it, the Hague Programme was an attempt to map out the steps needed to meet particular problems. The policy pre-

17 Adrian Fortescue, unpublished internal speech to the legal service of the European Commission in 2002.

18 European Commission, Communication from the Commission to the Council and the European Parliament, *A More Efficient Common European Asylum System: The Single Procedure as the Next Step*, COM(2004) 503 final, Brussels, 15 July 2004.

19 Note from the Presidency to Coreper/Council, 11122/04 of 9 July 2004.

20 *The Hague Programme – Strengthening Freedom, Security and Justice in the European Union*, Presidency Conclusions, Brussels, 4-5 November 2004, Council Document 14292/04 Annex 1.

scriptions of the Hague Programme were not, however, markedly different from those in the Commission's June 2004 Communication. Indeed, senior Commission JLS staff were active in assisting the Dutch government in their task of writing and promoting the Hague Declaration.

Based on the Hague Programme provisions, the Commission presented a Five Year Action Plan in May 2005, "in which the aims and priorities of this programme [would] be translated into concrete actions". It provided detailed proposals for EU action on terrorism, migration management, visa policies, asylum, privacy and security, the fight against organised crime and criminal justice.[21] The Hague Programme prioritised further development of cross-border police cooperation and amendment of the Convention implementing the Schengen Agreement. The Commission not only had a major role in the drafting of the Hague Programme, but remained the motor in its implementation and monitoring. There seemed little doubt that Member States now saw the Commission in the driving seat in this once purely intergovernmental sector.

The Commission adopted a proposal on the improvement of police cooperation between the Member States on 19 July 2005. The proposal provided a framework to improve information exchange between law enforcement authorities and strengthened structural and operational cooperation between them. It included the creation of a regulatory committee to assist the Commission by reviewing drafts of proposed measures. It was to consist of representatives of the Member States and to be chaired by the Commission.[22] On the same day, the Commission also adopted a Communication on ensuring greater security of explosives, detonators, bomb-making equipment and fire-arms[23] as part of its work in developing a coherent preventive strategy in the fight against terrorism. The Communication, which provides the state of play regarding security of explosives and makes a series of concrete recommendations, emphasises improving security arrangements along the production and supply chain, particularly during storage and transport.

In sum, therefore, the Commission has had a prime place as a facilitator and enabler in the EU fight against terrorism, even if as an institu-

---

21 European Commission, Communication from the Commission to the Council and the European Parliament, *The Hague Programme: Ten priorities for the next five years – The Partnership for European renewal in the field of Freedom, Security and Justice*, COM(2005) 184 final, Brussels, 10 May 2005.

22 European Commission, Press Release IP/05/970, Schengen Area – The Commission proposes to facilitate cross border surveillance and "hot pursuit" between Member States, Brussels, 19 July 2005.

23 European Commission, Communication from the Commission on *Measures to Ensure Greater Security in Explosives, Detonators, Bomb-making Equipment and Fire-arms*, COM(2005) 329 final, Brussels, 18 July 2005.

tion it does not have the technical expertise and has been obliged to have recourse to outside assistance, for example by the independent agency set up with the assistance of the EU's Joint Research Centre at Ispra in Italy to work on the technical aspects of anti-terrorism, such as explosives research.

8. External Relations and Internal Implications

An additional Commission obligation in the Hague framework included a joint obligation with High Representative Javier Solana to present by the end of 2005 a strategy "covering all external aspects of the Union policy on freedom, security and justice". Following 9/11, the external aspects of JLS expertise were initially only used to a limited extent in the numerous contacts with third-countries. There was little formal interaction between JLS and CFSP bodies, and CFSP *démarches* dealing with terrorism in third-countries were often not always as infused with the JLS dimension of EU action as they might have been if effective coordination had been the rule.[24] New, comprehensive anti-terrorism cooperation structures with third-countries were initially only developed with the US, though other important partners such as Japan and the Russian Federation followed later, as the G8 became closely involved. There was clearly an initial gap. There was no overall strategy for the fight against terrorism similar to that already in place since 1997 – through specific action plans – for the fight against organised crime. The following months and years saw the Commission at first hastily bundling together measures which lacked coordination, and which were subject to numerous *ad hoc* changes,[25] and then concentrating on a coordinated approach to the interaction between external and internal security. However, despite the amount of practical work involved, the Commission kept a low political profile. When the post of EU Counter-Terrorism Coordinator was created in 2004, the first incumbent, Dutch politician Gijs de Vries, was placed in the Council, reporting to the High Representative for CFSP, rather than in the Commission where the staff, financial resources and Commissioner Vitorino would have been an efficient policy focus. De Vries was subsequently replaced by a senior official in the Council of Ministers, Gilles de Kerchove, reinforcing the

---

24 David Spence, "The evolving role of foreign ministries in the European Union: Conduct of European Union affairs", in: Brian Hocking and David Spence (eds.), *Foreign Ministries in the European Union. Integrating Diplomats* (Houndmills: Palgrave Macmillan, 2005).

25 Jörg Monar, "The European Union's role in the fight against international terrorism: An evaluation in the light of the response to 11 September 2001", in: Georges Vandersanden (ed.), *Mélanges en hommage à Jean-Victor Louis* (Brussels: Éditions de l'Université Libre de Bruxelles, 2003), Vol. I, pp. 337-354.

impression of the Member States attempting to keep this policy area in their own camp.

9. The Implications of the Treaty of Lisbon

As the Irish referendum of June 2008 rejecting the Lisbon text demonstrated, deciding, ratifying and implementing it was not a forgone conclusion. The 2008 referendum was debated on issues that touched Irish sensitivities but whose connection to the Treaty were tenuous. The referendum which took place in Ireland on 2 October 2009 fortunately reversed the first vote after guarantees were introduced into the text to alleviate Irish fears.

The new Treaty sensibly abolishes the outdated notion of the "pillars" introduced at Maastricht, since the European Union now has legal personality. JLS is now in one single title (Title V) of the Treaty on the Functioning of the European Union (TFEU), and all policies, JLS included, fall under the Community method unless otherwise stated. Co-decision and qualified majority voting become the rule, with certain exceptions, particularly in the field of border control, asylum, immigration, Eurojust and Europol. There will be so-called "emergency brake" provisions in certain cases of judicial cooperation in criminal matters – to protect Member States' concerns in this sensitive area to allow them to block proposals and refer them to the European Council if they believe they affect some fundamental aspect of their criminal justice system. In cases where this right is taken up, the co-decision mechanism is suspended.

The Charter of Fundamental Rights became legally binding with Lisbon, but only in so far as its provisions apply to acts of the institutions or agencies of the Union and to Member States when implementing Union law. This is subject to certain derogations in the case of the United Kingdom and Poland; a protocol stipulates that the Charter does not extend the powers of the Court of Justice or the national courts of these countries to judge whether there have been breaches of the Charter.

The Court of Justice has been granted jurisdiction over what was the residual "third pillar" (criminal justice), though with some exceptions. There is an opening in the Treaty for the establishment of a European Public Prosecutor's Office to prevent fraudulent use of EU funds and to fight corruption. However, on the restrictive side, the United Kingdom, Ireland and Denmark have extended their existing opt-out provisions in the current first pillar fields to judicial cooperation in criminal matters and police cooperation. This latter policy area also has some transitional provisions; infringement proceedings, for example, will not apply for up to five years from the date of entry into force of the Treaty.

There are also some general provisions which do not fall exclusively into the JLS policy area but which will nevertheless affect its functioning and that of the responsibilities of the Commission. One of these is the strengthening of the role of national parliaments, which must be informed of all legislative proposals and are empowered to issue reasoned opinions on the issue of subsidiarity. The Commission receives a heavy additional workload. The principle of participative democracy where "a citizen's initiative" to propose legislation can be taken upon collection of at least a million signatures, is now possible, though it is almost certain that JLS policies will, at some point, be the target of these new provisions.

10. The Third JLS Programme under the Swedish Presidency – The Stockholm Programme

In the summer of 2009, in preparation for its Presidency, the Swedish government announced a new five year phase for the development of JLS policies. The aim, in the words of the Swedish authorities, is to "define the framework for EU police and customs cooperation, rescue services, criminal and civil law cooperation, asylum, migration and visa policy". The Commission's reaction (or perhaps pre-emption), was a Communication of their own setting out its vision of what should happen in the next five years.[26]

The political priorities are stated to be: promoting citizens' rights (bearing in mind the binding nature of the Charter of Fundamental rights in the Lisbon Treaty except for the opt-out countries), easing the anomalies in conflicting justice systems (which is implemented would have a major impact on private international law in Europe), protecting the citizen by improving security and what is termed "a more integrated society for the citizen", meaning policies on asylum and immigration that guarantees solidarity between the Member States and partnership with non-Union countries. The Communication states that "there should be a closer match between immigration and the needs of the European labour market, along with targeted integration and education policies". Commission President Barroso, commenting on the Communication laid particular emphasis on immigration, but it should be recalled that the Member States have never showed great enthusiasm for a common immigration policy especially regarding economic migration. On the other hand a second phase common asylum policy and systems is politically realistic and will almost certainly be proposed.

---

[26] European Commission, Communication from the Commission to the European Parliament and the Council, *An Area of Freedom, Security and Justice serving the citizen*, COM(2009) 262 final of 10 June 2009. See also Council Document 1648/1/09 REV 1 of 25 November 2009.

The Commission has given further examples of the kind of proposals that is envisaging, for example a comprehensive scheme to ensure better data protection, abolishing intermediate procedures for enforcing court proceedings between Member States, an exchange programme for police officers, strengthening procedural guarantees for criminal proceedings, creating an information system to improve information flows between police forces and increased research for security technologies.

The real difficulty facing all parties in this policy debate is how to obtain a balance between citizens' rights and protection of society, especially against terrorism, which is why its advocates consider the Charter of Fundamental Rights to be of such prime importance. Civil rights groups have already expressed concern at the tone and content of the emerging Stockholm programme and it will take all the political skills that the incoming Commission can muster to make acceptable proposals which satisfy both governments and civil society.

11. External Components of JLS Policy

There is hardly a JLS policy area that does not have an external component requiring negotiation and cooperation, both with individual third-countries and in multilateral fora. There is therefore a linguistic irony in the fact that Justice and Home Affairs issues are far from being confined within the borders of the enlarged EU. Enlargement itself has been a major exercise for the Union and the Commission. It is an unfinished process, both in the sense that there are other countries to follow and that, for the new Member States, there are transitional provisions, especially relating to migration.

The speed with which the Union embraced working together with the United States and other countries clearly illustrates the salient and rapidly expanding external dimension of JLS. To facilitate transnational cooperation in Justice and Home Affairs, a Commission official from DG JLS was appointed to the Commission's Delegation in Washington in 2003; similarly, a senior official in the US embassy to the EU in Brussels has been focussing full-time on EU JLS developments.[27] Transatlantic cooperation has been "extremely positive", with Commission officials in regular contact with their counterparts at the US Homeland Security Department and the State Department. The Commission has also played an important role in negotiating an agreement with the US on air passenger data, despite resistance from the European Parlia-

[27] Pascaline Winand, "The US Mission to the EU in 'Brussels D.C.', the European Commission Delegation in Washington D.C. and the New Transatlantic Agenda", in: Eric Philippart and Pascaline Winand (eds.), *Ever Closer Partnership. Policy-Making in US-EU Relations* (Brussels: P.I.E. Peter Lang, 2004, 3rd ed.).

ment on data protection grounds. The agreement required airlines to forward electronically to US Immigration Services an advance passenger list with passport and credit card details for checking prior to the aircraft landing on US soil. Following the London bombings in July 2005, the Council called on the Commission to put forward a proposal for an EU airline passenger name record system by October 2005.[28]

The Commission also led discussions with the Chinese government on human rights and illegal immigration from China, as well as the discussions on re-admission agreements which it had either negotiated or had a mandate to negotiate in the future. To prevent money laundering, Commission officials have since its inception been involved in the work of the Financial Action Task Force (FATF), an OECD organisation with primary responsibility for developing a world-wide anti-money laundering framework. Cooperation on the financing of terrorism has been enormously improved since 9/11, achieving a high degree of sophistication.[29] In cooperation agreements with third-countries in general, there is now always a JLS component and there are corresponding texts inserted in all international agreements on trade and other matters as a matter of principle.[30] Commission officials are also active in the United Nations and other international bodies, including the follow-up to the Global Commission on International Migration, launched by Secretary General Kofi Annan in December 2003, and in regular briefings to the UN's Counter Terrorism Committee. The Commission, together with the Counter-Terrorism Coordinator, is also encouraging the Union to continue its dialogue with relevant regional organisations and with its Euromed partners.[31]

After Amsterdam, JLS became mainstream activity, both within the EU and in the EU's relations with the outside world. As Fortescue put it in 2002, it "entered the consciousness of other services that the Commission now had a new full-scale Directorate-General dealing with a new area, whose work would certainly impinge on theirs".[32] Some powerful DGs such as External Relations and Development have not

---

28 Council of the European Union, Press Release of Extraordinary JLS Council Meeting, 13 July 2005.

29 Note to the European Council, 16-17 June 2005. Submitted by the Presidency and the EU Counter-Terrorism Coordinator.

30 This was also the case for the negotiations on the transit arrangements through EU territory for citizens of Kaliningrad.

31 Global Commission on International Migration; Migration in an international world; New directions for action, Geneva 2005; Note to the European Council, 16-17 June 2005. Submitted by the Presidency and the EU Counter-Terrorism Coordinator.

32 Adrian Fortescue, Justice and Home Affairs DG Moving into the Mainstream of European Commission, interview given for the European Commission Website 2002.

only been obliged to accommodate this new policy area, but they have also tried to claim some jurisdiction over it, a fact not unnoticed by the Commission's international partners. In some instances, third-countries have exploited perceived differences of opinion within the Commission's services. Clearly, demonstrating a lack of coherence damages the Commission's negotiating position and undermines its credibility. In this regard, the Commission proposal of 11 June 2003 for a regulation establishing a programme for financial and technical assistance to third-countries in the area of migration and asylum[33] was a significant advance, for it led to enhanced inter-service cooperation, higher visibility for JLS within the "RELEX family" and a concerted effort to make third-countries aware of the harmonised nature of JLS issues within the EU.

12. Technology-based Tools and Justice and Home Affairs

The Commission has already financed and developed two out of three major data systems to help manage aspects of border control policy: SIS and Eurodac. The Schengen Information System (SIS),[34] which entered its second phase in 2006, allows national authorities access to data on persons and property to ensure the smooth running of open borders between Member States taking part in the Schengen Agreement. Thirteen Member States participate in the SIS, but there was only capacity for a further five, hence the need for "SIS II". Norway and Iceland, as part of the Nordic Group of states, which already had a passport free zone prior to the accession of Sweden and Finland, also take part, as does Switzerland since 2008. The Commission was responsible for developing the SIS II, cooperating closely with Member States, the Council, the European Parliament and a Joint Supervisory Authority. It will also be in charge of its operational management, crucial for the implementation of the European Arrest Warrant and the Dublin Conventions. Finally, the Commission foresees the possibility of transferring SIS II personal data to third-countries or international organisations subject to the appropriate legal instruments.[35]

---

33 Communication on 'Integrating Migration Issues into the EU's External Relations', COM(2003) 355.

34 European Commission, Communication from the Commission to the Council and the European Parliament, *Development of the Schengen Information System II*, COM(2001) 720 final, Brussels, 18 December 2001.

35 See the European Commission Proposal for a Council Decision on *the establishment, operation and use of the second generation Schengen information system (SIS II)* presented by the Commission, COM(2005) 230 final, Brussels, 31 May 2005.

In the field of asylum, the Eurodac[36] system covers the fingerprinting of asylum seekers so that multiple applications can be traced at the touch of a button. All Member States are members of the system, as again are Norway and Iceland. The separate Visa Information System (VIS), on which the principles were adopted by the Council in February 2004, involves the exchange of data on visa applications aimed at helping consular authorities fight fraud, facilitate checks by carriers (especially for airlines), prevent "visa shopping", facilitate the administration of the "Dublin 2" Regulation on countries of first asylum, and help identify undocumented persons.[37] Political agreement on the VIS was reached in June 2007. However, there were complex technical issues still to be solved and the VIS was not operational before the end of 2009.

Clearly, Justice and Home Affairs is a complex policy area. Efficient policy-making must rely on unambiguous data and policy monitoring. A report by the Migration Policy Unit at University College London was commissioned in 1996 to report to the Commission on the requirements for information in the field of migration. The report highlighted the need for accessible data for policy-makers. It subsequently led to the creation of a network including the majority of Member States, for the exchange of data and its analysis. The network, known as the European Migration Network, is not managed by the Commission, but the Commission did choose the management institute responsible and forms one of its hubs. By providing greater clarity in the field, the Commission thus contributed to better output. The Commission also chairs a committee for the exchange of information between Member States on asylum trends. Known as Eurasil, its task was previously undertaken in the Council framework.

All these sophisticated instruments require a high degree of expertise in computer operations for which the Commission has engaged personnel and set up a specialised unit. The Commission is thereby becoming the focal point of a technological revolution in control of the movement of persons potentially in breach of either Member States' or EU legisla-

[36] Council Regulation (EC) No. 2725/2000 of 11 December 2000. In 2004, Eurodac successfully processed 232,205 fingerprints of asylum seekers, 16,183 fingerprints of people crossing the borders irregularly and 39,550 fingerprints of people apprehended while illegally on the territory of a Member State. Figures show that in 2004, the number of asylum applications has decreased while the number of registered irregular entrants has increased. The number of checks of illegally present persons has also more than doubled in 2004, see European Commission, Press Release MEMO/05/214, *EURODAC guarantees effective management of the Common European Asylum System*, Brussels, 21 June 2005.

[37] Council of the European Union, Press Release C/05/187, *Extraordinary Council meeting, Justice and Home Affairs*, Brussels, 13 July 2005.

tion. As discussed below, use of these technologies clearly calls for adequate provisions to uphold civil liberties, for which the Commission has prepared new rules and administrative arrangements on data protection principles in the field of law enforcement as requested by the extraordinary JLS European Council in July 2005.

13. The Current Responsibilities of JLS

The Directorate-General for JLS administers a bewildering array of policies, legislative proposals and ongoing projects including a hugely increased budget arising from the Financial Perspectives (that is budgetary provisions of the Commission agreed by the Council) 2007-2113.

In its Communication from the Commission to the Council and the European Parliament reporting on the implementation of the Hague Programme (COM/2007/373 final), the Commission set out its current work programme for JLS. The subjects covered include fundamental rights and data protection, a strategy on drugs, citizenship, asylum, immigration and border policy, legal migration, integration of third-country nationals, the fight against illegal migration, visa policy, electronic systems for border control, anti-terrorism measures, prevention of organised crime, police and customs cooperation and civil justice cooperation. Within these categories, there is a range of administrative documents, communications to the Council and Parliament and legislative proposals to draft and monitor the process and finally transposition into national law and compliance.

In the sensitive field of illegal migration the Commission has undertaken a number of its own initiatives and has a small team working on the issue. The Commission produced a Communication on policies for illegal migration in 2006,[38] a Return Action Programme and a Directive on Common Standards and Procedures for the return of illegal migrants.[39] Illegal migration needs to be controlled in line with international humanitarian standards and the parallel commitment to finding common solutions to asylum and legal economic migration.

---

38 European Commission, Communication from the Commission on *Policy priorities in the fight against illegal immigration of third-country nationals*, COM(2006) 402 final, Brussels, 19 July 2006.

39 European Commission Proposal for a Directive of the European Parliament and of the Council on *common standards and procedures in Member States for returning illegally staying third-country nationals*, COM(2005) 391 final, Brussels, 1 September 2005.

14. The Commission's evolving Administrative Structures for JLS

As with EPC, administrative and management changes were made to match expanding policy commitments. In 1995, the Commission had set up a Task Force on Justice and Home Affairs consisting of some twenty officials within the Secretariat General, *de facto* as a largely autonomous group. The custom of placing a new policy area such as this in the Secretariat General is more than just symbolic. The Secretariat General is the nerve centre of the Commission and the funnel through which proposals pass. Although it is placed under the direct authority of the President of the Commission, in the case of JLS between 1995 and 1999, the new Task Force reported to the Swedish Commissioner, Anita Gradin, rather than to the Secretary General or to the Commission President. Gradin was responsible for progressively garnering the confidence of the Member States, though the Secretariat General provided the administrative strength on which to build the new responsibilities.[40]

In May 1999, the entry into force of the Treaty of Amsterdam transformed the Task Force on Justice and Home Affairs into a fully-fledged Directorate-General of the Commission under the Portuguese Commissioner Antonio Vitorino. The establishment of the new DG was amply justified by the scope of the new Treaty. Amsterdam recognised that the model for JLS should not be a carbon copy of the other intergovernmental arm of the Union, the Common Foreign and Security Policy. If the new policy area were to be effective, it would need different instruments – directives (in JLS "framework decisions") and not simply the joint actions that had been a feature of both policy areas in the Maastricht framework. In addition, it would need more staff. Increased Commission responsibilities justified Vitorino's call to the Council to allocate 250 posts to JLS, a substantial increase over what had become 70 officials in the Task Force. In practice, it took two years to reach even 220, despite Heads of State and Government making it clear that JLS would become a major new area of activity and the workload having tripled by then.[41] Whether this can be attributed to the reluctance of the Council in general to increase the budgetary allocation for posts or the internal wrangling in the Commission over job allocations is difficult to tell.

---

40 Hans G. Nilsson, "The Justice and Home Affairs Council", in: Martin Westlake and David Galloway (eds.), *The Council of the European Union* (London: John Harper, 2004), p. 124.

41 Adrian Fortescue, Justice and Home Affairs DG Moving into the Mainstream of European Commission, interview given for the European Commission Website 2002.

While Adrian Fortescue[42] was content that "money became available", in the Byzantine workings of the Commission, "money" did not mean human resources, and an almost skeleton staff was obliged to shoulder the considerable new responsibilities; a fact which lead to substantial frustration and left some important tasks undone or placed on the back burner. In mid-2003, DG JLS changed its structure to four Directorates (up from the original three) involving 17 policy units.[43]

Since September 2009, the DG comprises six Directorates with 26 policy units, an audit unit and a reinforced team of assistants to the Director-General.[44] The total staff number has grown to 481.[45] The reasons for the expansion and reorganisation are clear. Given the workload and compared with other departments, this is a more workable format. Most importantly, in the structure of the new Commission appointed in November 2009, the portfolio will be split between Commissioner Cecila Malmström who will be responsible for internal security, migration and borders and Commissioner Viviane Reding who will take charge of fundamental rights, citizenship and justice. The split has been long anticipated and will make the workload less onerous. There will, however, be a need for close coordination between the two commissioners on the lines of the RELEX commissioners at present.

15. Future Perspectives: The evolving Nature of the Commission Role in JLS Policies and the Stockholm Programme

Maastricht and Amsterdam clearly constituted tentative steps towards creating genuine Union JLS policies, but the failure of the Constitutional Treaty and the drafting of the Lisbon Treaty provided confirmation to the Commission that the problems which confront Member States are considered so daunting that recourse to the supranational approach of the Community method was essential if progress were to be achieved, and this notwithstanding the marked reluctance of the UK and Ireland to participate in instruments relating to external borders, asylum and immigration, using opt-in provisions (mainly for asylum issues) only when they seemed to their advantage.

42 Adrian Fortescue, unpublished internal speech to the legal service of the European Commission in 2002.

43 The Directorates at the time were A: General Affairs, B: Immigration, Asylum and Borders, C: Civil Justice, Rights and Citizenship, and D: Internal Security and Criminal Justice.

44 See the organigramme of the DG JLS in the annex.

45 Source: European Commission, distribution of officials and temporary agents by Directorates-General and categories (all budgets), last update 1 December 2009.

Yet, the cause of further integrated policy in JLS has been well served over the years. The Commission long argued that one of the most important aspects of a European Constitution would be the abolition of the "pillar" structure and the extension of the Community method to the full range of JLS matters. This was effectively achieved by the Lisbon Treaty. The pillar structure was originally hailed as a great triumph, heralding the creation of the European Union to replace the European Community. Despite its commitment to intergovernmentalism, it did allow the measured development of a less intergovernmental approach to JLS over a period of twelve years during which the Commission promoted the JLS agenda, the Community method and its own prerogatives at the same time. The new Financial Perspective described above should give a substantial boost to JLS activities, not least in its external dimension. This will raise the Commission's international profile, if only because it manages the funds. Comparison with the initial phases of the Task Force in 1994 is striking; officials then had to persuade other departments to allocate small amounts for JLS issues from their own funds.

The Commission runs the Vienna-based Fundamental Rights Agency formerly the Monitoring Centre on Racism and Xenophobia set up in 1998[46] and the European Drugs and Drug Addiction Monitoring Centre in Lisbon, established in 1994.[47] In addition, Europol has become a full agency of the EU. In each of these fields, the Commission plays a vital part in the analysis of the technical and legal information required for informed policy-making at the European level. In addition, the Commission's role in the "scoreboard" mechanism was crucial. It reinforced both the Commission's watchdog role and its right of initiative, and it gave the Commission considerable leverage, by regularly highlighting failures and successes.[48] Member States and interested NGOs knew exactly where responsibility lay for lack of progress – the former through participation in Council working groups and the latter via their extensive lobbying. As a result, Member States and NGOs now increasingly turn to the Commission to find solutions to tricky political issues, and the Commission representative is a key member of the JLS Counsellors' Group, a Council forum for preparing the senior Council working groups that report to the JLS ministers via the hierarchical chain of

[46] Established by Council Regulation (EC) No. 1035/97 of 2 June 1997. It is currently in the process of being transformed into the EU Agency for Fundamental Rights (EP Resolution 26 May 2005).

[47] Established by Council Regulation (EEC) No. 302/93 of 8 February 1993.

[48] See http://ec.europa.eu/comm/justice_home/doc_centre/scoreboard_en.htm for the link to scoreboard.

Council meetings.[49] Generally speaking, in European affairs, the more complex issues become, the more the Member States turn to the Commission for advice and information.

At the end of 2009 it was clear that, building on the achievements of the Tampere and Hague Programmes, significant progress had been achieved. Internal border controls had been removed in the Schengen area and the external borders of the EU were now managed in a more coherent manner. Through the development of the global approach to migration, the external dimension of the EU's migration policy now focused on dialogue and partnerships with third-countries, based on their mutual interests. Significant steps had been taken towards the creation of a European Asylum System. European agencies such as Europol, Eurojust, the Fundamental Rights Agency and Frontex had reached operational maturity in their respective fields of activity. Cooperation in civil law was meanwhile facilitating the everyday life of citizens and law enforcement cooperation was providing for enhanced security. Yet, more needed to be done. A new multi-annual programme to be known as the Stockholm Programme, for the period 2010-2014, was negotiated during the second half of 2009 for adoption by the European Council in December 2009. The Stockholm Programme – whose final version was not yet available at the time writing – will propose further promotion of the Area of Freedom, Security and Justice as a single area in which fundamental rights are protected in line with the Charter of Fundamental Rights. For example, the exercise of freedoms and citizens' privacy must be preserved beyond national borders, especially by protecting personal data. In particular, allowance will be made for the special needs of vulnerable people, and citizens must be able to exercise their specific rights to the full, even outside the Union. Priority will now to be given to mechanisms that facilitate people's access to the Courts, so that they can enforce their rights throughout the Union. It will aim at improving cooperation between legal professionals, and to mobilise to put an end to barriers to the recognition of legal acts in other Member States. The Stockholm Programme will provide for the development of an internal security strategy in order to further improve security in the Union and thus protect the lives and safety of European citizens. The strategy should be aimed at strengthening cooperation in police matters and law enforcement and making Europe more secure. In addition, the development of a forward-looking and comprehensive European migration policy will be deemed a key policy objective for the European Union. Well-managed migration could be beneficial to all stakeholders. The European Pact on Immigration and Asylum was the

49 For further details on the JLS Counsellors' Group, see the chapter by Hans G. Nilsson and Julian Siegl in this volume.

basis for further development in this field. Europe needed a flexible and demand-driven labour immigration policy, responsive to the needs of Member States' national labour markets. People in need of protection have to be ensured access to legally safe and efficient asylum procedures, and illegal migration had to be controlled. Importantly, Stockholm will also underline the importance of the external dimension of the EU's policy in the Area of Freedom, Security and Justice and the need for increased integration of JLS policies into the general policies of the European Union.

In the light of the Stockholm Programme, the Commission will be expected to present an Action Plan in 2010 translating the Stockholm Programme into concrete action with a clear timetable for adoption and implementation with a mid-term review of the implementation before June 2012.

16. Conclusion

This chapter has outlined how the Commission demonstrated its commitment to its JLS mission. It consulted widely on the issues arising before Tampere, before The Hague and in preparation of Stockholm. It published official Communications and discussion papers and held public debates before drafting legislation. And, it did all this with minimal staffing, yet fully respecting the Amsterdam schedule and the guidelines of the European Council in Tampere. The agreement to the Hague Programme reached at the European Council of 4-5 November 2004, and its successor the Stockholm programme has demonstrated that EU instruments and policies were now viewed positively by Member States and the Commission was clearly a key component in this success. Armed with the tools in the Lisbon Treaty, the Commission is now equipped to deliver more of what the public seems to desire in the field. JLS policies are highly visible and despite the brickbats, this text has shown how the Commission is the main architect of EU action. While the Commission will doubtless continue to be constrained by the reluctance of some Member States to allow the EU to deal with certain sensitive issues, there is a risk of disaffection by a public hitherto purportedly committed to Europeanisation of policy in this politically contested area. Much now depends on the success or failure of the Lisbon Treaty arrangements and the Stockholm programme.

Annex: organigramme DG JLS (last update: 16/09/2009)

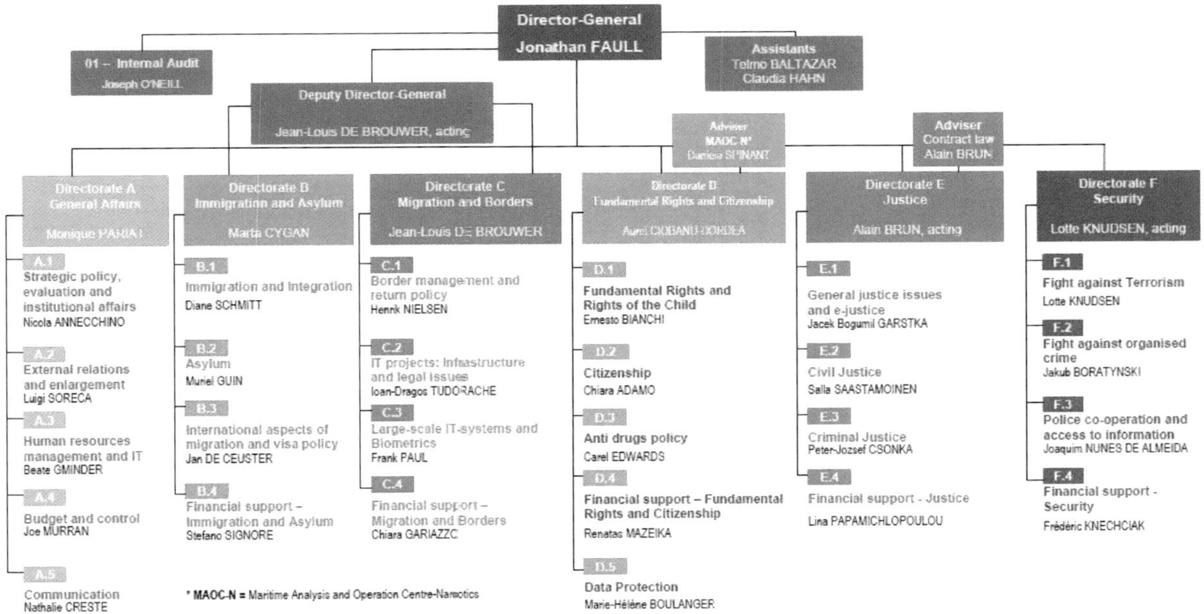

CHAPTER 4

The Evolving Role of the European Parliament in the AFSJ

Emilio DE CAPITANI*

1. Introduction

This chapter will focus on the main factors that influenced the growing role of the European Parliament in the domain of Justice and Home Affairs (JHA) since the beginning of the 1980s. In the same period the European Community and thereafter the European Union were progressively involved in JHA related policies till to the more ambitious objective to transform the European Union in an Area of Freedom, Security and Justice (AFSJ).

Not surprisingly the increasing political dimension of these policies has as a direct result to strengthen the parliamentary institution by so confirming a virtuous circle which can, hopefully, cover the democratic gap at European Union level notably in the AFSJ policies as denounced on 30 June 2009 by the German Constitutional Court.

Our aim is to highlight the main institutional dynamics of what we see as a three phased evolution when:

(a) in the first phase (before the entry into force in 1987 of the Single European Act) the European Parliament was practically unable to influence the final content of legislative proposals which were drafted, negotiated and concluded between the Council and the Commission;

(b) in a second transitional phase (from the 1987 Single European Act to the entry into force in 1999 of the Treaty of Amsterdam) the European Parliament engaged in a strong political interaction with the Commission and its first direct serious bilateral negotiations with the Council in the framework of the first co-decision procedures; and

(c) in this current phase (from 1999 to the possible entry into force of the Treaty of Lisbon) the Parliament has been able to influence also the agenda-setting of the other institutions and their working methods as the final content of the EU legislative proposals notably when issues, such

* The content of the present article is under the full responsibility of the author and does not engage in any way the position of the institution.

as the promotion and protection of fundamental rights or the issue of security and justice, are at stake.

Obviously some institutional dynamics prevailing in one phase can survive in the following, notably when the European Parliament is called to play different roles (as co-decider or as a simple consultative body) as still happens in the AFSJ domain. Yet, it is our understanding that there is a clear evolution in the general decision-making process which can hardly be reversed or continue to accept exceptional decisional regimes.

This evolution has already been anticipated by the lobbies who attend more and more frequently the parliamentary premises and have been recently followed by the press who, for the first time in the recent European Parliament elections, did not present this institution as no more than a "would-be" democratic assembly but as a real political and legislative player.

As confirmation of this trend this chapter will focus on a rather recent phenomenon; the so-called "first reading agreement". This agreement already covers more than two thirds of the co-decision procedure and is where the European Parliament plays the role of a protagonist.

2. The First Phase: When the European Parliament was out of the Picture (before the Single European Act (1987)

It is well-known that in the first three decades since the adoption of the founding Treaties the questions related to Justice and Home Affairs as well to the protection of fundamental rights were considered outside the scope of the Treaties and a domain jealously preserved by the Member States against the intervention of the European institutions. Before the 1980s the cooperation by Member States in the field of free movement of persons, Justice and Home Affairs (including immigration and asylum) were non-existent, or on a very low level except for the part concerning free movement of workers. But even for these cases, although Article 235 of the EEC Treaty[1] could have given some possibilities to develop a free movement policy of the EU citizens, founded on

[1] It is the "implicit powers" clause (currently Art. 308 of the TEC) according to which "If action by the Community should prove necessary to attain, in the course of the operation of the common market, one of the objectives of the Community, and this Treaty has not provided the necessary powers, the Council shall, acting unanimously on a proposal from the Commission and after consulting the European Parliament, take the appropriate measures".

the passive freedom of obtaining services[2] it was not possible to reach the required unanimity between the Member States.

During that period the Member States were more willing to build their cooperation outside the EEC legal framework in the form of intergovernmental cooperation (such as for TREVI in 1975, CELAD, Ad Hoc Group Immigration etc.), by limiting the involvement of the EU institutions to the presence of the Commission representatives at their meetings. It has to be noted that for the European Parliament the situation was frustrating even in the EEC legal framework where it was only rarely consulted and erratically informed by the other institutions. Furthermore, consultation of the Parliament was more close to a formality than a sign of a serious political dialogue.

As a matter of fact at that time in the institutional legislative arena, the Council and the Commission practically worked as closed partnership. They would cooperate on every legislative dossier for decades on a daily basis. The Commission officials would work in the Council working groups, and the ministerial representatives were the core of the Committees working for the Commission when the latter implemented Council decisions (9/10 of the binding acts adopted by the Commission).

This situation went back to the time of the 1965 Merger Treaty which imposed that "[...] The Council and the Commission shall consult each other and shall settle by common accord their methods of cooperation".[3] Following this Treaty provision, the internal rules of the two institutions were (and still are) drafted in a way that allowed them to influence each other's agenda if they so wished.

Needless to say, such daily cooperation between the officials of the Commission and the Council has created, along the decades, a sort of administrative culture of complicity. Obviously this culture, for the good and for the bad, could strongly influence the decision taken respectively at a political level by the commissioners and by the ministers. The proof of such an influence was (and still is) that less than only 20% of the Commission and Council decisions required a political discussion by the Council ministers or by the commissioners. Therefore, the real negotiations for shaping European compromises were (and to my understanding

2 As it was suggested by the jurisprudence of the ECJ (in the sense that the persons who wanted to use services could travel to another Member State to use those services provided).

3 Art. 15 of the "Merger" Treaty, currently the first paragraph of Article 218 of the EC Treaty.

still are) the result of the intelligence and determination of some thousands of civil servants in the Commission and in the Council.[4]

The European Parliament, on the contrary, was formally and even physically apart in the daily game of the legislative negotiations. Whilst the Council and the Commission worked in Brussels, the Parliament met in Strasbourg and Luxembourg. Consequently, it was difficult for MEPs to meet a member of the other institutions outside the rare, formal occasions when an intervention in the plenary was required notably by the President or by a member of the Commission. There was virtually no way to include a minister of the Council Presidency in a committee meeting. Additionally, the internal rules of the Council make only a very limited and formal reference to the relations with the European Parliament.[5]

As Council and Commission officials shared (and share) the same working space, it was at these times occasionally difficult to understand which institution was the real originator of messages to the European Parliament relating to the definition of European strategies for example, and even of replies to parliamentary questions. Such lack of transparency towards the European Parliament was even greater in the internal preparatory works of the Council decisions. The Council General Secretariat prevented internal officials and ministerial representatives from having the opportunity to share preparatory documents and information with institutions other than the Commission. This administrative culture of the "*arcana imperii*" would soon be challenged after the negative result of the Danish referendum on the Maastricht Treaty in 1992 but for the entirety of the 1980s and 1990s the European Parliament and civil society was cut out from the daily practical work of the other institutions.

This situation was particularly frustrating for an institution which was directly elected since 1979 but had the feeling to be practically

---

4 According to Sabino Cassese the credibility of the EU administration founded on public competition is comparable to the excellent one of the French *Hautes Écoles* which was designed on the system that formed the highest bureaucracy representatives in the Chinese Empire.

5 Council Decision of 15 September 2006 adopting the Council's Rules of Procedure (2006/683/EC, Euratom), *O.J.*, No. L 285 of 16 October 2006, p. 47. Rules of Procedure as last amended by Council Decision of 8 December 2008 (2008/945/EC, Euratom), *O.J.*, No. L 337 of 16 December 2008, p. 92, Art. 26, Representation before the European Parliament: "The Council may be represented before the European Parliament or its committees by the Presidency or, with the latter's agreement, by the following Presidency or by the Secretary-General. The Council may also be represented before those committees by its Deputy Secretary-General or senior officials of the General Secretariat, acting on instructions from the Presidency. The Council may also present its views to the European Parliament by means of a written statement".

irrelevant and not taken seriously into account by the two other institutions as well as by the public opinion and the press who presented the Strasbourg assembly more as a virtual than a real actor. To overcome this situation – as other national Parliaments had done before in the history – the European Parliament engaged then with the other institutions in a sort of institutional "guerrilla warfare" with the aim to strengthen its role starting by using its relatively large budgetary powers as well by engaging procedural quarrels linked with the protection of its prerogative to be fully consulted on the future binding acts of the European Economic Community.

The European Parliament was keen on the ECJ jurisprudence according to which the consultation of the EP is "an essential procedural requirement" (Case 138/79, *SA Roquette Frères v Council* [1980]) failure to comply constitutes ground for annulment as

> [...] the effective participation of the Parliament in the legislative process of the Community, in accordance with the procedures laid down by the Treaty, represents an essential factor in the institutional balance intended by the Treaty. Such power reflects the fundamental democratic principle that the people should take part in the exercise of power through the intermediary of a representative assembly.

Building on this favourable orientation of the ECJ the EP started by asking for more and more information on the background of the proposals, by delaying the adoption of its opinion and by requiring a new consultation every time that new substantial elements were added by the Council to the Commission proposal after the first opinion of the European Parliament.[6]

With all these initiatives the European Parliament was *de facto* challenging the seriousness of the other two institutions and pretending the loyal cooperation by the other institutions as required by the Article 10 TEC (ex Article 5). To be frank not all the political and legal challenges launched by the European Parliament were always strongly founded so that in one case the Court of Justice ruled against the European Parliament delaying tactic by recalling that the Council has the right to act if the Parliament does not deliver its opinion by the prescribed deadline without any particular reason.[7] Apart from this "incident", in other significant cases, the Court of Justice supported the European Parliament's willingness to play a more credible role in the EC decision-making process and recognised in a landmark case the EP's "right to

---

6 On the Council obligation to reconsult the EP, see Case C-65/90, *European Parliament v Council* [1992].

7 In Case C-65/93 of 30 March 1995, *European Parliament v Council* (Art. 43 EEC Treaty – Obligation to consult the Parliament.), ECR I-00643, 1995.

stand" before the Court[8] when its prerogatives were at stake. Similarly it recognised that the European Parliament had the right to challenge the Commission by an action for failure to act according to the Article 175 of the EC Treaty (currently Article 232 of the TEC) as the Commission was delaying the presentation of a legislative proposal required by the Treaty.[9]

In its jurisprudence in favour of the only directly elected European institutions, the Court of Justice was in fact fleshing out a more general political move shared by several Member States who wanted to upgrade the political dimension of the European Community as well as its internal ways to work and the balance of powers between the institutions. A clear message in this direction was the adoption by the European Council in Stuttgart, on 19 June 1983 of the "Solemn Declaration on European Union". With this text the Head of States and Governments expressed, among several other priorities, their willingness "[…] to strengthen and develop European Political Cooperation […]" and "[…] to promote, to the extent that these activities cannot be carried out within the framework of the Treaties […]" the need for an "[…] approximation of certain areas of the legislation of the Member States in order to facilitate relationships between their nationals" as well as for "[…] a common analysis and concerted action to deal with international problems of law and order, serious acts of violence, organized international crime and international lawlessness generally". In the same Solemn Declaration the Head of State and Government recognised that the participation of the EP in the decision-making process should have been strengthened and even extended if only on an optional basis, on some highly political domains where such a consultation was not formally required by the Treaty.[10] Needless to say, this new political vision gave the opportunity to the European Parliament to adopt on 14 February 1984 a report of Altiero Spinelli who proposed a fully fledged new draft Treaty (even if it was only of political nature) on the European Union.

---

8 In Case 70/88, *Parliament v Council* (*Chernobyl*), it was shown that the EP was entitled to challenge the Council and the Commission where its prerogatives were directly affected.

9 By this judgement the CJCE stressed that "[…] the fact that the European Parliament is at the same time the Community institution whose task is to exercise a political review of the activities of the Commission, and to a certain extent those of the Council, is not capable of affecting the interpretation of the provisions of the Treaty on the rights of action of the Institutions. Accordingly the European Parliament has the capacity to bring an action for failure to act".

10 In Case 165/87, *Commission v Council* [1988], the ECJ recognised the validity of such optional consultations.

3. The Transitional Phase: From the Cooperation to the Co-decision with the Council (from the Single European Act to the Amsterdam Treaty)

It would then have been necessary to wait for the Single European Act (February 1986) to see the implementation of some of the Stuttgart Declaration innovations. The main objective of the Treaty being the creation by 1 January 1993 of a Single Market without internal borders. This Treaty extended the policies for which the unanimity in the Council was abandoned by strengthening at the same time the association of the EP with the "cooperation" procedure. Even if the Treaty was much less ambitious than the draft Treaty proposed by the European Parliament, its innovations were successful and allowed for the realisation of a space without internal borders for services, capitals and goods. For the freedom of movement of people it appeared immediately clear that it would have been politically impossible to build on some articles (such as the Article 7a TEC, 100a TEC, etc.) and declarations (on Article 7a TEC) a Community area even with the necessary compensatory measures in the JHA domain. Faced with the deadlock of some Member States others launched, outside of the Community framework, the Schengen Cooperation which would had been after 1999 the core of the future cooperation inside the European Union.

The EP reacted to the innovations of the Single European Union with a fundamental revision of its internal rules of procedures by re-launching the inter-institutional game. Being aware of its impossibility to influence adequately the Council, it focused its pressure on the Commission to bring her closer to the EP or, at least, in a more neutral position where it could really play its role of guardian of the Treaty and of an honest broker between the EP and the Council.

The main elements which placed pressure on the Commission were, on a negative side, the power of the EP to vote a motion of censure (Article 144 of the EEC Treaty and Article 201 of the EC Treaty[11] and on a positive side the possibility to influence its nomination by the governments of the Member States as announced in the Stuttgart Decla-

---

[11] Art. 201: "If a motion of censure on the activities of the Commission is tabled before it, the European Parliament shall not vote thereon until at least three days after the motion has been tabled and only by open vote. If the motion of censure is carried by a two-thirds majority of the votes cast, representing a majority of the members of the European Parliament, the members of the Commission shall resign as a body. They shall continue to deal with current business until they are replaced in accordance with Article 214. In this case, the term of office of the members of the Commission appointed to replace them shall expire on the date on which the term of office of the members of the Commission obliged to resign as a body would have expired".

ration where an opinion of the EP Bureau was foreseen.[12] It is worth noting that even the Single European Act did not change the appointment procedure decided at the very beginning by the Member States. A formal association of the EP with the appointment of the Commission would only come in 1993 with the Maastricht Treaty, and only the Lisbon Treaty, if ratified, will give the final word to the EP and thereby establish a direct relation between the EP and the Commission.

3.1. How to bring the Commission closer to the Parliament...

In the daily legislative work the European Parliament's strategy to bring the Commission closer was achieved by amending on 16 January 1986 its internal rules[13] with notably three different changes.

The first one was aimed to push the Commission to choose for its legislative proposal as often as possible a legal basis allowing the association of the EP in cooperation with the Council instead of the simple consultation. A systematic check of the legal basis by the Legal Affairs Committee was (and still is) foreseen in the rules. This move opened the "legal basis" saga even if, as a matter of principle, the choice of the legal basis for a measure must rest on objective factors which are amenable to judicial review so to avoid the situation of the EC violating the principle of attribution, according to which it can legislate only when it is specifically authorised by the Treaty. The point is that the legal definitions in the Treaties are often rather vague and some policies could cover different and sometimes conflicting objectives. This could open the way to multiple solutions in shaping the legislative proposals with an impact also on the possible majority in Council or the level of participation of the Parliament. It is worth noting that in another landmark case, *Titanium Dioxide*,[14] the Court made clear that in presence of a concurrent possible legal basis, solutions which should be avoided were those that

[12] "2.3.5 Before the appointment of the President of the Commission, the President of the Representatives of the Governments of the Member States seeks the Opinion of the enlarged Bureau of the European Parliament. After the appointment of the members of the Commission by the Governments of the Member States, the Commission presents its programme to the European Parliament to debate and to vote on that programme".

[13] On a report of Sir Christopher Prout member of the Petitions and Rules Committee.

[14] See Case C-300/89 of 11 June 1991, *Commission of the European Communities v Council* – Directive on waste from the titanium dioxide industry. The Court declared (emphasis added) "2. Where an institution's power is based on two provisions of the Treaty, it is bound to adopt the relevant measures on the basis of the two relevant provisions. However, where, as in the case of Article 100a of the Treaty, one of the enabling provisions requires recourse to the cooperation procedure provided for in Article 149(2) of the Treaty, on conclusion of which the Council may act by a qualified majority provided that it intends accepting the amendments proposed by the Parliament and put forward by the Commission, and the other provision, as in the case of

> [...] would divest the cooperation procedure of its very substance, the purpose of that procedure being to increase the involvement of the European Parliament in the legislative process of the Community. That participation reflects a fundamental democratic principle that the peoples should take part in the exercise of power through the intermediary of a representative assembly.

The second, more "Machiavellian" move, was the provision for a double plenary vote on each legislative proposal to open a negotiation space by which to obtain, if necessary, substantial amendments of the Commission proposal (and accessorily change the text on the Council table). According to the EP rules the first vote is aimed at adopting, modifying or rejecting the Commission proposal. At the end of this first vote the political will of the Parliament is established and could start (if the EP *rapporteur* so wishes) a political negotiation with the Commission to convince to change, totally or partially, its proposal. If the Commission accepts to do so the original proposal will be modified not only for the Parliament but notably for the Council which, according to the Treaty (current Article 252 TEC) is bound by the Commission proposal and can change it substantially only by a unanimous vote and a reconsultation of the Parliament. In more simple terms, through the double vote the EP uses its new "privileged" relation with the Commission to influence the Council which was the real target of this move on the chess board. In fact, according to the cooperation procedure the Council could practically ignore the EP amendments but then needs to adopt the proposal by unanimity – unless the Commission changes the text again. But a new amendment by the Commission against the vote of the EP will become practically and politically impossible because the text will be resubmitted to the EP. By doing so the Commission was placed in an uncomfortable position and the Council was no longer able to obtain practically everything, as it was before.

The third move of the Parliament was to engage the two other institutions in the negotiation of the legislative programme. The explicit aim of such an exercise was apparently innocent and even sensible as a clear calendar made it possible to organise the different "readings" of the Parliament and of the Council required notably by the cooperation

Article 130s, requires the Council to act unanimously after merely consulting the European Parliament, use of both of them as a joint legal basis would divest the cooperation procedure of its very substance, the purpose of that procedure being to increase the involvement of the European Parliament in the legislative process of the Community. That participation reflects a fundamental democratic principle that the peoples should take part in the exercise of power through the intermediary of a representative assembly. It follows that in such a case recourse to a dual legal basis is excluded and that it is necessary to determine which of those two provisions is the appropriate legal basis".

procedure. The impact of this transparency would therefore have been less freedom of movement against the other institutions. At that time this would have been unconceivable for the Council who still considered itself the master of its own agenda. On the contrary, the Commission and particularly Commissioner Sutherland, considered that a clearer planning would have strengthened the right of legislative initiative of the Commission by establishing a minimum level of "discipline" and predictability in the work of the European Parliament. The experience which followed showed interesting results even though they were very different to what each institution was expecting. The Council became trapped in its internal six-month working plan and the Presidencies were increasingly dependent on the calendar of the new Commission proposals and of the Parliament votes. The Commission established a strict internal planning by regularly informing the other institutions which raised more and more requests of information on the preparatory phase of the Commission proposal. The only institution which remained paradoxically free in its agenda (out of the deadlines established in the Treaty) was the EP who now had all the information needed to press the Commission and at the same time the Council Presidencies to agree the priorities to be debated in the following six months. EP influence on the other institution's agendas became progressively clearer even if no mention of it was made in the internal rules of the Council or Commission.

All this institutional progress in the "Community" domain were unfortunately not transposable in the framework of the so-called "European Political Cooperation" (EPC) covering the EU external and internal security (as outlined in 1983 by the Stuttgart Solemn Declaration and formalised at Treaty level by the Single European Act). Since then, and in parallel with the corresponding practice followed within the Political Committee of the European Parliament where, four times a year, the foreign affairs minister of the Council Presidency informed the MEPs of the major subject of the external policy (EPC), the Legal Affairs Committee was – even if on a less regular basis – informed by a Presidency minister of interior or of justice about the negotiations and achievements such as the definition outside the EC of the first phase of the Schengen cooperation after the signature of the Schengen Convention in 1985. A "contact-procedure"[15] was also established in 1990 after pressure from the EP between the Presidency of the Council (Justice and Home Af-

15 In practice, the President in office of the Council would meet a designated Vice-President of the Parliament (and some members of the Committee on Legal Affairs of the EP) in order to listen to the views of the EP. The discussions, although well prepared by the EP, were behind closed doors and very often the minister responsible was not very open.

fairs) and the Legal Affairs Committee of the EP. In practice, the President in office of the Council met a designated Vice-President of the Parliament (and some members of the Committee on Legal Affairs of the EP) in order to listen to the views of the EP. According to some MEPs who had participated in these meetings, the debates, although thoroughly prepared by the EP, were held behind closed doors and very often the minister responsible was rather reticent and elusive.

3.2. The Maastricht Treaty and the Third Pillar

All these procedures where more theoretical than substantial and they were substantially upgraded only after the entry into force of the Maastricht Treaty (1993). This Treaty was in fact the first serious answer to the problems raised by the fall of the Berlin Wall, by the pressure of the economic globalisation and by the increasing intra-community movement of persons. It created the European Union, launched the process for the Euro, made an explicit reference to the protection of fundamental rights (as already acknowledged for years by the ECJ) established a European Citizenship as well as a cooperation between the Member States in the fields of Justice and Home Affairs (the so-called "third pillar").[16] From an institutional point of view the main achievement of the Treaty was the creation of the so-called "co-decision" procedure where the European Parliament was (at last!) placed on the same level as the Council in several important domains of the Community competences. This was a historical moment for the institution, the members and the external world, as the European Parliament was finally, for the good or for the bad, in the centre of the political scene. After some initial tentative attempts by the General Secretariat of the Council to present the new procedure as a sort of strengthened "cooperation" of the EP in the adoption of a Council decision,[17] it was accepted that the European Parliament should be treated by the Commission at the same level as the Council. In the new framework the Commission preserved its right of initiative and was to become more and more the "honest broker" between the other two institutions but also progressively losing the control of the content of the proposal to the extent Council and Parliament developed a closer cooperation.

The dialogue between the three institutions soon became very highly thought of and the European Parliament apparently played its cards very

[16] The policies covered by the "third pillar" in the Maastricht Treaty, Title VI TEU, were listed in Art. K.2 TEU.

[17] The Treaty, which makes a clear reference to the "consultation" and "cooperation" procedure, avoids calling it a "co-decision" procedure, but following a truly byzantine and warped style refers to this procedure with the formula "The Council acting in accordance with the procedure referred to in Article 251 of the Treaty […]".

well if at the end of the legislature the Council Presidency recognised that the intervention of the MEPs constituted a real added value for the entire process bringing new ideas, new interests and more transparency in the decision-making process of the European Community. From the date of the entry into force of the Maastricht Treaty (1 November 1993) and the end of the fourth legislature (mid 1999) 153 acts were adopted in co-decision. It is interesting that for more than one third (38%) it was necessary to convene the conciliation committee foreseen by the Treaty and that in more than 60% of the cases it was possible to reach an agreement at the stage of the second reading of the European Parliament. The meetings between MEPs, ministers and commissioners became increasingly frequent and the direct intervention of the "political authorities" downgraded, for the good or the bad, the role of the officials of the Commission and of the General Secretariat of the Council. This happened although the latter tried by any means to limit the space of manoeuvre of the Presidency by continually recalling its duty to preserve the confidentiality of the internal negotiations of the Council and moreover the need not to reveal the names of the national delegation potentially interested to be a part of the qualified majority needed to adopt the act or part of the minority which can block its adoption.

It soon became clear therefore that the confidentiality rules which had been applied for decades in an hierarchical organisation such as the General Secretariat of the Commission or of the Council would not resist in a political dialogue where each Council Presidency was keen to obtain as soon as possible a result, every commissioner, minister or *rapporteur* was keen to be the first to reveal the impact of its role in the legislative procedure. Lobbyists and journalists started to place pressure on the MEPs, and the LIBE Committee multiplied the public hearings where issues formerly negotiated in the working groups of the Council or of the Directorate-General of the Commission where publicly debated and notably voted.

Faced with this Copernican revolution in regards to how the European legislation could be shaped, the European Parliament decided to establish a full parliamentary committee responsible for the policies linked to "Justice and Home Affairs". Created in January 1992, the Civil Liberties Committee (LIBE)[18] tried, as a first priority, to flesh out the

---

[18] The following Chair persons, took initiatives to further develop the institutional position of the EP and of the LIBE Committee:

1992-1994, Amedée Turner;

1994-1995, António Vitorino;

1995-1997, Luís Marinho;

1997-1999, Hedy d'Ancona;

1999-2001, Graham Watson;

obligation established in the Article K.6 of the new Treaty according to which:

> The Presidency and the Commission shall regularly inform the European Parliament of discussions in the areas covered by this Title. The Presidency shall consult the European Parliament on the principal aspects of activities in the areas referred to in this Title and shall ensure that the views of the European Parliament are duly taken into consideration.

Therefore, the Council and Commission, notwithstanding all the developments between the EU institutions in the same period within the co-decision related domains, resisted the pressures of the LIBE Committee and refused to consider these Treaty obligations as comparable to the obligations to consult or inform the European Parliament in the Community "pillar". The formal excuse was that, even if the Treaty referred to the Council, the initiatives came in fact from the Member States in an intergovernmental framework[19] so that the Council was unable to collect more than the very weak documentation sent to the EP or give complementary information on the draft Joint Positions or Joint Actions or Conventions foreseen by Article K3 of the EU Treaty.

Faced with such a lack of cooperation from the other institutions and to the impossibility to challenge it before the Court of Justice (as the third pillar was explicitly excluded by the Treaty from the competence of the ECJ) LIBE decided to re-focus its activity on the annual political debate on Justice and Home Affairs. Those very lively debates were extensively reported in the press and gave support to the Committee in it's strive to develop community action.

But the main focus of the LIBE Committee was on the protection of fundamental rights within the EU. Formally this move was founded on an explicit reference in Article 6 TEU and on a phrase in Article K.2, first paragraph[20] as well as on the practice already followed by the EP External Affairs Committee who held an annual debate on the respect of human rights outside the EC. Politically this initiative regarding the

2001-2003, Ana Palacio;

2003-2004, Hernandez Mollar;

2004-2005, Jean Louis Bourlanges;

2005-2007, Jean Marie Cavada;

2007-2009, Gérard Deprez;

2009-…, Juan Fernando López Aguilar.

19 In fact even the Commission was often not informed of the background.

20 Art. K.2(1) TEU: "The matters referred to in Article K.1 shall be dealt with in compliance with the European Convention for the Protection of Human Rights and Fundamental Freedoms of 4 November 1950 and the Convention relating to the Status of Refugees of 28 July 1951 and having regard to the protection afforded by Member States to persons persecuted on political grounds".

protection of fundamental rights by the Member States themselves was at that time considered somewhat provocative and rash, not only because the Member States considered themselves beyond reproach in these domains (notwithstanding the hundreds of judgements of the Strasbourg Court showing the contrary) but moreover because this kind of debate would lift to the European level a lot of divisive questions from the national level.

The first LIBE *rapporteur* on this subject was Karel de Gucht[21] who had already been in 1989 the *rapporteur* in the Committee on Legal Affairs and Citizens' Rights for the first Catalogue of Human Rights adopted by the European Parliament.[22] Needless to say that the reports on fundamental rights became the periodic occasion of very lively debates in plenary and of political debates and initiatives by the other institutions. In particular by a resolution of 18 January 1994 the European Parliament reiterated the request to promote the Community accession to the European Convention on Human Rights,[23] and on 26 April 2004 the Council decided to ask the formal opinion of the Court of Justice on this subject. Therefore on 28 March 1996 the Court of Justice after a strong re-affirmation of the importance of the fundamental rights in the EU legal system considered that the accession by the EC "[…] would be of constitutional significance and would therefore be such as to go beyond the scope of Article 235. It could be brought about only by way of Treaty amendment". (Opinion 2/94)

4. From the Treaty of Amsterdam (1999) to the Treaty of Lisbon: The EP Contribution to the European AFSJ

One and half years later (2 October 1997) the Member States signed the Treaty of Amsterdam by which the European Union proclaimed to be founded on fundamental rights (Article 6 TEU) and stressed its objective "to maintain and develop the Union as an Area of Freedom, Security and Justice […]" (AFSJ) (Article 2 TEU). Due mainly to UK opposition it was impossible to amend the Treaty to allow the accession to the ECHR, but consistent with the objective of transforming the EU in an AFSJ the new Treaty transferred new powers to the European Union, strengthened the measures in favour of the European Citizenship (transparency, data protection) against any form of discrimination (Article 13 TEC), integrated the cooperation of Schengen, transferred

---

21 See the EP Resolution of 11 March 1993 on respect for human rights in the European Community published in *O.J.*, No. C 115 of 26 April 1993, p. 178.

22 See the EP Resolution of 12 April 1989 on the Declaration of Fundamental Rights and Freedoms published in *O.J.*, No. C 120 of 16 May 1989, p. 51.

23 *O.J.*, No. C 44 of 14 February 1994, p. 32.

some policies from the third pillar to the "Community" regime (migration, asylum, external borders, judicial cooperation in civil matters). Such an ambitious evolution had only been possible at the price of accepting ambiguous formulations, evolutionary clauses, complex and tricky compromises mirrored in 13 Protocols, 51 Declarations adopted by the Conference and 8 Declarations by Member States.

To understand why the Member States were pushing so hard towards a political union and why there was so much emphasis on the founding principles and values one should recall not only the determination expressed by Chancellor Kohl and President Chirac "[...] to put the finishing touches to the formation in Europe of a homogeneous space, where freedom of movement will be guaranteed by a common approach" but, moreover, that in the same period the European Union was negotiating its biggest enlargement with ten new Member States (some of them only recently re-instituted as liberal democracies). The Member States, building on the criteria set in Copenhagen for the accession negotiations, decided upon the creation in the EU Treaty of a political mechanism to preserve the decision-making process of the Union in case one of a serious and persistent breach by a Member State of principles founding the Union. By so doing (quite surprisingly) the Member States were developing at the highest level an exercise that the European Parliament hand launched only some years before.

Therefore it was clear that once created these monitoring mechanisms would have covered also the founding Member States which were from then on, also in these sensible domains no more "above any reasonable doubt". Per se, such a move meant no more than to align the EU Member States with their responsibilities before the Strasbourg Court or in the framework of the implementation of the Article 52 of the ECHR when the violation of fundamental rights would have been at stake. *De facto*, as the following experience showed even the very existence of this mechanism inside the EU created some big embarrassment between the EU Member States.[24]

Needless to say the most difficult issue was the protection of fundamental rights as there was no agreed definition common to all the Member States nor an internal EU interpreting mechanism (as even after Amsterdam the Court of Justice was excluded from the second pillar policies and a substantial part of the third pillar) nor the possibility for the EU to invoke the Strasbourg Court as the EU was not a contracting party of the ECHR.

---

[24] There were several cases were the mechanism of Article 7 TEU has been invoked (even if never formally launched) such as the case for the Haider case, ECHELON, the Media Pluralism, or the CIA flights, and in many parliamentary resolutions.

To find a pragmatic even if transitional solution for the citizens and the institutions some weeks before the entry into force of the Treaty the European Council launched in Köln, with the support of a EP resolution, the process which led to the proclamation in December 2000 of the Charter of fundamental rights.

Faced with the ambitious but fragile perspectives opened by the Treaty of Amsterdam the European Parliament decided to become a driving force in shaping the future EU action in the AFSJ and to turn the other Community and Union policy into a tool to promote and not only protect fundamental rights. It is worth noting that from the very beginning of the legislature the European Parliament (on initiative of its AFCO and LIBE Committees) made clear to the other institutions that it considered the development of the EU as an AFSJ much more than a simple consolidation of the policies previous listed in the administrative formula of "Justice and Home Affairs".

According to the EP vision the AFSJ was to be a more ambitious political objective focused on the fundamental rights of the individual and on a more general vision of the European public order where the EU institutions and the national authorities act in a multilevel and legally integrated framework.[25] The LIBE Committee and the Political Groups submitted to the plenary several resolutions[26] stressing this message to the European Council and to the Member States in the perspective linked of the preparation and implementation of the first multi-annual programme for the AFSJ (Tampere 1999).

---

25 This was the implicit message in the revision of the competencies of its LIBE Committee as Committee responsible for the freedom security and justice related policies area (AFSJ) complemented by the policies on transparency, data protection and the fight against discrimination. Contrary to what was (and is) foreseen in the internal distribution of competencies in the Council and in Commission these policies even if not formally cited by the Treaties have been considered by the European Parliament as essential elements for the development of the AFSJ.

26 Such as the Resolution recalled in para. 43 of the European Council Conclusions in Cologne on 3 June 1999, "The European Council calls attention to the action plan for the creation of an area of freedom, security and justice, which it approved in Vienna, and calls upon the institutions to press ahead swiftly with the action plan's implementation. It welcomes the fact that the European Parliament has approved a Resolution on the Vienna action plan and gave due consideration to this subject at a conference with Members of Parliament from the Member States on 22 and 23 March 1999. The results of the conference will be taken into consideration when the European Council establishes the political guidelines for future European justice and home affairs policy at its extraordinary meeting in Tampere on 15 and 16 October 1999"; and the Resolution on the extraordinary European Council meeting on the area of freedom, security and justice, Tampere, 15-16 October 1999 adopted at the beginning of the legislature on 16 September 1999. Minutes Part II, Item 10(b), *O.J.*, C 54 of 25 February 2000, pp. 93-94.

Despite their high political level (and somehow rhetorical) declarations in the following years, the European Parliament and the other institutions were confronted with several internal and external challenges which made evident the different cultures and approaches. Some of these challenges are, ten years later, still sources of tension and political misunderstandings and some others (more linked with the internal procedural machinery) will only be settled by the Treaty of Lisbon (if and when it will enter into force).

4.1. How to Better Monitor the Respect of the Founding Principles of the EU (Article 6 and 7 TEU)

Since the entry into force of the Treaty of Amsterdam the "sanctions mechanism" foreseen by the Article 7 of the TEU as well the "alert system" (inserted by the Treaty of Nice in the same context), have been evocated on several occasions but never formally activated for several reasons, the main being that the institution which was more vocal in this context was never able to obtain the support of the political groups representing at least two thirds of the Members of the EP as required by the TEU.

In two cases a majority was reached to establish temporary parliamentary committees in charge of further (political and not formal) inquiries.

The first case was linked with the global secret interception system called "Echelon" which became a subject of public debate thanks to a study by the European Parliament and a public hearing of the LIBE Committee.

After several contradictory declarations and some embarrassed positions adopted by the Council Presidency[27] as well as by the UK Prime Minister who invoked the right for his country to take all the initiatives necessary to preserve its economic well-being, the Parliament created a temporary committee that submitted a report one year later without being able to obtain all the information it was seeking for. The Temporary Committee report was adopted by the Plenary (367 votes in favour, 159 against and 34 abstentions) on 5 September 2001 (only few days before the 9/11 terrorists attacks) and it ascertained the existence of this

[27] On 3 April 2000 the Portuguese Council Presidency, opening a debate in the European Parliament, stressed that the EU could not accept the existence of a telecommunications system irrespective of national laws and fundamental rights, and expressed the hope that the Council would reach a political agreement on the question of interception of communications. On behalf of the European Commission, Mr. Erkki Liikanen stressed that national security fell within the competence of Member States, and drew attention to the non-transposition into national law of the 1995 Data Protection Directive.

world-wide spy network dubbed "Echelon" led by the United States and associating also a member of the EU (UK). When presenting his report to the Parliament, Gerhard Schmid stressed how gruelling the task had been for the Temporary Committee. He brushed aside the idea that all telecommunications systems in Europe were being spied upon as this was physically impossible. Between the 44 recommendations the resolution recommends the widespread use of date encryption and urges the EU institutions to set the example. Therefore, it should be noted that Amendments 6 and 28, which called on Germany and the United Kingdom to stop allowing US intelligence-gathering services to eavesdrop within their borders, was rejected by a large majority.

The second case was on the alleged use of European countries by the CIA for the transportation and illegal detention of prisoners. Again, the decision to create a Temporary Committee was taken after a first debate in the LIBE Committee founded on revelations in the US and European press as well on the parallel inquiry by the Council of Europe Assembly and moreover of a formal inquiry of the Council of Europe Secretary General according to Article 52 of the ECHR. It is also worth noting that the Commission formally wrote to the EU Member States to ascertain if there was ground for an Article 7 of TEU initiative.

On 14 February 2007 the European Parliament adopted (382 votes in favour, 256 against with 74 abstentions) a report drafted by Giovanni Claudio Fava (PES, IT) which deplored the passivity of some Member States in the face of illegal CIA operations, as well as the lack of cooperation from the EU Council of Ministers. In addition, it considered that it was wholly unacceptable that the Council should first have concealed and then, at Parliament's request, only supplied piecemeal information on the regular discussions held with senior officials of the US government, asserting that this was the only available version. These shortcomings of the Council implicated all Member State governments[28] since they have a collective responsibility as members of the Council. Parliament also expressed its concern about the omissions in the statements made to the Temporary Committee by the Council and its Secretary General regarding the Council's discussions and knowledge of the methods used by the United States in its campaign against terrorism. It

---

28 The national governments specifically criticised by the report for their unwillingness to cooperate with Parliament's investigations are those of Austria, Italy, Poland, Portugal and Britain. The report also gave detailed evidence of investigations of illegal rendition or CIA flight cases involving Bosnia, Cyprus, Denmark, the Former Yugoslav Republic of Macedonia (FYROM), Germany, Greece, Ireland, Romania, Spain, Sweden and Turkey.

deplored the fact that the Council was unable to supplement the evidence already possessed of the Temporary Committee.[29]

Faced with the difficulties in establishing a neutral assessment of the state of fundamental rights as described by the Charter of Nice in each EU Member State the European Parliament, in its 2000 resolution,[30] took into account a suggestion of the Cologne 1999 European Council to set up a Fundamental Rights Agency[31] and proposed the creation, as a preparatory measure, of a network of independent experts. The network started its work soon after and its contribution was very much appreciated by the members of LIBE. Furthermore, only three years later on 12 and 13 December 2003 at the European Council, a decision was taken to convert the European Monitoring Centre on Racism and Xenophobia into a Fundamental Rights Agency.

In 2005 the European Parliament, after a LIBE hearing on the subject,[32] called the Commission to submit a legislative proposal to establish the new Agency. It asked that the proposal be based on co-decision between the Parliament and the Council to give the possibility to the legislators of a better shaped structure, better working methods and an increased role for the Agency. The EP objective was to build the Agency as a sort of a new authority, acting like the European data protection supervisor foreseen by Article 286 TEC, and which could be at the same time independent and willing to help the EU legislator in its legislative work and to obtain from the Member States all the necessary information when protection of fundamental rights may be at stake.

It is worth noting that even the Council Legal Service considered this to be a sensible and legally founded strategy, but this was not the position of the Commission. The Commission (probably with the support of several Member States) insisted on a simple data-collecting Agency and,

---

29 Parliament also questioned the real substance of the post of EU Counter-Terrorism Coordinator occupied by Gijs de Vries, since he was unable to give satisfactory answers to the questions raised by the Temporary Committee. It was of the opinion that a revision and strengthening of his competence and power, as well as the increased transparency and monitoring of his activities by Parliament must be undertaken in the near future. Parliament also criticised the lack of cooperation evinced by the Director of the European Police Office (Europol), Max-Peter Ratzel, and expressed its deep concern about the refusals of the former and current Secretaries General of NATO, Lord Robertson and Jaap de Hoop Scheffer, to appear before the Temporary Committee.

30 See http://www.europarl.europa.eu/sides/getDoc.do?pubRef=-//EP//TEXT+TA+P5-TA-2001-0401+0+DOC+XML+V0//EN.

31 See "46. The European Council takes note of the Presidency's interim report on human rights. It suggests that the question of the advisability of setting up a Union agency for human rights and democracy should be considered".

32 See http://www.europarl.europa.eu/hearings/20050425/libe/programme_en.pdf.

by claiming that the future Agency should also cover policies not covered by co-decision, it submitted a proposal to be adopted unanimously by the Council after a simple consultation of the EP.

Not surprisingly the final mandate of the Agency as defined by Council Regulation (EC) No. 168/2007 of 15 February 2007 was then narrowed down and did not cover the most sensible areas of judicial and police cooperation in penal matters and prevented the Agency from establishing single EU country reports.

The result was (and is) so absurd that even the Council one year later consulted the Agency on a draft legislative proposal which fell into the area of police cooperation in penal matters (the so-called "EU-PNR" proposal). A revision of the Agency mandate, or at least of its working methods and Action Plan, will probably be needed after the entry into force of the Lisbon Treaty and of the Charter of Fundamental Rights which require a more stringent verification of the future legislative proposal against the definition set out in the Charter.

4.2. Promoting and not only protecting Fundamental Rights

In a particular case, the difficult question of the compatibility between traditional economic liberties and the impact of fundamental rights was raised. It was the case dealing with the protection of Media Pluralism in the EU (and notably in Italy) in accordance with Article 11 of the European Charter of Fundamental Rights proclaimed in Nice in December 2000. On this subject, the LIBE Committee submitted a general resolution to the EP plenary[33] in which it considered that where Member States fail to take appropriate action, the Union has a political, moral and legal duty, within the limits of its powers, to guarantee media pluralism.

The EP considered that following an explicit judgement of the Italian Constitutional Court, there were sufficient grounds for concern to justify a comprehensive examination of the situation and the presentation of appropriate legislative proposals by the Commission. It took three years for the Commission to submit a statement (16 January 2007) on this subject and to declare that it was "appropriate for the Commission to continue to monitor the situation closely", but that there were not enough elements to justify a formal legislative initiative. On 25 September 2008 (on proposal of its Committee on Culture), the EP adopted a new resolution on media pluralism[34] which asked the Commission to

33 See http://www.europarl.europa.eu/oeil/FindByProcnum.do?lang=en&procnum=INI/2003/2237.

34 See http://www.europarl.europa.eu/sides/getDoc.do?type=TA&reference=P6-TA-2008-0459&language=EN&ring=A6-2008-0303.

establish some objective indicators of risk of violation of pluralism but did not raise again the possibility of an EU intervention in case of difficulties in a Member State.

4.3. The EP as Robin Hood and the Council as the Sheriff of Nottingham? (The interinstitutional saga of "data protection" and "data availability" in the PNR and SWIFT cases)

Last but not least the more notorious example of the different approaches taken by the EU institutions has been the question of data protection when personal data are needed for security purposes, notably in the aftermath of 9/11. It is worth mentioning that only two months after this horrific event the European Parliament was the only EU institution who dared raise profound reservations about the impact of certain measures taken by the USA in the framework of the "war on terror", such as the Patriot Act and the US President's executive order on military tribunals. On this occasion the EP notably demanded:

– not to limit in a disproportionate manner data protection standards (even if under a sunset clause) on electronic surveillance provisions;

– not to admit any discrimination between third-country and non-third-country citizens that would be contrary to the ECHR;

– to guarantee the protection of fundamental rights as regards the monitoring of communications between a prisoner and an attorney;

– the procedural guarantees to a fair trial, as consolidated by the European Court of Human Rights.[35]

---

[35] See EP Resolution on EU judicial cooperation with the United States in combating terrorism accessible http://www.europarl.europa.eu/sides/getDoc.do?pubRef=-//EP//TEXT+TA+P5-TA-2001-0701+0+DOC+XML+V0//EN&language=EN. According to this text the EP considered "... that the US Patriot Act, which discriminates against non-US citizens, and President Bush's executive order on military tribunals are contrary to the principles established above;

3. Considers that, such being the legal situation, legal problems could arise from the fact that the USA considers terrorists as war criminals, whereas this is not the case in the EU; considers that, therefore, no extradition could be allowed to the US from Member States for people who are to be tried before military tribunals;

4. Expresses concern at the fact that the President's executive order does not specify the limits on the court's jurisdiction, makes no provision for the presumption of innocence and the right to an impartial judge and, above all, allows sentences, including capital punishment, to be decided by a two-thirds majority;

5. Reiterates its request for a complete abolition of the death penalty in the USA and reminds Member States that they are bound not only on the basis of their individual ratification of Protocol 6 of the ECHR but also as members of the Union, in accordance with Article 6 of the Treaty; a general EU-USA agreement cannot therefore be reached; extradition cannot take place if the defendant could be sentenced to death;

The main concern of the EP was to avoid the fight against terrorism justifying EU initiatives legalising massive data collection without previously being shaped by the European legal framework for data protection when public security is at stake (as Directive 95/46 is not applicable in this domain). The EP wanted to avoid the creation of a false feeling of security and moreover possible abuses as Article 8 of the ECHR allows for limitations of personal freedoms as far as these are compatible in a democratic society. According to the understanding of the EP, in democracies citizens should be allowed to control the institutions and not only the reverse.

Moreover, it seemed bizarre to the MEPs to endorse, at an EU level, a mass collection of ordinary European citizens data when the same Member States were unwilling to share the data on criminals, terrorists and EU agencies, and, at least at that time, lacked the expertise for analysing the terrorism threat. It took in fact years after 9/11 before the Council was able to agree on the so-called "Swedish Initiative" which granted a minimum level of sharing information between EU Member States security and intelligence services.

Before this background one can understand why, in the following years, the EP was the first institution which asked for the transformation of Europol into a true EU Agency, was able to conclude in three months time the agreement on the EU Directive on data retention, strongly supported the interconnection of criminal records and the inclusion at the EU level of the Prüm Convention (allowing the transfer between security services of the fingerprints of researched or convicted criminals DNA). All these projects encountered resistance inside the Council even if they were a clear improvement in terms of the mutual trust between security services at an EU level.

Yet the European Parliament was extremely reluctant in giving its support to data mining or profiling initiatives such as the systematic collection of personal data other than the ones needed to check the identity of a passenger already known as a terrorist or a dangerous criminal. The "*casus belli*" I would like to refer to is the protection of the personal data of airline passengers travelling to the United States (PNR). After 9/11 the US took the strategic decision to prevent and combat terrorism by pooling both criminal investigation techniques when searching for a known terrorist (FBI) and the technique of detecting potential terrorists based on intelligence and sifting through ever-

6. Requests that expulsion or deportation proceedings should not be used as "disguised" extradition proceedings, and calls on the EU to guarantee European data protection standards that are proportionate, effective and of limited duration and to ensure that no mandatory retention of data be allowed, which would undermine rights and guarantees;"

growing volumes of data (CIA). In particular, it demanded (and still demands) to be given all the data on airline passengers at the time the ticket is booked, for a dual purpose: a) to check their identity; and b) to check how dangerous they might be. While the first objective is perfectly logical and even indispensable, if only to compare against check-lists of terrorists or criminals in the national databases, the second objective seemed to Parliament to be more sensitive and disproportionate in relation to the implementation planned by the US authorities. It would indeed mean to systematically give access to information such as e-mail addresses, credit card numbers, membership of clubs or parties, dietary preferences, lists of flights made and with whom.

For years after March 2003, members of the Commission and Council were pushing to obtain the support of the Parliament and this support was not given for the lack of factual elements showing the effectiveness and the proportionality of these kinds of measures.

It is worth recalling that in a memorable hearing on 14 May 2007, in the presence of the national parliaments and of the US Homeland Security Secretary Chertoff, Vice-President Lambrinidis reacted to the pressure of Minster Schäuble to give up on the PNR by claiming the good faith of the LIBE members by saying

> [...] I do feel frustrated sometimes because I get the sense that we act in the Parliament like the Robin Hood, running around protecting data and we tend to treat you like the Sheriff of Nottingham as you were the only people who care about police measures and all that stuff. This is not true but you do get this impression [...] We still do not have, as you know, the minimal procedural guarantees for defendants although for five years now, we have the European arrest warrant, [...] [for] data protection in the third pillar, [...] we don't know where it is going to go [...] It wouldn't have hurt the Council to make some statement on the extraordinary renditions issue. It was a big issue, Parliament had a huge debate on it.

4.4. The EP-Council Relation: Not only Tensions but also an increasing Loyal and Fruitful Dialogue with the growing Phenomenon of the "First Reading Agreements"

In spite of the previous examples, the dialogue between the European Parliament and notably the Council was mainly characterised by an increasing trust in many other domains of the AFSJ.

This could be proved by the figure of more than 80% agreements in first reading on AFSJ related co-decision procedures during the last legislative term (2004-2009). As it is confirmed by the last activity report[36] of the European Parliament delegation to the Conciliation Committee, since 2004 following notably the December 2004 "*passerelle*" decision[37] the co-decision procedure was applied to "[...] most legal acts regarding borders, visas, asylum, illegal migration and civil law cooperation".[38] Compared to the previous legislative term (1999-2004), the number of co-decisions of the main committee responsible for this area (the LIBE Committee) rose sensibly from 8 to 38 procedures.

The same report highlights that very significant developments took place since the last legislature regarding the stage of conclusion. During the sixth legislature 72% of files were concluded at first reading, 22.9% at second reading[39] and 5.1% in conciliation. This contrasts strongly with the figures for the previous legislatures (see diagram below).

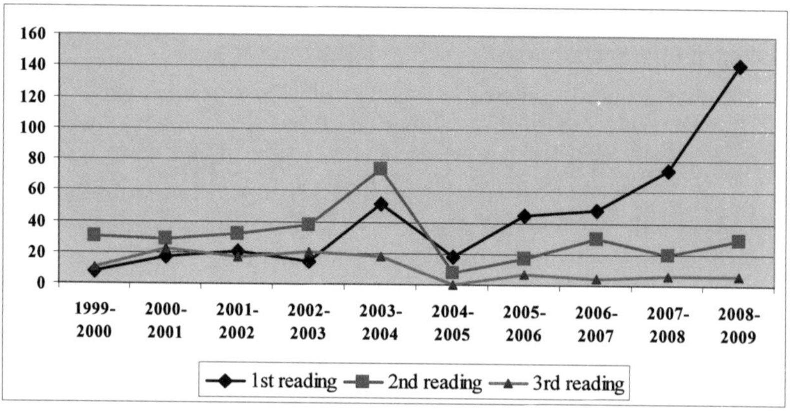

Figure 1: Evolution of the stage of conclusion 1999-2009 (Files adopted between 01.05. and 30.04. each cycle, except for 2008-2009 – all files included) (Source: EP)

---

36 Accessible at the following address: http://www.europarl.europa.eu/code/ information/activity_reports/activity_report_2004_2009_en.pdf.

37 Council Decision of 22 December 2004 providing for certain areas covered by Title IV of Part Three of the Treaty establishing the European Community to be governed by the procedure laid down in Article 251 of that Treaty (2004/927/EC), *O.J.*, No. L 396 of 31 December 2004.

38 For a first analysis of the increased co-decision powers in this area and the role of the LIBE Committee see part I.4 of the Conciliations and Codecision Activity Report 2004-2006; available as the previous reports under http://www.europarl.europa.eu/code/information/activity_en.htm (in the following "Midterm Report 2007").

39 In 10.8% of cases common positions were approved by Parliament without amendments ("early second reading agreement"), 12.1% went into a "classical" second reading.

Turning to the specific domain of AFSJ related policies, the figure of 72% of first reading agreements rises to 84%. This shows an even stronger will of the Council to reach a political agreement with the European Parliament as soon as possible.

It is worth noting that the move towards a closer institutional and political dialogue started in 2001 on two LIBE reports dealing with the domains of transparency[40] and data protection,[41] which were highly controversial and where, on paper, the two institutions seemed to be more apart than in other more technical domains. As a matter of fact, for these two specific cases there was strong pressure on the institutions to reach an agreement. In the first case, 1 May 2001 was the deadline established by the Treaty of Amsterdam to define the principles on transparency and confidentiality to be applied by the three legislative institutions[42] and 1 January 1999 was the deadline to establish "an independent supervisory body"[43] to protect the data in the EU institutions. LIBE negotiated the first proposal (data protection) with the COREPER I (which is the one in charge of the Internal Market legisla-

---

40 Regulation (EC) No. 1049/2001 of the European Parliament and of the Council of 30 May 2001 regarding public access to European Parliament, Council and Commission documents, *O.J.*, No. L 145 of 31 May 2001. see: http://eur-lex.europa.eu/LexUriServ/LexUriServ.do?uri=CELEX:32001R1049:EN:HTML.

41 Regulation (EC) No. 45/2001 of the European Parliament and of the Council of 18 December 2000 on the protection of individuals with regard to the processing of personal data by the Community institutions and bodies and on the free movement of such data, *O.J.*, No. L 8 of 12 January 2001. See: http://eur-lex.europa.eu/LexUriServ/LexUriServ.do?uri=CELEX:32001R0045:EN:HTML.

42 Art. 255 TEC:

"1. Any citizen of the Union, and any natural or legal person residing or having its registered office in a Member State, shall have a right of access to European Parliament, Council and Commission documents, subject to the principles and the conditions to be defined in accordance with paragraphs 2 and 3.

2. General principles and limits on grounds of public or private interest governing this right of access to documents shall be determined by the Council, acting in accordance with the procedure referred to in Article 251 within two years of the entry into force of the Treaty of Amsterdam.

3. Each institution referred to above shall elaborate in its own Rules of Procedure specific provisions regarding access to its documents".

43 Article 286 TEC:

"1. From 1 January 1999, Community acts on the protection of individuals with regard to the processing of personal data and the free movement of such data shall apply to the institutions and bodies set up by, or on the basis of, this Treaty.

2. Before the date referred to in paragraph 1, the Council, acting in accordance with the procedure referred to in Article 251, shall establish an independent supervisory body responsible for monitoring the application of such Community acts to Community institutions and bodies and shall adopt any other relevant provisions as appropriate".

tive procedures) and the second with COREPER II (at ambassadors' level) which was dealing for the first time with these kinds of files and negotiations.

Why has there been such an astonishing increase in the "first reading agreements" since 2004? The EP delegation report cited above explains the trend with six (sometimes complementary) reasons:

a) the possibility to conclude in the first reading following a simple majority vote in Parliament;

b) "[...] the greater number and better contacts between the institutions whose representatives now start talking to each other routinely very early in the procedure";

c) the higher number of uncontroversial and rather technical proposals;

d) the objective, perceived or political urgency of proposals presented by the Commission also seems to play a role;

e) the Council Presidencies being more and more eager to reach quick agreements during their Presidencies and they seem to favour first reading negotiations for which the arrangements are much more flexible than in later stages of the procedure;

f) last but not least, because since the enlargement of 2004 it seems to become increasingly difficult to find a Council position among the now 27 Member States and an early input of the Parliament can be seen as a factor facilitating the Council's internal consensus-building.

I will add to these reasons the fact that in first reading there is no deadline as it is the case for all the phases following the Common position of the Council.

With the entry into force of the Lisbon Treaty this trend will inevitably amplify in the AFSJ domain as co-decision will be extended to judicial and police cooperation in penal matters, to legal migration and a new legal basis will be created for integration etc. It is worth looking closer at the impact of this phenomenon and the way the institutions behave with regards to relations between them and the external world. No one can doubt that for the European Parliament the co-decision in the penal and security area will be a new important challenge as long as these domains are (and remain) jealously protected by the Member States – which also keeps the intervention of the European Commission at the lowest possible level.

Also, after Lisbon, the interinstitutional dialogue should be no longer be anecdotic and frustrating as Article 295 TFEU asks the three institutions (and not only the Council and Commission) to establish common agreements:

> The European Parliament, the Council and the Commission shall consult each other and by common agreement make arrangements for their cooperation. To that end, they may, in compliance with the Treaties, conclude inter-institutional agreements which may be of a binding nature.

If these agreements are fairly negotiated it will be more than likely that the current trend of the first reading agreements will be reinforced. This has already happened since the 2004 enlargement when the growing role of the European Parliament has been accompanied by an increasing difficulty of the EU Council to build, between more than twenty-seven Member States, a qualified majority or to control several possible potential blocking minorities.[44] The Council found its way out from possible blockade by pushing the European Parliament towards an agreement at its first reading of the co-decision procedure (as is possible since the entry into force of the Treaty of Amsterdam). It has to be noted that from a formal point of view a "first reading agreement" requires only a simple majority in the EP, a qualified majority in Council and the Commission's support to the Council qualified majority.[45] It should not be surprising that under such flexible conditions the first cases of "first reading agreements" took place already in 2001 in the AFSJ.[46]

What happens during the "first reading agreements"? – Formally all the political negotiations take place in the framework of the EP's preparatory works which are virtually convened in the same working space. They bring together the Member States represented in the Council working groups, the Council Presidency as spokesperson from the Council side, the Commission and the EP *rapporteur*/shadow *rapporteurs* who refer back to their political groups.

During these preparations, different political dynamics take place: on one side the EP tries to build its simple majority between the political groups and define a political orientation which can be supported by a qualified majority in the Council. Complementary to that move national representatives in the Council try to influence the position of the EP's political groups by invoking a sort of national solidarity.[47]

---

44 The enlargement did not have the same effect in the EP as the number of political players has remained practically the same as well as the possible political combinations to build a majority.

45 Otherwise according to Art. 250 TEC the unanimity of the Council will be required.

46 The first cases of "first reading agreement" have been Regulation (EC) No. 45/2001, *op. cit.* and Regulation (EC) No. 1049/2001, *op. cit.*

47 It has also to be noted that when issues in the AFSJ are particularly complex the EP does not really launch the negotiations with the Council before the representatives of the Member States have had their own "*tour de table*" and raised the reservations of each country on the draft legislative text.

The weight of national interests in the EP is not as heavy as it is in the Council so that there is a strong chance that a possible compromise between the initial positions of the Commission, the Council and the Parliament can take shape. This "third way" is very often opened by external interventions such as independent authorities at European and national level (such as the European Data Protection Supervisor, the Fundamental Rights Agency, the UNHCR, the Article 29 Working Group, Europol, Eurojust, etc.), the national parliaments, academic experts (such as the Odysseus network for migration policies), the civil society representatives (Amnesty International, Statewatch, Human Rights Watch, etc.) and even lobbyists who take advantage of the public debates in the parliamentary committees to give their own view of the situation in the Member States and to try to influence the position of the political groups.

Needless to say, some external interventions have sometimes questioned the viability of the data on which a Commission or a Member State legislative initiative was based and even the impact assessments of the Commission (which in principle should motivate in an objective way all the possible alternatives) have not always been considered conclusive or satisfactory. In some cases, the European Parliament following the US Congress example, launched its own alternative impact assessment. This move was mirrored by the Council which recently requested the Fundamental Rights Agency to draw up a neutral assessment of the Commission's proposal on the EU PNR system. In some cases the European Parliament has even conducted several visits in the Member States to ascertain the real conditions of the reception of asylum seekers in different EU countries by visiting several reception centres and meeting the local regional and national authorities as well as the NGOs and the migrants themselves.

5. Looking Forward: The Need to Strengthen the Principle of Loyal Cooperation at the EU and the National Level

Faced with this evolution in the decision-making process, the proliferation of alternative sources of information and moreover the proliferation of the parliamentary hearings and public debates, alternative solutions to the original Commission proposals could emerge.

This increasing transparency and openness could not be limited to the work of the European Parliament, and the pressure from the Treaty of Lisbon for a stronger and loyal dialogue between the institutions of the legislative trilogue should be more than welcomed.

If well implemented, Article 295 TFEU could break down the current separations between the three institutions and not only between the Council and Commission as it is currently foreseen by Article 218 TEC – see above) to establish common agreements:

> The European Parliament, the Council and the Commission shall consult each other and by common agreement make arrangements for their cooperation. To that end, they may, in compliance with the Treaties, conclude interinstitutional agreements which may be of a binding nature.

At the same time the public debates in the European Parliament push the national parliaments to scrutinise their government's representatives, and it becomes more and more difficult for the national administrations to escape questions on their positions in the working groups of the Council related to new legislative proposals. As is shown by several inquiries at national level, the direct and indirect dialogue between European and national parliamentarians make it increasingly clear, at a national level, what is really at stake in Brussels and bring national parliamentarians to ask for progressively more comparative studies between the Member States themselves.

At the crossroads of all these contacts and reciprocal influences, the "traditional" way of interaction between the institutions and Member states in the implementation of the EU policies become more and more outdated and formalist.

It is therefore hardly defendable before an ordinary EU citizen, and not compliant with the principle of loyal cooperation outlined in Article 10 TEC, that fifty years after the entry into force of the founding Treaties the Commission should still be obliged to launch every year dozens of infringement procedures for the simple fact that the Member States did not notify the national measures implementing the EU/EC rules which in principle should be public as these rules affect the EU citizens' freedoms.

This situation will be even less acceptable after the entry into force of the Treaty of Lisbon notably as far as the AFSJ related policies will be concerned. The Lisbon Treaty emphasis on fundamental rights, the explicit reference to democratic principles (Articles 9 to 12 TEU) and to the enhanced role of political parties as well as to the European citizenship (Articles 18 to 25 TFEU) together with the decision to place the individual at the centre of the new European Union will be worthless if everything can be jeopardised by the resistance of the national and even European administrative bodies and procedures.

It is worthwhile to consider how far the European institutions could go following the new EU obligation to "[…] observe the principle of the equality of its citizens, who shall receive equal attention from its institutions, bodies, offices and agencies" (Article 9 TUE).

As far as the Member States are concerned it will not be only a question of acting in loyal cooperation with the EU (ex Article 10 TEC and Article 4 of the new TEU) but also to actively build a common project where each national judiciary and national parliament[48] could play a "European" role in the interest of the citizen itself enjoying at the same time the national and European citizenship.

Obviously in this new legal framework a peculiar role will be played by national parliaments which, according to Article 12 TEU shall "[...] contribute actively to the good functioning of the Union" notably when AFSJ policies are at stake.

It is worth noting that in the recent years the position of the European and national parliament is coming closer together notably on sensitive issues like the PNR, the CIA flights and the Framework Decision on terrorism. It is more and more frequent that at a national level the positions, or at least the arguments raised during the European Parliament debates, are mirrored. The presence of permanent national parliament's representatives in the EP premises, new informatics tools and networks (even if not comparable to the ones linking together European and national administrations) are all elements of a new virtual working area which can evolve in a inter-parliamentary "Agora".

Several signs notably in the AFSJ show that the period of the institutional liturgies between the parliaments of Europe is drawing to an end and that some national parliamentarians are progressively more comfortable in approaching problems from a European point of view. This evolution could be strengthened by the creation of the a "joint evaluation system" foreseen by Article 70 TFEU according to which

> Without prejudice to Articles 258, 259 and 260 [Commission infringement procedures and Court judgements], the Council may, on a proposal from the Commission, adopt measures laying down the arrangements whereby Member States, in collaboration with the Commission, conduct objective and impartial evaluation of the implementation of the Union policies referred to in this Title by Member States' authorities, in particular in order to facilitate full application of the principle of mutual recognition. The European Parliament and national Parliaments shall be informed of the content and results of the evaluation.

This mechanism, which will associate closely the European and national parliaments in the political evaluation of the AFSJ related policies, could become even more credible if the European and national

[48] According to a consolidated ECJ jurisprudence national judges should consider "European judges" when interpreting and applying the EU rules.

parliaments will connect it with the more specific evaluation of essential tools involved in the implementation of these policies such as Europol and Eurojust (as foreseen by Article 85 and Article 88 TFEU). Measuring political objectives with concrete figures and listing the analysis of the same phenomenon from a national and a European perspective will be an essential asset to measure the real impact of the EU policies and enhance the mutual trust between parliamentarians – and with them the political forces at European and national level.

A stronger link between the European and national parliament is of the utmost importance notably in the AFSJ domain as this could improve the democratic legitimacy of the overall European Union, as strongly emphasised by the German Constitutional Court in 1993 with its Maastricht "*Urteil*"[49] and repeated, with even stronger words with its judgement of 30 June 2009.

A question could therefore arise: has the EU democratic deficit been increased between 1993 and 2009, or on the contrary, has the European Parliament's appearance on the scene with the co-decision procedures changed the perspective? As I tried to demonstrate in this chapter, from a democratic point of view these two different periods are fundamentally different.

If the level of democracy can be measured by taking as a criterion the possibility for the citizens to influence the content of the legislation, there is no doubt that the intervention of the EP has fundamentally changed the way decisions are taken at the EU level. Until 1993 there was practically no way for anybody who was not associated with the dialogue between the Council and the Commission to influence the content of the legislation. Obviously these institutions have also their own strong contacts with civil society but everything is filtered by their internal organisational logic: the rationale of a multinational bureaucracy in the Commission and the skilled diplomacy in the Council.

After no less than 858 co-decision procedures, the European Parliament has now brought other disrupting elements to previous EU ways such as a transparent debate and confrontation with thousands of democratic and verifiable votes (while the culture of the other institutions remain a hierarchical decision-making process in the Commission and the consensus building in the Council).

The experience of the last decade, notably after the 2004 enlargement, shows that the parliamentarian method had some collateral positive effects on the ways in which the other institutions work by bringing more transparency to the position taken by the national delegations

[49] Decision of the German Federal Constitutional Court of 12 October 1993, 2 BvR L 134/92 and 2159/92.

inside the Council or confronting the Commission services with alternative impact assessments on a given issue.

It is true that from a traditional point of view this growing role of the European Parliament takes shape without the parallel formation of a "European" government as neither the Commission nor the Council could play this role. But the absence of a real European government means that consequently, in the European Parliament, the political majorities can be built issue by issue and by the nominal vote each European citizen can verify the behaviour of the elected.

There is, however, to my understanding, an essential need for the legislator and the EP in particular. Both often greatly need independent assessments of the situations where essential interests of the citizens could be at stake. Nobody can underestimate the role played in this perspective by the Court of Justice, the Court of Human Rights and notably the National Constitutional Courts. But this role is not available when legislation is taking shape (contrary to what happens for instance in France with the *Conseil Constitutionnel*). Such an independent support could in fact be extremely helpful in the AFSJ domain in which major issues are at stake and where the risk of exploitation for partisan political quarrels either at national or European level is all the bigger. The creation of the European Data Protection authority has played an essential role in these years even if on several occasions the institutions have not followed its opinion. As these opinions were public, the citizens had the opportunity to make their own judgement.

Will this approach be developed after the entry into force of the Lisbon Treaty, for instance in the case of the Union's Fundamental Rights Agency? It will soon be known as it will be the case for the other objectives of the AFSJ which will be decided by the European Council when it adopts the Stockholm Programme in December 2009.

CHAPTER 5

Casual but Smart

The Court's New Clothes in the Area of Freedom, Security and Justice (AFSJ) after the Lisbon Treaty

Vassilis HATZOPOULOS

1. Introduction

Unintended as it was, the European Court of Justice (ECJ) has played an extremely important role in the construction of the Area of Freedom Security and Justice (AFSJ). The AFSJ was set up by the Treaty of Amsterdam in 1997 and only entered into force in May 1999. The fact that this is a new field of EU competence, poses afresh all the fundamental questions – both political and legal – triggered by European integration, namely in terms of: a) distribution of powers between the Union and its Member States; b) attribution of competences between the various EU Institutions; c) direct effect and supremacy of EU rules; d) scope of competence of the ECJ; and e) extent of the protection given to fundamental rights. The above questions have prompted judicial solutions which take into account both the extremely sensible fields of law upon which the AFSJ is anchored, and the EU's highly inconvenient three-pillar institutional framework.[1] This structure is on the verge of being abandoned, provided the Treaty of Lisbon enters into force.

The ECJ is the body whose institutional role is to benefit most from this upcoming "depilarisation", possibly more than that of the European Parliament.[2] However spectacular this formal boost of the Court's competence, the changes in real terms are not going to be that dramatic. This apparent contradiction is explained, to a large extent, by the fact

1 For a systematic account of the Court's case-law in this field see Vassilis Hatzopoulos, "With or without you... Judging politically in the field of area of freedom, security and justice", *European Law Review*, Vol. 33, No. 1, 2008, pp. 44-65; see also Henri Labayle, "Architecte ou spectatrice? La Cour de Justice de l'Union dans l'Espace de liberté, sécurité et justice", *Revue Trimestrielle de Droit Européen*, Vol. 42, No. 1, 2006, p. 1.

2 For a general assessment of the jurisdictional role of the Court after the entry into force of the Lisbon Treaty see Floris de Witte, "The European Judiciary after Lisbon", *Maastricht Journal of European and Comparative Law* 15, 2008, pp. 43-54.

that the Court has in many ways "provoked", or even "anticipated", the depilarisation of its own jurisdictional role, already under the existing three-pillar structure.

Simply put, under the new – post-Treaty of Lisbon – regime, the Court will have full jurisdiction over all AFSJ matters, as those are going to be fully integrated in what is now the first pillar. Some limitations will continue to apply, however, while a special AFSJ procedure will be institutionalised. Indeed, if we look into the new Treaty we may identify general modifications to the Court's structure and jurisdiction affecting the AFSJ (section 2), modifications in the field of the AFSJ stemming from the abolition of the pillar structure (section 3) and, finally, some rules specifically applicable to the AFSJ (section 4).

2. General Modifications to the Court's Jurisdiction, affecting the AFSJ

The Lisbon Treaty, compared to previous EC/EU Treaties, innovates as to its own structure. It consists of three parts, all having equal legal value: a) the very brief Treaty of European Union (TEU) introduces the basic structure and principles of the EU; b) the more extensive and technical Treaty on the Functioning of the European Union (TFEU) describes in detail the various policies and functions of the EU; and c) the long series of protocols further detail several issues. The Court's jurisdiction is dealt with in all three parts of the new Treaty.

2.1. The Court's Tripartite Constitution

The most visible modification introduced by the Lisbon Treaty concerns the very structure of the Court, now renamed "Court of Justice of the European Union" (CJEU).[3] Changes in this respect are twofold:

First, the division between the Court of First Instance (CFI) – renamed "General Court" and the (higher) "Court of Justice" – is being reinforced. True to its new name, the General Court, is to become the main jurisdictional body of the EU, hearing at first instance all actions, but preliminary rulings and infringement proceedings against Member States (Article 256(1) TFEU). Hence, annulment proceedings between the institutions, which have been quite common in the field of AFSJ,[4]

---

3 See Art. 19 EU, Arts. 251-281 TFEU and Protocol No. 3.

4 See e.g. Case C-170/96, *Commission v Council, air transit visas* [1998] ECR I-2763; Case C-160/03, *Spain v Eurojust* [2005] ECR I-981; Case C-257/01, *Commission v Council, visa policy* [2005] ECR I-345; Case C-176/03, *Commission v Council, sanctions for the environment* [2005] ECR I-7879; Joined Cases C-317 & 318/04, *European Parliament v Council, PNR* [2006] ECR I-4721; Case C-540/03, *EP v Council, Family reunification* [2006] ECR I-5769; Case C-77/05, *Commission v Council, sanctions for the environment*, judgement of 23 October 2007, not yet reported; Case

would no longer be heard by the Court, but on appeal. Compared to individual actions (which already are in the jurisdiction of the CFI), annulment proceedings between the institutions are more likely to bear on important institutional questions. Therefore, the more detailed and rigorously reasoned judgements of the General Court – occasionally reviewed by the Court of Justice – would be likely to increase visibility and to better the understanding of the issues raised by the AFSJ. All the above, however, is put into a provisory halt by Article 51 of Protocol No. 3 on "the Statute of the CJEU" which creates a very important derogation to the general rule of Article 256(1) TFEU. In the statute it is made clear that annulment actions and actions for failure to act brought by the Member States or by the institutions against the Parliament, the Council and the Commission, remain under the exclusive jurisdiction of the CJEU. Therefore, until such time as the European Parliament and the Council modify Article 51 of the Court's Statute,[5] the above apparent change in the Court's jurisdiction is only forthcoming and hypothetical. The General Court, nonetheless, will be hearing annulment (and failure to act) proceedings against the newly recognised defendants: the European Council and the Agencies and Bodies of the EU.[6]

Second, Article 257 TFEU provides that Specialised Courts may be attached to the General Court, according to the ordinary legislative procedure. This may prove highly relevant for the AFSJ, for at least four reasons. Firstly, individuals are being recognised a standing for annulment and failure to act proceedings, both for asylum and immigration issues (current Title IV EC) and for police and judicial cooperation issues (current Title VI EU).[7] Moreover, admissibility conditions of such standing are being extended.[8] Secondly, the preliminary competence of the Court is being generalised and extended to all jurisdictions of all Member States.[9] Therefore, an important increase of AFSJ cases reaching the docket of the CJEU is to be expected.[10] Thirdly, an urgency

C-133/06, *Parliament v Council, asylum procedures directive*, judgement of 6 May 2008, not yet reported.

5 Such a modification may be adopted according to the ordinary legislative procedure, following a proposal by the Court or the Commission and in consultation with the other body; see Art. 281 TFEU.

6 See section below on "Passive legitimation: new institutions subject to the Court's control" in this chapter.

7 See section below on "Regular plaintiffs admitted to introduce annulment proceedings" in this chapter.

8 See section below on "Active legitimation: individual plaintiffs admitted more extensively" in this chapter.

9 See section below on "Generalisation of preliminary rulings" in this chapter.

10 For a thorough discussion of the additional charge of the Court arising from AFSJ cases see House of Lords (EU Committee), 10th Report 2007-2008, The Treaty of

procedure is provided specifically for AFSJ cases, where a person in custody is involved.[11] Fourthly, it has been forcefully been put forward that judging in the field of AFSJ, especially in cases involving criminal law, requires special expertise, which the Judges of the General Court and the Court of Justice may be lacking.[12] These four factors together may, if overload does in fact materialise, eventually lead to the creation of a specialised AFSJ Court.

2.2. Expanded Admissibility in Annulment Proceedings

2.2.1. Passive Legitimation: New Institutions subject to the Court's Control

Article 263 TFEU, provides that the Court "shall also review the legality of acts of bodies, offices or agencies of the Union intended to produce legal effects *vis-à-vis* third parties". Similarly, Article 265 TFEU provides for failure to act proceedings against such bodies. Both provisions use a wide formulation which includes all acts and, presumably also, all kinds of bodies, no matter their legal status. The only limitation introduced by the new provision is that of the intent of the author of the act. Therefore, jurisdictional immunity is no longer afforded to players actively participating in shaping and/or implementing EU policies. Two categories of new litigants are especially relevant for the AFSJ.

Firstly, the European Council: this body started up as an informal and purely intergovernmental forum for the exchange of political views as far back as 1969. It got formally institutionalised by the 1992 Treaty of Maastricht as the only new institution pertaining to the EU – as opposed to the pre-existing EC institutions. Since its institutionalisation, the European Council has fully dominated cooperation in the second pillar (common foreign and security policy). It has also played an extremely important role in the third pillar (immigration etc. / Justice and Home Affairs) even after its partial "communitarisation" by the 1997 Amsterdam Treaty. This boost of the European Council's role in the field of the AFSJ is not only symptomatic of the general trend towards intergovernmentalism[13] and the hyper-activity of the European leaders (the European Council was meant to meet twice – or more – every year, but in fact it has been meeting an average of 6-8 times). It is also, and to

---

Lisbon: an impact assessment, *HL Paper* 62-I (London: Her Majesty's Stationary Office, 13 March 2008), p. 127ff.

11 See section below on "Urgency procedure" in this chapter.

12 See House of Lords 10th Report, *op. cit.*, p. 129ff.

13 See recently Spyros Blavoukos, Dimitris Bourantonis and George Pagoulatos, "A President for the European Union: a new actor in town?', *Journal of Common Market Studies*, Vol. 45, No. 2, 2007, pp. 231-252, at 237.

a large extent, due to the fact that the Treaty provisions on the AFSJ only provide powers for the EC (Title IV EC) and the EU (Title VI EU), but not the ends to which such powers should be used. This gap has been filled up by the European Council's meeting in special sessions, most importantly in Tampere (1999) and The Hague (2004).[14] Therefore, the European Council has been playing a "semi-constituant" role in the field of AFSJ. The role of the most supranational body has been further strengthened by the fact that until the end of 2004 the Council of Ministers has been deciding alone (or merely in consultation with the Parliament under the EC Treaty), based on unanimity. Only in December 2004 the Council decided to switch, starting from January 2005, to the co-decision procedure and this only in respect of the less contentious matters of visas, asylum and illegal (as opposed to legal) immigration.[15] Under the Lisbon Treaty co-decision and qualified majority in the Council will become the standard decision-making procedure, while the Treaty itself will contain some general aims to be achieved in the AFSJ. The projected President of the European Council, however, is expected to strengthen the role of this Institution.[16]

Secondly, the AFSJ is one of the fields in which new EU agencies develop and flourish.[17] Europol, Eurojust, CEPOL (European Police College), Frontex (European Border Management Agency), FRA (Fundamental Rights Agency) are only some of the agencies involved in the

---

14 This point is clearly being made by Philippe De Bruycker, "L'émergence d'une politique européenne d'immigration", in: Philippe De Bruycker (ed.), *The Emergence of a European Immigration Policy L'émergence d'une politique européenne d'immigration*, Academic Network for Legal Studies on Immigration and Asylum Law in Europe, Réseau académique Odysseus, (Bruxelles: Bruylant, 2004), pp. 1-95.

15 See Council Decision of 22 December 2004 (2004/927/EC), *O.J.*, No. L 396 of 31 December 2004. For the scope of this Decision see Case C-133/06, *Parliament v Council*, asylum procedures Directive, not yet reported, delivered on 6 May 2008.

16 See Blavoukos e.a., *op. cit.*

17 In general for agencies see Edoardo Chiti, "The emergence of a Community administration: the case of European agencies", *Common Market Law Review*, Vol. 37, No. 2, 2000, pp. 309-343; Ellen Vos, "Reforming the European Commission: what role to play for EU agencies?", *Common Market Law Review*, Vol. 37, No. 5, 2000, pp. 1113-1134; Xénophon Yataganas, "Delegation of regulatory authority in the EU, the relevance of the American model of independent agencies", *Jean Monnet Working Papers*, No. 3/01, 2001; Giandomenico Majone, "Delegation of regulatory powers in a mixed polity", *European Law Journal*, Vol. 8, No. 3, 2002, pp. 319-339; Paul Craig, "The constitutionalisation of Community administration", *European Law Review*, Vol. 28, No. 6, 2004, pp. 840-864; Matthew Flinders, "Distributed public governance in the EU", *Journal of European Public Policy*, Vol. 11, No. 3, 2004, pp. 520-544; Damien Geradin and Nicolas Petit, "The development of Agencies at EU and national levels: conceptual analysis and proposals for reform", 23 *Yearbook of European Law*, 2004, pp. 137-197; see also the Commission communication COM(2002) 718 final of 11 December 2002.

management of the AFSJ.[18] These agencies do not, in principle, issue binding acts. Therefore, their action is only subject to some kind of "principal-agent" supervision by the institution to which they are attached (i.e. the Commission or Council),[19] as well as to indirect control by the European Parliament and the ombudsman. It is not, however, subject to judicial review. Moreover, the "acts" they issue do not fall within the typology of those currently provided for in Articles 230 EC (first pillar) or 35(7) EU (third pillar), which the ECJ does have competence to review. This has led the Court to hold in *Spain v Eurojust* that, unless otherwise provided in their founding acts, no annulment proceedings are possible against the acts of such agencies.[20] This finding, grounded on a narrow reading of the "rule of law" principle, creates an uncomfortable situation, since the agencies play an ever increasing role in the administration and every day running of the AFSJ. Moreover, the Court's findings in *Spain v Eurojust* seem indirectly infirmed by the more recent judgements in *Gestoras, Segi* and *Kadi,*[21] where the Court opted for a much wider application of the "rule of law" principle.

Next to the agencies, there are also several other "bodies" or "offices" involved in the design and management of the AFSJ. The High Level Group on Asylum and Migration (created in 1998) is hierarchically the most important, but one should not forget the SCIFA (Strategic Committee on Immigration, Frontiers and Asylum) and the, the CIREFI (*Centre d'Information de Réflexion et d'Échange sur les Frontières et l'Immigration*), the EURASIL, the European Migration Network, the Immigration Liaison Officers Network, to state just a few. These bodies

---

18 For the acts instituting these agencies see the Europol Convention of 26 July 1995, *O.J.*, No. C 316 of 27 November 1995; Council Decision of 28 February 2002 (2002/187/JHA), *O.J.*, No. L 63 of 6 March 2002; Council Decision of 20 September 2005 (2005/681/JHA), *O.J.*, No. L 256 of 1 October 2005; Council Regulation (EC) 2007/2004 of 26 October 2004, *O.J.*, No. L 349 of 25 November 2004; Council Regulation (EC) 168/2007 of 15 February 2007, *O.J.*, No. L 53 of 22 February 2007, respectively.

19 With few exceptions, supervision is essentially indirect and operates mainly through a) the nomination/revocation of members and/or of the board of managers and/or of the Director of the agencies; b) control over their financial resources and their use; c) a yearly report submitted to the supervising institution and (more often than not) to the European Parliament.

20 Case C-160/03, *Spain v Eurojust* [2005] ECR I-2077. The question arose as to whether the terms and conditions (concerning the linguistic qualifications of the participants) for the selection of personnel for Eurojust could be challenged by a Member State (i.e. a privileged applicant). The Court answered in the negative. It maintained that the rule of law is sufficiently protected by both the individual right of participants to challenge the terms of the selection procedure before the CFI, and the right of Member States to intervene in the proceedings.

21 For which, see the analysis below in the section on "Active legitimation: individual plaintiffs admitted more extensively" in this chapter.

play essentially consultative and/or preparatory role and therefore their "acts" are unlikely to "produce legal effects *vis-à-vis* third parties", in the sense of Article 263 TFEU. It may not be altogether excluded, however, that a "strategic plan" adopted by the High Level Group affects individual rights through some "return policy", nor that some of the other body's activities impairs the status of some "third party".

Last but not least, the broad way in which Article 263 TFEU is drafted, seems to be encompassing also Funds. It should be remembered that an important series of funds is already active in the AFSJ: the European Refugee Fund, the External Borders Fund, the Return Fund, the Integration Fund.[22] Their acts could be challenged in the future, essentially by the privileged plaintiffs (i.e. the Member States, the Council and the European Parliament), probably as a way to controlling their functioning.

2.2.2. *Active Legitimation: Individual Plaintiffs admitted more Extensively*

Article 263 TFEU introduces yet another considerable extension of the Court's competence for annulment proceedings. The standing of individual plaintiffs is formally extended to cover not only acts "addressed to that person or which [are] of direct and individual concern to them" but also against "a regulatory act which is of direct concern to [them]" provided it does not entail any implementing measures. This replaces the current much more restrictive formula (Article 230 EC), whereby individual plaintiffs may only oppose "decisions" addressed to them or "regulations and decisions" addressed to other persons, provided they are of direct "and individual" concern to the plaintiffs. The fact that annulment proceedings may be brought not only against formal "decisions" but against any act affecting individual rights, irrespective of its formal qualification, does not constitute an innovation and corresponds to longstanding case law of the Court.[23]

Of more interest is the fact that "individual concern" is being dropped as a prerequisite for the admissibility of individual annulment proceedings against regulatory acts.[24] In this respect the Court's case-

---

22 Decision 573/2007/EC, 574/2007/EC and 575/2007/EC of 23 May 2007, *O.J.*, No. L 144 of 6 June 2007, respectively.

23 See Case 22/70, *Commission v Council, ERTA* [1971] ECR 263 and, more recently, Case C-57/95, *France v Commission, Pension Funds Communication* [1997] ECR I-1627.

24 New problems are expected to arise out of this provision of the Lisbon Treaty, as no definition is given in the Treaty of what constitutes "a regulatory act".

law has ebbed and flowed.[25] It is, however, in the recent terrorist cases, borderlining between the AFSJ and the CFSP (Common Foreign and Security Policy) that the Court has uncovered the lengths to which it is ready to go in order to ensure that acts affecting individual rights do not evade judicial control. In *Gestoras pro Amnestia* and *Segi*,[26] the President of the CFI had declared inadmissible an action in damages against the EC institutions for having placed some individuals and organisations on the list of presumed terrorists. The Court, confirming on this point the CFI, started by recognising that the system of judicial protection foreseen by the Treaty for the third pillar is incomplete compared to that of the first pillar and that no action in damages lies outside the latter.[27] It went on, however, to hold that by virtue of Article 6 EU the Union is based on the rule of law and the respect of fundamental rights.

> It follows that the institutions are subject to review of the conformity of their acts with the treaties and the general principles of law, just like the Member States when they implement the law of the Union.[28]

In consequence, the Court found that all acts (under all pillars) which have the effect of directly affecting individual rights may be brought before the ECJ by way of a preliminary question, even if this is not expressly provided for in the relevant Treaty provision. They may also be challenged by the privileged applicants (EC institutions and Member States) in accordance with Article 35(6) EU.[29] And since individual plaintiffs are not eligible to bring annulment actions against acts of the second or third pillar,

> it is for the Member States and, in particular, their courts and tribunals, to interpret and apply national procedural rules governing the exercise of rights of action in a way that enables natural and legal persons to challenge before the courts the lawfulness of any decision or other national measure relating to the drawing up of an act of the European Union or to its application to them.[30]

---

25 The last episode in the Court's jurisprudence is the remarkable judgement in Case C-50/00 P, *Unión de Pequenos Agricultores* [2002] ECR I-6677.

26 Case C-354/04 P, *Gestoras pro Amnestia* and Case C-355/04 P, *Segi*, both delivered on 27 February 2007; for these two cases see E. Meisse in *Europe*, No. 4, 2007, comm. 110, pp. 24-25.

27 *Gestoras pro Amnestia*, *ibid.*, para. 50.

28 *Gestoras pro Amnestia*, *ibid.*, para. 51; and more recently Case C-303/05, *Advocaten voor de Wereld*, judgement of 3 May 2007, para. 45.

29 *Advocaten voor de Wereld*, *ibid.*, para. 55.

30 *Advocaten voor de Wereld*, *ibid.*, para. 56. In this respect this judgement operates a clear reversal of the Orders of the CFI, where it was maintained that individuals have no remedy against a common position, either under EU or under national law. The same restrictive solution has also been adopted by the French Conseil d'État, in its

Therefore, based on the rule of law approach, the Court partly reviewed the procedural arrangements of the Treaty,[31] in order to ensure that any act producing legal effects is subject to a) judicial review and b) its own preliminary jurisdiction. In this way the Court, at a time when the content of the Lisbon (then named Reform) Treaty was being actively negotiated under the auspices of the German Presidency, sent a clear message highlighting the gaps of legal protection existing in the current institutional constellation and pushed for extending individual plaintiffs' rights.[32] This has also led to the introduction, in the Lisbon Treaty, of Article 275 TFEU, whereby by derogation to the general rule that CFSP measures are immune to the Court's jurisdiction, the Court will have competence to review "the legality of European decisions providing for restrictive measures against natural or legal persons adopted by the Council".[33]

---

judgement in case *Dispans c/ Ministre de l'Intérieur*, 11-12-06, AJDA 2007, p. 421; for this French case see D. Simon in (4/2007) *Europe*, comm. 108, p. 23.

31 Concerning generally the role of the rule of law in the AFSJ see also Catherine Dauvergne, "Sovereignty, migration and the rule of law in global times", *Modern Law Review*, Vol. 67, No. 4, 2004, pp. 588-615.

32 See on this aspect of the ECJ's case law, Hatzopoulos, "With or without you…", *op. cit.*, pp. 47-50. This trend of interpreting the law in order to accommodate the need for protection of fundamental individual rights, was further pursued, in a very spectacular way, in the Court's judgement in *Kadi*, see Joined Cases C-402/05 P and C-415/05 P *Kadi & Al Barakaat* [2008] ECR I-6351. On this very important judgement see Jean d'Aspremont and Frédéric Dopagne, "*Kadi*: The ECJ's reminder of the elementary divide between legal orders", *International Organizations Law Review*, Vol. 5, No. 2, 2008, available at http://ssrn.com/abstract=1341982; Gráinne De Búrca, "The EU, the European Court of Justice and the International Legal Order after *Kadi*", *Harvard International Law Journal*, Vol. 1, No. 51, 2009, also available as Fordham Law Legal Studies Research Paper No. 1321313 at http://ssrn.com/abstract=1321313; Anthony Dawes and Bjørn Kunoy, "Plate tectonics in Luxembourg: The *ménage à trois* between EC law, international law and the European Convention on Human Rights following the UN sanctions cases", *Common Market Law Review*, Vol. 46, No. 1, 2009, pp. 73-104; Guy Harpaz, "Judicial review by the European Court of Justice of UN 'smart sanctions' against terror in the *Kadi* Dispute", *European Foreign Affairs Review*, Vol. 14, No. 1, 2009, pp. 65-88; as well as the case note of the judgement by Andrea Gattini in *Common Market Law Review*, Vol. 46, 2009, "The EU, the European Court of Justice and the International Legal Order after *Kadi*"; Jean-Paul Jacqué, "Primauté du droit international versus protection des droits fondamentaux", *Revue Trimestrielle de Droit Européen*, No. 1, janvier-mars 2009, pp. 161-179.

33 Further on that see section below on "CFSP acts" in this chapter.

2.3. Enhanced Infringement Proceedings

Compliance with EU law is also addressed by the Lisbon Treaty. In particular, Commission infringement proceedings against Member States are facilitated in two ways, aiming at putting pressure onto recalcitrant States through the accelerated imposition of fines:

Therefore, recidivist States, who insist on not complying with a (first) judgement of the Court, may be brought before the Court for a second time without a fresh reasoned opinion being served to them (compare Article 260(2) TFEU with Article 228(2) EC). More importantly, where a Member State is pursued by the Commission for the non-transposition of a directive (i.e. a straight forward and easily ascertainable infringement), then the latter may require the imposition of fines, already in the first proceedings brought before the Court.[34]

3. Specific AFSJ Modifications to the Court's Jurisdiction linked to the "Depilarisation"

3.1. Generalisation of Preliminary Rulings

The single most important consequence, in terms of the Court's jurisdiction, stemming from the abolition of the three-pillar structure, is the generalisation of the Court's preliminary jurisdiction. As things stand today there is a double limitation in the way the Article 234 EC procedure applies in the field of the AFSJ. In the first pillar (Article 68(1) EC), preliminary questions are only open to jurisdictions "against whose decisions there is no judicial remedy", not to all jurisdictions.[35] Worse still, in the third pillar, Article 35 EU, provides for a twofold limitation. First, Member States are not subject to the preliminary jurisdiction of the Court unless they have made a declaration to that effect. To date, only sixteen Member States have made such a declaration.[36] Second, Article 35 EU – contrary to Article 234 EC or even

---

34 This new possibility is criticised by part of the doctrine (see e.g. S. Peers in the House of Lords 10th Report, *op. cit.*); our guess is that this possibility will be useful as a means to exert pressure to Member States, but will be used by the Commission only in the most flagrant violations.

35 For a very critical account of this Treaty provision see Cédric Cheneviere, "L'article 68 CE – rapide survol d'un renvoi préjudiciel mal compris", *Cahiers de Droit Européen*, No. 5-6, 2004, pp. 567-589. See also the Commission Communication, COM(2006) 346 final of 28 June 2006, where it proposes that Article 234 EC should also become plainly applicable in the field of Asylum, Immigration and Visas.

36 According to Art. 35 EU Member States are free to make a declaration as to whether they accept the Court's preliminary jurisdiction and, in the case that they do, whether all – or only higher – jurisdictions should have access to the Court. It is remarkable that out of sixteen Member States who have submitted declarations, only two have limited the access of their tribunals to the ECJ. The remaining fourteen include coun-

68 EC – only provides for the interpretation by the Court, of secondary legislation and not of the Treaty provisions themselves.

These differences, however, have been considerably "played down" by the Court. The judgement of the Court in *Pupino*[37] was delivered in preliminary proceedings initiated by an Italian jurisdiction, under Article 35 EU, in relation to a framework decision in the field of criminal law. Before answering the substantive issues raised by the referring jurisdiction, the ECJ had to reject some admissibility claims put forward by some of the intervening Member States. In doing so, the Court made it clear that the preliminary procedure provided for by Article 35 EU is governed by the same interpretative rules (concerning the qualification of the referring body as a "court", the clarity and necessity of the question referred to the Court etc.), as that of Article 234 EC.[38] The same tendency was also pursued in the more recent judgement of the Court in *Gestoras pro Amnestia*, with the effect of furthering the parallelism between the first and the third pillars.[39]

The second difference identified above, concerning the Court's (lack of) jurisdiction to interpret the Treaty provisions of the third pillar, has been addressed by the Court in the judgement in *Advocaten voor de Wereld*.[40] In a judgement delivered by the Grand Chamber, with the intervention of no less than ten Member States (the conclusions of which were, for once, followed by the Court) the Court upheld the validity of the Council's Framework Decision which established the European Arrest Warrant.[41] A Belgian NGO contested before the Belgian Courts the legality of the law which transposed into national law the aforementioned framework decision. One of the intervening states in the proceedings before the Court deemed the preliminary question

tries such as: Austria, the Benelux countries, the Czech Republic, Finland, France, Germany, Greece, and Italy. It is also worth noting that there is no official document enumerating Member States which have submitted a declaration and that the number of declarations informally brought to the attention of the present author differs from the one the British House of Lords refers to in its 10th Report, *op. cit.*, p. 125, where it is stated that fourteen Member States have made declarations.

37 Case C-105/03, *Pupino*, judgement of 31 May 2005.

38 According to Art. 35 EU, Member States are free to make a declaration as to whether they accept the Court's preliminary jurisdiction and, in the case that they do, whether all – or only higher – jurisdictions should have direct access to the Court. It is remarkable that out of sixteen Member States who have submitted declarations, only two have limited the access of their tribunals to the ECJ. The remaining fourteen include countries such as: Austria, the Benelux countries, the Czech Republic, Finland, France, Germany, Greece, and Italy.

39 *Gestoras pro Amnestia*, *op. cit.*

40 *Advocaten voor de Wereld*, *op. cit.*

41 Council Framework Decision of 13 June 2002 (2002/584/JHA), *O.J.*, No. L 190.

inadmissible in that it (indirectly) required the Court "to examine Article 34(2)(b) EU, which is a provision of primary law not reviewable by the Court".[42] The Court remained unconvinced by this argument, as well as by the stark difference of wording of the above-mentioned Treaty provisions. It held that:

> Under Article 35(1) EU, the Court has jurisdiction [...] to give preliminary rulings on the interpretation and validity of, *inter alia*, framework decisions, which necessarily implies that it can, even if there is no express power to that effect, be called upon to interpret provisions of primary law [...] where [...] the Court is being asked to examine whether a framework decision has been properly adopted on the basis of that latter provision.[43]

Therefore, the Court has reshaped its preliminary competence in the third pillar in parallel with that of the first. Not only has it extended its jurisdiction to all acts of secondary legislation (see *Gestoras pro Amnestia* in relation to common positions),[44] but it has also interpreted the Treaty provisions themselves, of a Treaty deemed "intergovernmental" (see *Advocaten voor de Wereld*).

Article 267 TFEU now provides for a single preliminary procedure covering all issues of the current first and third pillar. This is compulsory for all Member States and for all jurisdictions and does not require any prior declaration or other formality. Further, both primary and secondary law may be subject to the Court's interpretation. A special fast-track procedure is provided for in the last paragraph of Article 267, for cases stemming from the AFSJ, where "a person in custody" is involved.[45] As a consequence of the above "generalisation" of the Court's preliminary jurisdiction, the special competence of the Court (provided for in Article 68(3)) to give interpretative judgements on the request of the Council, the Commission or any Member State is being dropped.

3.2. Regular Plaintiffs admitted to introduce Annulment Proceedings

A second important change in the Court's jurisdiction, already mentioned, relates to annulment proceedings. It has already been explained that passive legitimation has been extended to cover the European Council and the agencies, bodies etc. It has also been said that individual plaintiffs are more largely admitted to introduce annulment proceedings, as an individual concern is no more required where a regulatory act

---

42 *Advocaten voor de Wereld*, *op. cit.*, para. 17.

43 *Advocaten voor de Wereld*, *ibid.*, para. 18.

44 *Gestoras pro Amnestia*, *op. cit.*

45 For which see section below on "Urgency procedure" in this chapter.

requiring no transposition is at stake. These are important changes for both the matters currently falling under the first and under the third pillar. However, for third pillar issues "depilarisation" makes the change all the more important.

This is so because, as it now stands, Article 35(6) EU provides only for annulment proceedings to be brought by a Member State or the Commission. In other words, only privileged plaintiffs – and then again not all – can initiate annulment proceedings. The fact that no annulment proceedings are possible for individuals has been highlighted – and indeed stigmatised – by the Court itself in its judgement in *Gestoras pro Amnistia* and *Segi.*[46] It is true that in these judgements the Court did find a way to secure the "rule of law" principle. This, nonetheless, was both "indirect" and "imperfect". "Indirect", because it was through the intermediation of Member States that the Court sought to guarantee that individuals have rights of action. Indeed, the Court held that Article 6 EU obliges Member States, when implementing EU law, to

> interpret and apply national procedural rules governing the exercise of rights of action in a way that enables natural and legal persons to challenge before the courts the lawfulness of any decision or other national measure.

"Imperfect" because, while opening up their dockets to European AFSJ cases, the national jurisdictions are supposed – according to the Court – to have access to the preliminary rulings of the Court. This, however, ignores the fact that only sixteen Member States have made declarations under Article 35(2) and that plaintiffs in national proceedings can never force their way to Luxembourg.

The abolition of the pillars by the Lisbon Treaty will, for the first time, make it possible for individual plaintiffs – and privileged plaintiffs other than the Member States and the Commission – to bring annulment proceedings in the fields of judicial cooperation in criminal matters and police cooperation. Indeed, the indirect and imperfect way devised by the Court to comply with the "rule of law" principle (above) should only be seen as an "interim" solution, on the way to some more acceptable institutional setting. Already under the current indirect fertilisation of the EU by the grand ECHR principles and the oblique control the ECtHR exerts over the functioning of the EU,[47] it is unclear whether the Court's judgements in *Segi* and *Gestoras pro Amnistia* would satisfy

---

46 See e.g. *Gestoras pro Amnestia*, *op. cit.*, para. 50.

47 See ECtHR judgement in *Bosphorus International*, application No. 45036/98, judgement delivered on 30 June 2005. See annotation by Douglas-Scott in *Common Market Law Review* (2006), pp. 243-254. See also, by the same author "A tale of two Courts; Luxembourg, Strasbourg and the growing European Human Rights Acquis", *Common Market Law Review* (2006), pp. 629-665.

Article 6 ECHR. After the full accession of the EU to ECHR, provided for in the Lisbon Treaty, the opening up of "third pillar" annulment proceedings to individual plaintiffs seems a one way road.

3.3. Infringement Proceedings against Member States

Further to the extension of individual rights *vis-à-vis* the institutions, the "depilarisation" also strengthens the role of the Commission, not only as an initiator of EU legislation, but also as a watchdog for the proper application of such legislation. Under the current intergovernmental setting of the third pillar, the Commission may not bring infringement proceedings against Member States. Only other Member States can do so, provided however, that "such dispute cannot be settled by the Council within six months of its being referred to the Council by one of its members" (Article 35(7) EU). Existing solidarity between non-compliant peers, combined with the six month political interlude, have led to the *de facto* idleness of judicial enforcement in the third pillar.

This is going to change under the Lisbon Treaty since the Commission will recover its traditional enforcement role. In this respect the new, enhanced, powers of the Commission concerning infringement proceedings,[48] will be of utmost importance. By the same token, compliance in the field the AFSJ will be de-politicised, since negotiations in the Council will bear only on prospective legislation and will not be diluted by compliance issues. Indeed, the position of Member States in the field of AFSJ – in particular what is today the third pillar – will be fundamentally altered: from a situation where each Member State can negotiate around its veto and may, in impunity, indefinitively resist the application of EU rules it dislikes, States will now have to decide with qualified majority and be subject to strict compliance scrutiny by the Commission. This substantial departure from intergovernmentalism may be a partial explanation for the "emergency brake" procedures provided for by Articles 82(2) TFEU, 83(3) TFEU (judicial cooperation in criminal matters), 86 TFEU (European Public Prosecutor) and 87 TFEU (police cooperation). The precise mechanisms of the "emergency brakes" differ from area to area, but the basic idea is that any Member State which considers that a proposed legislative text affects fundamental aspects of its judicial system can refer the matter to the European Council and have the ordinary legislative procedure suspended. Such suspension may go on until such time as divergences are settled at the political level, or at least nine Member States decide to proceed with enhanced cooperation.

48 See section above on "Enchanced infringement proceedings" in this chapter.

3.4. Action in Damages against the EU

A further consequence of the depilarisation is that, henceforth, individual plaintiffs will have the right to claim damages for EU action in the field of police and judicial cooperation in criminal matters. The non-existence of such a claim under the current setting has been stigmatised by the Court in the *Gestoras* and *Segi* cases.

This newly acquired jurisdiction of the Court, however, is expected to be of limited importance for, at least, two reasons. First, future cases similar to *Gestoras* and *Segi* may not be successfully pleaded in the framework of a claim for damages. According to the Court's longstanding case-law a claim in damages is inadmissible where an annulment action could have the very same practical effects for the claimant. In other words, damage suffered because of an act imposing some kind of fine, freezing of funds or other pecuniary sanction, can only be remedied by the annulment of such act, but not through an action for damages.[49] Second, damages claims in a field where the EU decision-making is characterised by the exercise of important discretion and by restricted disclosure of relevant information and documents, will be very difficult to substantiate.

The "passive legitimation" of agencies, bodies etc.,[50] however, some of which may also develop operational activities (Europol, Frontex), may be a source of important damages claims.

4. Rules Specifically applicable in the AFSJ

Despite the "depilarisation" pursued by the Lisbon Treaty and the fusion of the first with the third pillar, some specific rules concerning the Court's jurisdiction are to be found in the new Treaty.

4.1. Public Order Derogation

Article 276 TFEU provides that:

> In exercising its powers [...] relating to the area of freedom, security and justice, the Court of Justice of the European Union shall have no jurisdiction to review the validity or proportionality of operations carried out by the police or other law-enforcement services of a Member State or the exercise of the responsibilities incumbent upon Member States with regard to the maintenance of law and order and the safeguarding of internal security.

---

49 Case 25/62, *Plaumann* [1963] ECR 201: a different solution would indirectly sidestep the two-month time-limitation for introducing annulment proceedings.

50 For which see section above on "Passive legitimation: new institutions subject to the Court's control" in this chapter.

This provision is directly issued from Article 35(5) EU as it now stands. It also finds its equivalent in the first pillar in current Article 68(2) EC. It is true that the latter (EC) provision seems to be limiting solely to the preliminary competence of the ECJ, while the former (EU) provision clearly introduces a general reserve to the Court's jurisdiction.

It remains that none of these provisions have ever been applied up till now, so only speculations may be made concerning the way in which they may be construed and applied in the future. Four ideas may, nevertheless, be put forward in this respect. First, the general "mainstreaming" of the AFSJ into the general EU structure is likely to lead to an extremely restrictive interpretation of this sovereignty reserve. Second, from the Court's case-law already in *Commission v Council, air transit visas* it would seem that, in an unspoken way, the ultimate judge of the *Komptenz Kompetenz* is the Court itself, and therefore any reserve thereto is subject to its own control.[51] Third, and in relation to the previous point, Article 276 TFEU reserve should be read in the light of the Court's terrorist case-law and the rule of law principle:[52] if individual plaintiffs are not offered minimal procedural guarantees under the national legal system, then the EU legal order should step in – on the face of the express exclusion described above – in order to offer some judicial control, at least indirectly, in the form of a preliminary ruling. The same logic has also prevailed in the Court's judgement in *Kadi*, in relation to international law: because the plaintiffs were not granted any defence rights in view of the adoption, against them, of smart sanctions by the UN Security Council, these plaintiffs should have access to the ECJ to control the legality of the EC acts implementing such sanctions.[53] Such a requirement seems all the more compelling in view of the EU's accession to the ECHR. Fourth, Member States whishing to stop some EU measure affecting their internal public order, are more likely to have recourse to the emergency brake clauses provided for in the Lisbon Treaty,[54] at the adoption level, rather than wait until such measures reach the Court.

---

51 For this and further cases see section below on "Urgency procedure" in this chapter.

52 See sections above on "Active legitimation: individual plaintiffs admitted more extensively" and "Regular plaintiffs admitted to introduce annulment proceedings" in this chapter.

53 Joined Cases C-402/05 P and C-415/05 P, *Kadi & Al Barakaat* [2008] ECR I-6351, paras. 319-326.

54 See section above on "Infringement proceedings against Member States" in this chapter.

4.2. Urgency Procedure

The generalisation of the Court's jurisdiction to cover all matters pertaining to the AFSJ will certainly lead to some (considerable?) increase of the Court's workload. In particular, the extension of preliminary references to all jurisdictions of all Member States[55] is likely to lead to greater delays in delivering preliminary rulings. Despite the successful efforts of the Court to limit the time necessary for delivering its judgements, the mean duration of a preliminary procedure before the Court was of 19.3 months in 2007.[56] Part of this delay is due to inelastic procedural requirements, linked to translation, to the time left to the Commission and the Member States in order to present their observations etc.

In order to accommodate these procedural requirements with the need to avoid lengthy detention periods,[57] the President of the ECJ has proposed to the Council a modification of the Court's own statute, in order to introduce a fast-track "interim" preliminary procedure specifically reserved to AFSJ issues.[58] From the two solutions put forward by the President of the Court, the Council opted for the one most respectful of Member States' rights (to the detriment of expediency and the rights of detainees). Council Decision 2008/79/EC[59] modified the Court's statute in order to shorten the duration of the written procedure.[60] Therefore, only the Member State concerned and the Commission (and the Parliament and Council if one of their acts are at stake) are allowed to present written observations, while intervening parties may only present oral observations. The five-member chamber specially competent for this procedure shall deliver its judgement shortly after hearing the Advocate General, while the exchange of documents shall be based essentially on the use of electronic means. This procedure is already

---

55 See section above on "Generalisation of preliminary rulings" in this chapter.

56 See the Court's Annual Report (2007) available at http://curia.europa.eu/jcms/jcms/Jo2_11035/?hlText=2007.

57 In this respect the ongoing negotiations for the adoption of the "return" Directive are highly topical, on which a political agreement in the Council has only been reached after three years of negotiations, on 5 May 2008.

58 Document 13272/06 of 28 September 2006. For a brief discussion of this document see the Editorial Comments in *Common Market Law Review*, Vol. 44, No. 1, 2007, pp. 1-7.

59 Council Decision of 20 December 2007 amending the Protocol on the Statute of the Court of Justice (2008/79/EC, Euratom), *O.J.*, No. L 24 of 29 January 2008.

60 See Elsa Bernard, "La nouvelle procédure préjudicielle d'urgence applicable aux renvois relatifs à l'Espace de liberté, sécurité et de justice", *Europe*, No. 5, 2008, pp. 5-8.

operational[61] and has been successfully used three times in 2008,[62] therefore, the last paragraph of Article 267 TFEU has no added value other than to offer a (not needed) constitutional grounding for it.

4.3. CFSP Acts

The Court's judgements in the "terrorist" cases[63] have shown how closely intertwined the acts pertaining to the AFSJ (first and third pillars) and those stemming from the CFSP (second pillar) may be. In this respect a new provision introduced into the Lisbon Treaty does merit a comment.

Article 275 TFEU specifically provides that the Court has no "jurisdiction with respect to the provisions relating to the CFSP nor with respect to acts adopted on the basis of these provisions". This general rule, however, is subject to two exceptions enumerated in the second paragraph of this same provision. Both exceptions are highly relevant for the AFSJ.

First, it is foreseen that the Court monitors the borderlines between CFSP and the other EU competences (see Article 40 TEU). This confirms and consolidates previous ECJ jurisprudence. At a time when the Court had no competence at all in the third pillar (i.e. before the entry into force of the Amsterdam Treaty, on May 1999), it held that it had jurisdiction to rule on the legality of a (third pillar) common action of the Council.[64] Such jurisdiction was necessary in order to ensure that first pillar competences were not violated. The same solution was later followed concerning the relationships between the second and third pillars. The recent cases concerning the imposition of "smart sanctions" (in the form of the "freezing" of assets) on persons, organisations etc. allegedly connected to terrorism, offer a vocal illustration of the Court's perception of the extent of its own jurisdiction. In this respect, the Court of First Instance (CFI) has delivered three series of important judgements[65] and, on appeal,[66] the Court another three.[67] The factual back-

61 See also the information and instructions provided by the Court's webpage http://curia.europa.eu/en/instit/txtdocfr/txtsenvigueur/noteppu.pdf

62 See Annual Report of the Activity of the ECJ, 2008, available at http://curia.europa.eu/jcms/upload/docs/application/pdf/2009-03/ra08_en_cj_stat.pdf, p. 100.

63 See among others the cases quoted above: Gestoras pro Amnestia; Segi; and Advocaten voor de Wereld, *op. cit.*

64 Case C-170/96, *Commission v Council, air transit visas* [1998] ECR I-2763.

65 Cases of the same date T-306/01, *Yusuf*; and T-315/01, *Kadi*, judgements of 21 September 2005, for which see Denys Simon and Flavien Mariatte, "Le tribunal de première instance des Communautés: Professeur de droit international? A propos des arrêts *Yusuf* et *Kadi*", *Europe*, chron. 12, 2005, p. 6; and the case note by Christian Tomuschat in *Common Market Law Review*, Vol. 43, No. 2, 2006, pp. 537-551; and T-253/02, *Ayadi* and T-49/04, *Hassan*, judgements of 12 July 2006, for which

ground of all five cases decided by the CFI is very similar.[68] In order to implement several UN Security Council resolutions the Council of the EU has adopted several common positions based on the second (and occasionally) third pillar. On the basis of these common positions, and for their implementation, several first pillar regulations and decisions have been adopted. In all cases, the plaintiffs asked for the annulment of the totality of the above acts. The CFI started by explaining that common positions of either the second or third pillar are, in principle, outside its control. It went on, however, to state that

> the Court of First Instance has jurisdiction to hear an action for annulment directed against a Common Position adopted on the basis of Articles 15 EU and 34 EU only strictly to the extent that, in support of such an action, the applicant alleges an infringement of the Community's competences.[69]

This approach was taken further and expanded in the two extremely important judgements of the Court, in appeal proceedings against an Order of the President of the CFI.[70] In *Gestoras pro Amnestia* and *Segi*

---

see Denys Simon and Flavien Mariatte, "Le 'droit' à la protection diplomatique: droit fondamental en droit communautaire?", *Europe*, chron. 11, 2006, p. 4; see also case T-228/02, *Mojahedines*, judgement of 12 December 2006, for which see the case note by Christina Eckes in *Common Market Law Review*, Vol. 44, No. 4, 2007, pp. 1117-1129; all the above cases are currently under appeal before the ECJ. For a general assessment of the relevant case-law see William Vlcek, "Acts to combat the financing of terrorism: common foreign and security policy at the European Court of Justice", *European Foreign Affairs Review*, Vol. 11, No. 4, 2006, pp. 491-507; also Martin Nettesheim, "UN sanctions against individuals – A challenge to the architecture of EU governance", *Common Market Law Review*, Vol. 44, No. 3, 2007, pp. 567-600; also Pétros Stangos and Georgios Gryllos, "Le droit communautaire à l'épreuve des réalités du droit international: leçons tirées de la jurisprudence communautaire récente relevant de la lutte contre le terrorisme international", *Cahiers de Droit Européen*, No. 3-4, 2006, pp. 429-481.

66 For all five cases, appeals are currently pending before the ECJ; the three appeal judgements already delivered by the ECJ concern previous orders by the President of the CFI.

67 Case C-229/05, *Ocalan* judgement of 18 January 2007; Case C-354/04 P *Gestoras pro Amnestia* and Case C-355/04 P, *Segi*, both delivered on February 27, 2007; for these two cases see E. Meisse in *Europe*, No. 4, 2007, comm. 110, pp. 24-25.

68 On similar facts and concerning the imposition of smart sanctions the CFI has actually delivered some more judgements and orders, of lesser importance, which are not discussed here; see for instance: Case (order) T-338/02, *Segi e.a.* [2004] ECR II-1647; Case (Order) T-299/04, *Selmani*, judgement of 18 November 2005; Case T-362/04, *Minin*, judgement of 31 January 2007.

69 *Mojahedines*, para 56. On these judgements see Alina Miron, "La jurisprudence du tribunal de première instance à propos de l'inscription sur les listes terroristes", *Revue du Marché Commun et de l'Union Européenne*, No. 511, 2007, pp. 526-531.

70 See *op. cit.*, Case (order) T-338/02, *Segi e.a.* [2004] ECR II-1647; Case (Order) T-299/04, *Selmani*, judgement of 18 November 2005; Case T-362/04, *Minin*, judgement of 31 January 2007. For these judgements see Abdelkhaleq Berramdane, "Les

the Court opened up the way for the judicial control of CFSP acts, as well as for their being the object of a preliminary reference.[71]

Most importantly, in *Kadi*, the Court held "the principles of liberty, democracy and respect for human rights and fundamental freedoms enshrined in Article 6(1) EU" to lie in the foundations of the Union, whereby it may not be derogated by virtue of any rule of the Treaty (such as Article 297) nor, indeed, by any rule of international law.[72] Therefore, limitations to the fundamental rights which stem from the three pillar structure of the EU are no more to be tolerated.

The above judgements of the Court also explain the second reserve to the general rule of Article 275 TFEU, whereby the Court does have jurisdiction to hear annulment proceedings against CFSP "decisions providing for restrictive measures against natural or legal persons".

5. Conclusion

It would be exaggerated to say that the Lisbon Treaty fundamentally changes the Court's jurisdiction. The single most important novelty of the new Treaty, the abolition of the pillar structure, does, nonetheless, have important consequences for the Court's role, especially in the AFSJ. Henceforth, the Court has full competence a) to deliver preliminary rulings (all jurisdictions of all Member States concerning all sources of EU law, both primary and secondary); b) to hear annulment proceedings introduced by individual plaintiffs against all acts of all the EU institutions and of other bodies, agencies etc.; c) to judge on infringement proceedings against Member States; and d) to hear claims for damages. By the same token, the hotly debated issue of EU competence to adopt criminal measures is emptied of any substance.[73] All these are new competences in the field of the AFSJ. Most of these developments, however, have been anticipated or at least, put into the agenda, by the Court already under the current institutional setting.

---

limites de la protection juridictionnelle dans le cadre du titre VI du traité sur l'Union européenne", *Revue du Droit de l'Union Européenne*, No. 2, 2007, pp. 433-446.

71 See *op. cit.*, Ocalan; *Gestoras pro Amnestia*; Segi.

72 Joined Cases C-402/05 P and C-415/05 P *Kadi & Al Barakaat* [2008] ECR I-6351, paras. 319-326, paras. 303 and 316.

73 Dealt with by the judgements of the Court in Cases C-176/03 and C-77/05, *op. cit.*; see in this respect Henri Labayle, "L'ouverture de la jarre de Pandore, réflexions sur la compétence de la Communauté en matière pénale", *Cahiers de Droit Européen*, Vol. 42, No. 3-4, 2006, pp. 379-428; and on a more critical tone, Anthony Dawes and Orla Lynskey, "The ever-longer arm of EC law: the extension of Community competence into the field of criminal law", *Common Market Law Review*, Vol. 45, No. 1, 2008, pp. 131-158.

Most interestingly, the judgements that the Court delivered in the field of AFSJ during these years have had a clear spill-over effect: they have paved the way for a more general strengthening of the Court's role in all other areas: the right of individual plaintiffs to initiate proceedings against acts of the European Council and of agencies, bodies etc., and this without (always) having to prove individual concern, are requirements stemming from the strong "rule of law" approach put forward by the Court in the AFSJ.

In its judgements in *Pupino*, the terrorist cases and the other cases discussed above, the Court recognises supra-constitutional status to some basic principles, strictly connected to the respect of individual rights. Such rights are not, according to the Court, modifiable at the free will of the Member States, and remain beyond their grasp. Such principles are inherent to the construction of any legal order having as its subjects (also) individuals and not only States. However, the accession of the EU to the ECHR requires these principles to be spelled out and to have a clearer scope. This is the essential input of the Lisbon Treaty in relation with regard to the AFSJ.

Part Three

The Special Structures

CHAPTER 6

Europol and the Architecture of Internal Security

Michael NIEMEIER & Marc André WIEGAND*

The European Police Office (Europol) is among the best-known institutions of police cooperation in the field of Justice and Home Affairs, the EU Treaty's third pillar. However, in addition to Europol numerous other institutions and structures have been created which are significant for European police cooperation.

The current EU structures of police cooperation are complex with occasionally overlapping responsibilities. They stem from the need to regularly adapt to a changing security situation, but also from political compromises between Member States. Against this background police cooperation has become one of the most dynamic areas in the EU since the early 1990s. But it is not free from inconsistencies: on the one hand there is the practical need for a constantly developing European cooperation across borders with "centralised structures" – as desirable in terms of integration – and on the other hand it is a policy area which is at the core of national responsibility and sovereignty.[1]

The following section (1) will briefly outline the history of the police structures. In section 2 this is followed by a description of the specific organisational structures of Europol including an outlook on possible future developments under the Treaty on the Functioning of the European Union (TFEU, Lisbon Treaty). Since the Lisbon Treaty will reform the entire structure of police cooperation, these developments will be addressed in a separate section (3) which in particular focuses on the planned committee for operational cooperation between Member States (COSI). Finally, section 4 will close with a brief outlook on the future of European police cooperation.

---

* The opinions expressed in this article reflect only the personal views of the authors.

1 Cf. Art. 33 TEU.

1. History of the Structures of Police Cooperation[2]

European police cooperation in the strict sense became part of primary legislation only with the Maastricht Treaty in 1993. The origins of the provisions of Article K TEU lie in the TREVI cooperation[3] initiated in the 1970s, which was consolidated, however, only in the mid-1980s to become the basis for the structure and contents of the Maastricht Treaty. The TREVI working groups[4] have been integrated as Council working parties into the third pillar of the EU Treaty (Justice and Home Affairs).

Under the Maastricht Treaty, the former TREVI senior officials groups were replaced by the K.4 Committee named after the relevant article of the Treaty.[5] This coordinating committee covered all areas of Justice and Home Affairs, i.e. police cooperation, customs, asylum, migration and judicial cooperation in criminal and civil matters. Member States were represented in this committee by the director-generals of the responsible ministries. For the individual policy areas steering groups accountable to the K.4 Committee and working parties accountable to the steering groups were established.[6] There were a number of reasons for setting up this new coordination structure in the first pillar (EC Treaty): a need for more coordination among working parties, the

---

[2] A general overview of the history of international and European police cooperation can be found in: John D. Occhipinti, *The Politics of EU Police Cooperation* (Boulder/London: Lynne Rienner Publishers, 2003), p. 239. For a conceptual analysis of European police cooperation see e.g. Jan Hecker, "Europäisches Verwaltungskooperationsrecht am Beispiel der grenzüberschreitenden polizeilichen Zusammenarbeit", *Europa und Recht*, No. 6, 2001, p. 826ff. and Ludo Block, *Decentralisation Trends in European Police Cooperation: Implications for Efficacy and Accountability*, Social Science Research Network (SSRN), April 2007.

[3] For more details on the history of TREVI Cooperation see Magali Sabatier, *La coopération policière européenne* (Paris: L'Harmattan, 2001), p. 58ff.

[4] Terrorism, training and technical knowledge, organised crime, Europol and TREVI EC 92 (Implementation of programme of action, Dublin, 1990).

[5] Art. K.4 of the EU Treaty (Maastricht): "1. A Coordinating Committee shall be set up consisting of senior officials. In addition to its coordinating role, it shall be the task of the Committee to: give opinions for the attention of the Council, either at the Council's request or on its own initiative; contribute, without prejudice to Article 151 of the Treaty establishing the European Community, to the preparation of the Council's discussions in the areas referred to in Article K.1 and, in accordance with the conditions laid down in Article 100d of the Treaty establishing the European Community, in the areas referred to in Article 100c of that Treaty. 2. The Commission shall be fully associated with the work in the areas referred to in this Title. 3. The Council shall…".

[6] For more details see Michael Niemeier, "The K.4 Committee and its position in the decision-making process", in: Roland Bieber and Jörg Monar, *Justice and Home Affairs in the European Union* (Brussels: European Interuniversity Press, 1991), p. 321.

sensitive area of internal security affecting national sovereignty and the responsible Member State ministers' wish to maintain a greater influence on work in Brussels. Another reason for this interim level might have been the sometimes strained relations between the responsible ministries for Justice and Home Affairs and the ministries for foreign affairs which coordinated this area as well through their ambassadors in COREPER. To a different extent, all revisions of the Treaty since 1993 have resulted in special structures in the third pillar due to these considerations.

In sum, since the area of police cooperation has been included in the EU Treaty there is an at least four-tier structure within the Council: working party, high-level coordinating committee (sometimes including steering committees), Committee of Permanent Representatives (ambassadors) and the Council of Ministers.

The voting procedures and instruments of police cooperation established by the EU Treaty followed the pattern of international law rather than the Community law of that time. Instruments introduced by Article K TEU included Joint Positions and Joint Actions which were not directly applicable in the Member States but required implementation. For the third legal instrument, the convention (Article K.3(2)(c) TEU) to become effective, all Member States had to ratify it, which sometimes caused significant delays in implementing a decision (e.g. in the case of Europol). Votes in the Council had to be unanimous (Article K.4(3) TEU), except for those on matters of procedure and measures implementing Joint Action which could be adopted by qualified majority.

The Commission (with its right to be consulted) and the European Parliament (with its right to be heard) played only a minor role. The Commission's "comitology committees" which under Community law served to implement Council decisions were not involved in third pillar matters. The Council and its working parties had to oversee the implementation of decisions themselves. Due to its limited scope of action in this field as compared to its strong competence in Community law ("motor of integration"), the Commission often found itself in a difficult position within the institutional triangle.

The European Court of Justice was responsible only for interpreting and applying conventions, and this solely if specifically provided for in the relevant convention.

Administrative costs of the third pillar were covered by the Community budget whereas in individual cases a unanimous decision had to be made on whether operational expenditures were to be financed from the Community budget or by the Member States according to a certain formula (Article K.8(2) TEU).

Finally, it should be noted that the Maastricht Treaty introduced police cooperation as a European issue, but since this cooperation was purely intergovernmental, the framework was much less binding than in traditional policy areas of the European Communities. Despite all exceptions, the integration of Justice and Home Affairs largely complied with the traditional forms of legislative and administrative cooperation within Brussels structures.[7] As usual, COREPER defined the necessary working structures for this policy area if not specified by the Treaty (e.g. Article K.4 Committee).[8] It was responsible for preparing the Council and ensured horizontal coordination with the other areas. The working parties were chaired by the acting Council Presidency. Within the Council Secretariat a new Directorate-General (H) for Justice and Home Affairs was created which is responsible for supporting the Presidency and ensuring continuity. A new Directorate-General for Justice and Home Affairs (JLS) was established also within the EU Commission.

In addition to introducing these legislative and administrative structures, Member States intended to improve operational cooperation. For this purpose, a European Police Office (Europol) was to be created based on the work of the *ad hoc* group on Europol in the TREVI framework. This group took up work in June 1992 and developed the basis for the forerunner to Europol, the Europol Drugs Unit (EDU) in Strasbourg,[9] before a convention was adopted by the Council and ratified by all Member States.

Europol has never been part of the Council structures but an independent international organisation based on an international treaty within the political framework of the EU Treaty's third pillar. However, with regard to significant decisions concerning Europol (e.g. budget, work programme, appointment of a director) the Europol convention refers to the procedures of the third pillar, i.e. Council decisions. This issue will be discussed in more detail in section II.1.

Until the Nice Treaty, the general functioning and structures of police cooperation did not change. By communitising the entire area of asylum and migration the 1997 Treaty of Amsterdam limited the re-

---

7 Barbe describes the third pillar as the "*antichambre du droit communautaire*", Emmanuel Barbe, *Justice et affaires intérieures dans l'UE* (Paris: La Documentation Française, 2002), p. 25.

8 Regarding COREPER Art. K.8(1) of the EU Treaty referred to Arts. 150-153 of the EC Treaty. Thus the general rules for COREPER and its relations to the Council became applicable also for the third pillar. In line with Art. 151(3) TEU the Council Rules of Procedure stipulate that COREPER is responsible for setting up working parties.

9 Cf. Henri-Michel Darnanville, *Europol* (Villeneuve d'Ascq: Presses universitaires du septentrion, 2002), p. 126.

sponsibilities of the Article 36 Committee, the successor of the K.4 Committee, to police and law enforcement cooperation.[10]

2. Organisational Structures of Europol[11]

2.1. Police in Europe – European Police

To better understand cooperation of police and judicial authorities, and in particular the European Police Office Europol, we first need to explain what Europol is *not* before describing the features of European police cooperation in a second step.

As a rule, negative definitions help gain a better understanding only if a positive definition of the subject has already been provided. However, there is a special and justified reason for choosing the opposite way in this chapter: since national legislations and citizens have a very precise idea of the police as an institution, we first need to move beyond the national perspective to fully comprehend the phenomenon of police cooperation at European level. Especially when talking about Europol as the "European Police Office" we need to explain that it is not a police office with tasks and powers similar to national police authorities. Hence, the title "Police in Europe" was chosen intentionally to contrast the term of "European police" which does not yet exist. Developments indicating the emergence of a true European police authority will be discussed at the end of this contribution.

But first we will give the aforementioned definitions starting with a comparison of Europol's work with the work of national police forces and public prosecutors, and other forms of international police cooperation. This will illustrate the current framework conditions for European police cooperation through Europol. At the same time, it will cast a light on pending issues regarding the role of the police which still require adequate solutions in the process of harmonising national legislation.

---

10 Regarding entry into the EU, controls of external borders as part of the Schengen Agreement and migration legislation were transferred to the first pillar where they are coordinated at the level of senior officials by SCIFA, the Strategic Committee on Immigration, Frontiers and Asylum. SCIFA was established by COREPER as a high-level coordination body in 1997 after the scope of the Article 36 Committee had been limited to police cooperation by the Amsterdam Treaty. For more details see Wenceslas de Lobkowicz, *L'Europe et la sécurité intérieure. Une élaboration par étapes* (Paris: La Documentation Française, 2002).

11 A general overview of Europol's organisational structures is given by Thomas Bernhard Petri, *Europol, Grenzüberschreitende polizeiliche Tätigkeit in Europa* (Baden-Baden: Nomos, 2001).

2.2. The Role of National Police Forces as compared to the Functions of the European Police Office

2.2.1. The Role of National Police Forces

Law enforcement by national police forces has two components: accountability to the public prosecutor's office and investigations in the framework of public prosecutor proceedings. These patterns developed in 19th century Europe when modern law enforcement structures emerged and were codified in different ways.

Whereas, for example, in France, the introduction of the *Code d'instruction criminelle* in 1808 established close organisational ties between the examining magistrate (*juge d'instruction*), the public prosecutor (*Procureur de la République*) and the criminal police, a general organisational link between the public prosecutor and the (criminal) police has never been established in Germany where the function of examining magistrate, which is common in the Romanic countries of the European Union, does not exist either. In practice, this difference is reflected, for example, in the public prosecutor's right to issue instructions to the police: in Germany, the public prosecutor has no general right to issue instructions to agencies and police officers but, pursuant to Section 161(1) of the Code of Criminal Procedure, must issue a request to the police who are then obliged to meet the request.

These different structural connections between police forces and public prosecutors in individual Member States also give rise to different views on the type of cooperation between Europol and Eurojust or the relation between Europol and a future European public prosecutor provided for by the Lisbon Treaty. At this stage, we would only like to touch on the issue of transferring national police structures to the European level but will get back to it in more detail later.

As mentioned earlier, participation of the police in the public prosecutor's investigations entails another function of national police forces. Provided a relevant court order has been issued, they are also allowed to exercise various coercive powers necessary to obtain information on planned or committed offences. These include, for example, the seizure of items relevant to the investigation, telecommunications surveillance and house searches. The exercise of these powers should always serve to obtain information on offences requiring intervention by the public prosecutor.

2.2.2. *Tasks and Activities of the European Police Office*

a. The Relation between National Police and Europol Tasks

From the overview given above we can identify two features characterising the law enforcement work of national police forces: On the one hand their accountability to the public prosecutor, which European countries handle differently, and on the other hand their coercive powers in criminal investigations.

When comparing these features with Europol, one can easily notice that neither of them applies to the European Police Office. There is neither a European Public Prosecutor[12] nor does Europol have coercive powers. The following sections will therefore deal with Europol's relation to national authorities. Based on these findings, section II.3 will take a look at future developments and structural changes in the work of Europol.

b. TEU Framework Provisions Regarding Europol's Tasks

The legal basis for the European Police Office is Article 29ff. TEU. Europol is first mentioned in Article 29 TEU whereas Article 30(1)(b) TEU defines the functions of Europol in the framework of police cooperation including

> the collection, storage, processing, analysis and exchange of relevant information, including information held by law enforcement services on reports on suspicious financial transactions, in particular through Europol, subject to appropriate provisions on the protection of personal data.

Moreover, Article 30(2)(a) TEU enables Europol

> to facilitate and support the preparation, and to encourage the coordination and carrying out, of specific investigative actions by the competent authorities of the Member States, including operational actions of joint teams comprising representatives of Europol in a support capacity.

Pursuant to Article 30(2)(b) TEU the Council shall

> adopt measures allowing Europol to ask the competent authorities of the Member States to conduct and coordinate their investigations in specific cases and to develop specific expertise which may be put at the disposal of Member States to assist them in investigating cases of organised crime.

Another relevant article is Article 33 TEU with its reservation clause: "This Title shall not affect the exercise of the responsibilities incumbent upon Member States with regard to the maintenance of law and order and the safeguarding of internal security".

---

[12] Eurojust does not function as European public prosecutor but like Europol is an instrument for coordinating Member State activities.

Considered together, these provisions determine the work of Europol as follows:

First, Europol has no own investigative and thus no coercive powers. These powers may be exercised only by the Member States, which consider them a core area of national sovereignty since they derive directly from the state's monopoly on the legitimate use of force.

Second, Europol's task is – in positive terms – "the collection, storage, processing, analysis and exchange of relevant information", which given Article 33 TEU does not imply independent investigations but rather secondary activities accompanying Member State investigations.

Third, Europol may support Member State investigations also in operational terms (in the framework of the aforementioned secondary activities).

c. Europol Convention: Task Description and Information Management Systems

Thus, Europol's overall focus is to collect, process and analyse information.[13] Since this does not give Europol independent powers to collect information, as explained above, Europol depends on the voluntary supply of data, namely data from the Member States, as Europol is an instrument to improve cooperation among EU Member States.[14] Needless to say, Member States do not have to share all their investigation data but only those with a cross-border dimension, i.e. those which affect two or more EU Member States and are instrumental for combating organised crime (cf. Article 2(1) of the Europol Convention). Only in those cases of crime information is exchanged via Europol.

In this respect, the Europol Convention[15] greatly differs from traditional national police law and law enforcement action. The provisions of the Europol Convention primarily focus on the exchange, processing and analysis of police information. To this end, Europol maintains two types of automated information systems: the Europol Information System (EIS, Articles 7 to 9 of the Europol Convention) and the Analysis Work Files (AWF, Articles 10 to 12 of the Europol Convention). In general terms, the structural difference between both systems can be described as follows: Data entered in the EIS refer to persons who are

---

13 This new dimension of European policing is discussed by Josef Aulehner, *Polizeiliche Gefahren- und Informationsvorsorge* (Berlin: Duncker & Humblot, 1998), p. 136ff.

14 However, Europol has concluded agreements on information-sharing also with various third-countries and other third parties.

15 Convention based on Art. K.3d of the Treaty on European Union on the establishment of a European Police Office (Europol Convention), *O.J.*, No. C 316 of 27 November 1995.

suspected of having committed an offence or who were convicted for an offence or who give reason to believe that they will commit offences which fall under the responsibility of Europol. Member States store data centrally in the EIS where they are available for law enforcement authorities. We will present the bodies entitled to transmit and access data in the next section when discussing the internal structure of Europol and its relation to the Member States.

The Analysis Work Files, which are at the heart of Europol's work, cover a broader range: they include also persons who may serve as witnesses during investigations or who actually were or might become victims of an offence, contacts and associates, and persons who can provide information on the offence. The analysis projects for which AWF are created are aimed not only at making data provided by the Member States available but also at linking them to gain insights into cross-border connections which Member States do not have. It can safely be said that the AWF represent the true added value of Europol's work since they not merely pool existing information but also generate new findings by linking existing material in the analysis process.

Given the high number of data transmissions and links, Europol faces the challenge of ensuring the effective channelling of the manifold communication flows and at the same time to prevent data from being misused and information incorrectly used or interpreted. The following section will describe the relevant provisions and thus lead us to the general internal structure of Europol and its relation to the EU Member States.

d. Data Transmissions to Europol

Data are entered in the Europol Information System by the "national units". In this respect, Article 7(3) of the Europol Convention generally states that "[t]he national unit in each Member State shall be responsible for communication with the information system". The term "national unit" is defined in Article 4(2) of the Europol Convention according to which it is "[…] the only liaison body between Europol and the competent national authorities" while "[r]elationships between the national unit and the competent authorities shall be governed by national law, and, in particular, the relevant national constitutional requirements".

Pursuant to Article 4(4) of the Europol Convention the tasks of the national units include:

1) [supplying] Europol on their own initiative with the information and intelligence necessary for it to carry out its tasks;

2) [responding] to Europol's requests for information, intelligence and advice;

3) [keeping] information and intelligence up to date;

> 4) [evaluating] information and intelligence in accordance with national law for the competent authorities and [transmitting] this material to them;
>
> 5) [issuing] requests for advice, information, intelligence and analysis to Europol;
>
> 6) [supplying] Europol with information for storage in the computerized system; [and]
>
> 7) [ensuring] compliance with the law in every exchange of information between themselves and Europol.

Thus, Article 4(4) of the Europol Convention specifies the general task of the national unit provided for in Article 4(2), i.e. to serve as a communication channel between the Europol Information System and the individual Member State, in astonishing detail. At first glance, the list of the national units' tasks and duties may even seem too detailed. However, the list is fully justified on the grounds that Europol has no powers to obtain information on its own. Precisely because Europol depends on information provided by Member States to reasonably fulfil its tasks, the tasks and duties of the national units with regard to Europol need to be very well defined. This becomes particularly clear when one looks at the requirement that national units must ensure compliance with the law in every exchange of information between Europol and themselves: since Europol has no own powers, it is not able to control compliance of the information exchange with the law. This clearly shows to which extent Europol is dependent on Member States and that there is little reason to speak of a true European police authority.

e. Liaison Officers

In terms of staff, the close connection to the Member States is reflected also by the liaison officers deployed to Europol. The legal basis for liaison officers is Article 5 of the Europol Convention. According to paragraph 3 of this article, liaison officers

> assist in the exchange of information between the national units which have seconded them and Europol, in particular by
>
> 1) providing Europol with information from the seconding national unit;
>
> 2) forwarding information from Europol to the seconding national unit; and
>
> 3) cooperating with the officials of Europol by providing information and giving advice as regards analysis of the information concerning the seconding Member State.

At the same time, liaison officers pursuant to Article 5(4) of the Europol Convention "assist in the exchange of information from their national units and the coordination of the resulting measures […]".

f. Retrieving Data

An important provision in this context is Article 5(5) of the Europol Convention: "[...] liaison officers [...] have the right to consult the various files in accordance with the appropriate provisions specified in the relevant Articles". What is the background of this provision and what is special about it? To answer this, we need to remember the special character of Analysis Work Files, namely that there is no general right to retrieve data. Data from Analysis Work Files are retrieved in a completely different way than data from the Europol Information System.

When reading Article 9 of the Europol Convention which governs the right to access the Europol Information System one can easily observe that the right to *enter* and the right to *retrieve* data are *symmetric*: national units have the right both to enter and retrieve data, and pursuant to Article 9(4) of the Europol Convention, Member States may even designate further authorities entitled to retrieve data. Therefore, it may be concluded that the intention is to give national authorities extensive access to data from the information system.

A different rule applies for the access to Analysis Work Files. According to Article 10(2) of the Europol Convention, an analysis group is established for each analysis project. The group includes Europol analysts and other Europol officials designated by the Europol Directorate as well as liaison officers and/or experts of the Member States. Although information on the individual analysis projects is submitted by the Member States, only Europol analysts are authorised to directly enter data into the file concerned and modify such data.

The Council Act of 27 November 2003 granted all participants of an analysis group the right to retrieve data from the Analysis Work File concerned. Until then, only analysts had been allowed to do so. By extending access rights, Member States' justified need for information was met. In practice, however, the possibilities to access Analysis Work Files are still limited. In October 2007, the Europol Management Board adopted rules on the practical implementation of Member State access according to which data should be retrieved from the Analysis Work Files with caution for two reasons. The first is that, as indicated earlier in this chapter, Analysis Work Files contain numerous sensitive data also from ongoing investigations of national law enforcement authorities. These ongoing investigations should not be put at risk by an uncontrolled retrieval and dissemination of information from the Analysis Work Files. The second reason is that information processed in an analysis project may reveal new connections to investigations or findings from other Member States. But, if individual data from an Analysis Work File are retrieved, the individual retrieving participant might not take into account these connections so that the information forwarded is based upon wrong premises and misinterpreted. The practical work of analysis groups therefore begins by determining the conditions and restrictions for data retrieval. This ensures that data are retrieved only to the extent considered reasonable by the participants of an analysis group.

Since information relevant for analysis is not submitted only by Member States but also by other organisations, Article 10(4) of the Europol Convention allows for the involvement of other institutions such as the bodies of the European Communities or the European Union, third-countries, international organisations or the International Criminal Police Organisation Interpol.[16] Pursuant to Article 10(9) of the Europol Convention, Europol may invite experts from these organisations to act as associates of an analysis group. To this end, an agreement on information exchange between Europol and the institution concerned must be in force, the association of experts must be in the interest of the Member States, the analysis work must directly affect the third-country or organisation, and all participants must agree on the associations of the experts.

g. The Index System

Given the restricted access to the Analysis Work Files on the one hand and the Member States' need for information from the analysis groups on the other, Member States need a way to examine whether relevant findings have been made in an analysis project without disclosing too many details of this project. For this purpose, the index system described in Article 11 of the Europol Convention was set up. Whereas other descriptions list the index system as the third information system besides the EIS and AWF, we did not include this system in our brief overview of information management systems above. To avoid misunderstandings, we would like to point out that although this is not incorrect in formal terms, the index system is only an annex system to the Analysis Work Files. Without the Analysis Work Files there would not be an index system.[17]

---

16 Compared with Europol, Interpol is more loosely organised, in particular since Interpol is not part of a supranational institution's legal framework as is the case for Europol and the EU. Regarding the role of Interpol cf. Nadia Gerspacher, "The roles of international police cooperation organizations", *European Journal of Crime, Criminal Law and Criminal Justice*, No. 13, 2005, p. 413; and Malcolm Anderson, *Policing the World. Interpol and the Politics of International Police Co-operation* (Oxford: Clarendon Press, 1989).

17 For this reason, the Europol Council Decision does not use the term "index system" but the term "index function". Cf. Art. 15 of the Council Decision of 6 April 2009

Pursuant to Article 11(2) of the Europol Convention the Director, Deputy Directors and duly empowered officials of Europol and liaison officers have the right to consult the index system. The index system must be such that it is clear to the liaison officer consulting it, from the data being consulted, that the files contain data concerning the seconding Member State. Access by liaison officers is defined in such a way that it is possible to determine whether or not an item of information is stored, but that it is not possible to establish connections or further conclusions regarding the content of the files. According to Article 11(3) of the Europol Convention the detailed procedures for the design of the index system are defined by unanimous decision of the Management Board.

2.2.3. *The Europol Management Board as a Strategic Body and the Operational Support of its Work*

The Europol Management Board has already been mentioned twice in connection with the specific working method of analysis groups and the index system. It became clear that Europol's work can only be fully understood if both the role and the decisions of the Management Board are taken into account. It is no exaggeration to say that without the decisions of the Management Board Europol's legal framework would merely be "law in the books". The Management Board has decisive influence on the interpretation and practical implementation of the legal basis.

The Management Board is based on Article 28 of the Europol Convention. We will not describe all 28 tasks of the Management Board in detail. They can be roughly summarised as follows: The most important provision is Article 28(1)(1) of the Europol Convention stipulating that the Management Board takes part "in the establishment of the priorities for Europol". It also supervises Europol and its structures, e.g. by taking part "in the appointment and dismissal of the Director and Deputy Directors" pursuant to Article 28(1)(11) and appointing "the financial controller" pursuant to Article 28(1)(17) of the Europol Convention.[18] Finally, the Management Board is usually involved when certain legal

---

establishing the European Police Office (Europol) (2009/371/JHA), *O.J.*, No. L 121 of 15 May 2009, p. 37.

18 However, the Management Board has no jurisdiction over the joint supervisory body which pursuant to Art. 24 of the Europol Convention is an independent body responsible for data protection and the right to privacy. In this respect, according to Art. 28(1) No. 8 of the Europol Convention the Management Board has only the right to deliver opinions on the comments and reports of the joint supervisory body. Regarding the appointment of the Director, the Management Board has also only the right to deliver an opinion; the appointment itself is effected by the Council pursuant to Art. 29(1).

provisions at EU level are to be transposed into detailed implementing provisions for Europol. In accordance with Article 28(2) of the Europol Convention the Management Board is "composed of one representative of each Member State" and pursuant to Article 28(9) of the Europol Convention meets "at least twice a year". Currently, the Management Board meets six times a year.

In sum, the Europol Convention already indicates that the Management Board is a body which provides Europol with direction and a basic structure. This is also emphasised by the definition of tasks of the Director who, according to Article 29(3)(2) is responsible for "day-to-day administration". The Management Board might thus be called Europol's strategic body. But since strategic decisions also need to be reviewed and cannot be made without taking into account operational needs of investigation authorities in the Member States, there is another body which is only marginally mentioned in Article 4(7) of the Europol Convention which states that: "The Heads of national units shall meet on a regular basis to assist Europol, at their own motion or on request, by giving advice". This is called the meeting of HENUs (Heads of Europol National Units). Concisely, it might be called an operational advisory body. It cannot make own decisions but should ensure that strategic decisions are in line with operational needs.[19]

2.3. *Further Developments*[20]

2.3.1. Towards Greater Independence for Europol

So far, Europol has been described as a police institution which supports Member States' law enforcement authorities and whose activities are determined by Member States. However, there are already some instruments indicating that Europol will strengthen its position and might gain more independence in the future. This includes the possibility of Europol officials to take part in joint investigation teams, the possibility of Europol to issue investigation requests to EU Member States and Europol's role as central office for combating euro counterfeiting.

---

19 In contrast, the European Police Chiefs Task Force (PCTF) covers a broader range of police cooperation issues but has no basis in a legal document. It was founded in 1999 (Tampere European Council) in order to create an operational body at a level equivalent to the Article 36 Committee (CATS). Therefore, the future of the PCTF is closely linked to COSI (cf. section 3.3).

20 See also Michael Niemeier, "Die Zukunft von Europol", *Integration*, July 2007, p. 292ff.; and also, "L'avenir d'Europol", *La Revue de la Gendarmerie Nationale*, No. 227, June 2008, p. 53ff.

a. Participation in Joint Investigation Teams

The Council Act of 28 November 2002[21] added Article 3a to the Europol Convention. According to this provision, Europol officials may participate in joint investigation teams as mentioned in Article 13 of the Convention on Mutual Assistance in Criminal Matters of 29 May 2000. The joint investigations teams are composed of representatives from justice and police authorities of at least two Member States who are assigned to investigate specific areas for a limited period of time (which may be extended upon approval of all parties involved).[22] The new element introduced by this instrument is that, compared to the previous framework of Europol's work, Europol officials may now work in an operational context, i.e. they may participate directly in investigations. However, in principle this does not contradict Europol's support function. Article 3a(1), last sentences clearly states that Europol officials must not take coercive measures and that their role is only to assist.

b. Requests by Europol to EU Member States

A more important new element is introduced by Article 3b which was added to the Europol Convention by the same legal act as Article 3a. Article 3b(1) of the Europol Convention allows Europol to request Member States "to initiate, conduct or coordinate investigations". If the Member States "decide not to comply with a request from Europol", they are obliged to inform Europol of the reasons for the refusal unless "to do so would harm essential national security interests; or [...] jeopardise the success of investigations under way or the safety of individuals". Although this provision does not give Europol any powers in the strict sense, it nevertheless represents a new approach since it gives Europol for the first time a more active role. Whereas Europol generally is dependent on data provided by Member States without having the possibility to intensify or accelerate this process, Article 3b of the Europol Convention at least creates an instrument which forces Member States to a certain extent to give reasons for not initiating investigations.

c. Central Office for Combating Euro Counterfeiting

Finally, Council Decision 2005/511/JHA of 12 July 2005[23] gave the European Police Office a decisive role in combating Euro counterfeiting

---

[21] *O.J.*, No. L 312 of 16 December 2002, p. 2.

[22] Art. 3a of the Europol Convention also refers to Framework Decision 2002/465/JHA of 13 June 2002. However, this Framework Decision was adopted only because the ratification process of the Convention on Mutual Assistance in Criminal Matters was unreasonably long. The Framework Decision became obsolete when the Convention entered into force on 23 August 2005.

[23] *O.J.*, No. L 185 of 16 July 2005.

by declaring it the central office in this field. The Decision ties in with the Geneva Convention of 20 April 1929 for the Suppression of Counterfeiting Currency. According to Article 12 of this Convention,

> In every country, within the framework of its domestic law, investigations on the subject of counterfeiting should be organised by a central office. This central office should be in close contact:
>
> (a) With the institutions issuing currency;
>
> (b) With the police authorities within the country;
>
> (c) With the central offices of other countries.

Finally, the central office should "centralise, in each country, all information of a nature to facilitate the investigation, prevention and punishment of counterfeiting currency". After the Euro was introduced as a common currency, the need arose to assign the role of central office to one institution instead of numerous national authorities. What is most interesting about this is that Europol as the central office is at the same time an investigative authority within the meaning of the Geneva Convention. Even if this does not give Europol true operational powers, it does nevertheless significantly strengthen Europol's position as any information on Euro counterfeiting is collected by Europol for analysis.

2.3.2. Europol Council Decision

So far we have discussed only existing legal provisions governing Europol activities. However, on 1 January 2010 the Europol Convention will be replaced by a new legal instrument. In late December 2006 the European Commission presented the "proposal for a Council Decision establishing the European Police Office (EUROPOL)"[24] dated 5 January which was discussed in the Council bodies and approved by the Council in its final agreed version on 18 April 2008.[25] Until its entry into force, the implementing provisions required by the Council Decision will have to be discussed and adopted.

---

[24] Council Document 5055/07 EUROPOL 2.

[25] Council Decision of 6 April 2009 establishing the European Police Office (Europol), *op. cit.* Negotiations took place in three stages: working party, Article 36 Committee (or CATS, *Comité de l'article trente-six*) and the Permanent Representatives Committee (COREPER – *Comité des représentants permanents*). Whereas the latter two bodies are mentioned in Article 36 TEU and Article 207 TEC, respectively, working parties are not expressly mentioned in primary legislation. Working parties are bodies at working level in which national delegations composed of officials come together to hold initial and thorough discussions on various subjects. Council working parties are established by COREPER through a procedural decision.

An alternative proposal of the Europol Council Decision has been presented by Jürgen Wolter, Wolf-Rüdiger Schenke, Hans Hilger, Josef Ruthig and Mark A. Zöller (eds.), *Alternativentwurf Europol und europäischer Datenschutz* (Heidelberg: C.F. Müller Verlag, 2008).

Replacing the Europol Convention by a Council Decision on the basis of Article 34 TEU was considered necessary because the ratification procedures of the previous three amending protocols took so long that the Europol Convention could be amended only with a delay. The instrument of a Council Decision will allow possible future amendments of Europol's legal framework to be adopted faster. The replacement causes only a few substantive changes. On the one hand, Europol's mandate, which has so far been limited to organised crime, will be extended to include any cases of serious crime affecting two or more Member States regardless of whether they are committed within structures of organised crime. On the other hand, Europol will be led from a purely intergovernmental form of cooperation closer to Community structures, e.g. Europol will not only be financed from the Community budget, but its officials will also be subject to the Community staff regulations.[26] Finally yet importantly, Article 10(2) of the Council Decision allows the establishment of a new system processing personal data.

2.3.3. Lisbon Treaty

Apart from the Europol Council Decision, the future development of Europol will greatly depend on the entry into force of the Lisbon Treaty. There are two important aspects:

According to Article 88(1) TFEU Europol's mission will be to

> support and strengthen action by the Member States' police authorities and other law enforcement services and their mutual cooperation in preventing and combating serious crime affecting two or more Member States, terrorism and forms of crime which affect a common interest covered by a Union policy.

The word "strengthen", which is not included in the current wording of Article 30 TEU, seems to be important in this context since it indicates that Europol might play a more active role in combating crime in the future.

---

26 This caused certain problems during consultations, but they have already been solved. Transposing Europol into the EU's legal framework was to ensure *first* that no additional costs will be incurred, *second* that the EC Protocol on Privileges and Immunities will not apply to Europol officials who participate in joint investigation teams, and *third* that Europol officials participating in joint investigation teams may receive, as has been done so far under Art. 3a of the Europol Convention, instructions from a national head of the investigation team despite the EC staff regulations. Council Regulation (EC) No. 371/2009 of 27 November 2008 amending Regulation (Euratom, ECSC, EEC) No. 549/69 determining the categories of officials and other servants of the European Communities to whom the provisions of Art. 12, the second para. of Art. 13 and Art. 14 of the Protocol on the Privileges and Immunities of the Communities apply, *O.J.*, No. L 121 of 15 May 2009, p. 1, now stipulates that Europol officials, who participate in joint investigation teams, are not granted any privileges or immunities.

One possible aspect of this role may be indicated by Article 86 TFEU which in its first paragraph states that the Council in order to combat crimes affecting the financial interests of the Union may by means of regulations establish a European Public Prosecutor's Office proceeding from Eurojust. Pursuant to Article 86(2) TFEU

> [t]he European Public Prosecutor's Office is responsible for investigating, prosecuting and bringing to judgment, where appropriate in liaison with Europol, the perpetrators of, and accomplices in, offences against the Union's financial interests, as determined by the regulation provided for in paragraph 1.[27]

Under Article 86(4) TFEU the European Council may, upon or after adoption of the regulation, "adopt a decision amending paragraph 1 in order to extend the powers of the European Public Prosecutor's Office to include serious crime having a cross-border dimension".

2.4. Europol and the Future European Public Prosecutor's Office: Remaining Questions

Taken together, all the described provisions which over the last years have strengthened and, after the entry into force of the Lisbon Treaty, will further strengthen Europol's position, reveal certain patterns which in the next years will influence policy discussions on Europol.

Obviously, Europol's functions have been carefully expanded over the last years. Since Europol officials are not allowed to take coercive measures, Europol's general task has continued to be the support of national police forces. Within the current legal framework only Article 3b of the Europol Convention, according to which Europol may request a Member State to initiate investigations, indicates that the European Police Office might play a more active role in the future.

However, as soon as a European Public Prosecutor's Office is established[28] in line with Article 86 TFEU, further discussions of Europol's role will ensue and this for two reasons:

1. If the European Public Prosecutor's Office is established, it will have the power to conduct independent investigations. If this is done in liaison with Europol as stipulated by Article 86 TFEU, the question will arise which powers Europol should be given in

---

27 In this context, the obvious question will arise whether OLAF should be dissolved as an independent agency while the European Public Prosecutor's Office and/or Europol would assume its functions.

28 Cf. Gregor Srock, Rechtliche Rahmenbedingungen für die Weiterentwicklung von Europol (Tübingen: Mohr Siebeck, 2006), p. 203ff.; Martin Engel, Befugnis, Kontrolle und Entwicklung von Europol unter Berücksichtigung des Vertrages über eine Verfassung für Europa (Hamburg: Verlag Dr. Kovacs, 2006), p. 155ff.

this context. This is particularly relevant given that according to Article 88(3) TFEU "[a]ny operational action by Europol must be carried out in liaison and in agreement with the authorities of the Member State or States whose territory is concerned". The use of coercive measures remains the exclusive right of the responsible national authorities. But the European Public Prosecutor's Office will insist on appropriate investigative instruments, so that Europol on the one hand must respect the national privilege to exercise coercive measures (as an expression of sovereignty and the state's monopoly on the legitimate use of force) and on the other hand will not be able to refuse requests from the European Public Prosecutor's Office for support – a choice between a rock and a hard place. A possible solution might be that in line with the idea behind Article 3b of the Europol Convention, Europol would request national police forces to initiate investigations.

2. In this case, however, another conflict might arise which is not relevant at the moment but was briefly addressed earlier when we described the relationships between national public prosecutors and police forces, namely how the relationship between the public prosecutor and police forces should be structured at European level. Should the police be strictly accountable to the public prosecutor as in France or be more independent as in Germany? How can judicial control of investigations be ensured and which role will national (examining) magistrates play?[29] At the moment, this issue is not pressing since Member State authorities conduct investigations in line with their national provisions even if they might be very different.

3. Future Structures of Operational Police Cooperation under the Lisbon Treaty and the Role of "COSI"[30]

By the Lisbon Treaty, which makes this policy area part of Community law, police cooperation will be subject to major changes for the first time since its inclusion in the EU Treaty of Maastricht. Although there

[29] Cf. Kerstin Degenhardt, *Europol und Strafprozess* (Fankfurt a.M.: Verlag Peter Lang, 2003); Sabine Gless, Rainer Grote and Günter Heine (eds.), *Justitielle Einbindung und Kontrolle von Europol*, (Freiburg/Br.: edition iuscrim, 2001).

[30] Even though it is not yet clear whether the Lisbon Treaty will enter into force, the possible new structure will be presented in this section. This would also be possible within the current legal framework of the Nice Treaty if COREPER adopted a decision. The French Presidency will submit relevant proposals in the second half of 2008 (as at July 2008).

are numerous exceptions,[31] this might be the beginning of a new stage of development since 1993, especially in terms of structure.

In the area of policing, the Treaty enhances the rights and the influence of the Commission, national parliaments and the European Parliament, but it no longer mentions the coordination level (K.4 Committee or Article 36 Committee) introduced by the Maastricht Treaty. Instead, Article 71 TFEU creates a committee for operational cooperation among Member States (*Comité pour la sécurité intérieure*, COSI).[32] This committee should "[...] ensure that operational cooperation on internal security is promoted and strengthened within the Union". To this end, it should "[...] facilitate coordination of the action of Member States' competent authorities".

Does this new standing committee represent a step towards abolishing the four-tier Council structure and establishing a three-tier structure familiar from Community law (working party, COREPER, Council of Ministers) or was the aim simply to anchor an insufficiently noticed element more visibly in primary legislation? Since the Intergovernmental Conference copied the provisions on police cooperation from the Constitutional Treaty unchanged, it might help to consult also the documents of the responsible working group of the European Convention.[33] Working group X responsible for Home Affairs states in its final report[34] that "[t]here is a broad acknowledgement amongst members of the Working Group that current operational collaboration lacks efficiency, transparency and accountability".

In spring 2003, the then French foreign minister de Villepin and his Spanish counterpart Palacio presented a proposal on "Strengthening operational police cooperation".[35] Referring to the measures and instruments provided by the Treaties of Maastricht and Amsterdam the authors stated that coherence and authority were lacking. They therefore recommended creating a committee for internal security (*Comité de*

---

31 In this context, some already speak of an "Amsterdamisation" of the Lisbon Treaty.

32 Art. 71 TFEU: "A standing committee shall be set up within the Council in order to ensure that operational cooperation on internal security is promoted and strengthened within the Union. Without prejudice to Article 240, it shall facilitate coordination of the action of Member States' competent authorities. Representatives of the Union bodies, offices and agencies concerned may be involved in the proceedings of this committee. The European Parliament and national Parliaments shall be kept informed of the proceedings".

33 For general information on the Convention's work see Michael Niemeier, *Die europäische polizeiliche Zusammenarbeit als Thema des Regierungskonferenz: Vorschlag des EU-Konvents*, in: ERA-Forum 3/2003, p. 99ff.

34 Final report of Working Group X of the Convention, CONV 426/02 (WGX 14) of 2 December 2004 at http://register.consilium.europa.eu/pdf/en/02/ cv00/00426en2.pdf.

35 CONV 600/03 CONTRIB 269 of 7 March 2003.

sécurité intérieure, COSI) on the model of the CFSP Political and Security Committee.[36] According to the ministers' proposal, the interior security committee should have two tasks:

- initiating and, if necessary, coordinating operations within the EU, and
- being responsible for operational measures to protect external borders. For this purpose, it should regularly evaluate external border security by using own experts, and ensure professional training and the interoperability of equipment. In case of insufficient controls, it should deploy units to the relevant border section and in case of crisis manage an operation, if authorised by the Council.

While respecting cooperation among Member States, the committee should coordinate measures at European level. The head of the committee should also be a member of the Europol Management Board. The committee should be composed of senior officials responsible for operational measures who are permanently based in Brussels. The head should be appointed by the Council and assigned to the Council Secretariat. The committee should not intervene in legislative discussions within the responsibility of the Article 36 Committee and SCIFA.

This proposal, which was submitted only a few days before the final discussions on the Area of Freedom, Security and Justice, has not been implemented. Its far-reaching operational powers would have significantly infringed on Member State sovereignty. It would also have been hard to explain how these powers were in line with the Member States' guaranteed responsibility for internal security and public order. During the plenary debate on 3 and 4 April 2003 general agreement was reached on the draft presented by working group X which proposed a more restricted scope of activity and did not address the composition of the committee.[37]

Noting that operational coordination at EU level was insufficient, working group X in its final report suggested that "a more efficient structure for the coordination of operational cooperation at high technical level be created within the Council". One of the working group's two "golden rules" was to "introduce, as much as possible, a separation between 'legislative' and 'operational' tasks".[38] Therefore, the commit-

---

36 Art. 25 TEU (Art. 38 TFEU).

37 Cf. CONV 677/03, p. 4 on Art. 5.

38 Cf. CONV 426/02, p. 4. The committee further explained: "There should be clearer distinction between legislation (legal instruments; legislative procedures; implementation; in large part to be aligned with the general procedures of Community law) and

tee suggested a standing committee be set up to strengthen operational cooperation in the Council by coordinating measures taken by the Member States' responsible authorities. The responsible EU institutions should be involved and the European Parliament be kept informed. In the final proposal of the Convention this text was adopted with only some minor editorial changes.[39]

The Intergovernmental Conference adopted the proposal without changes as Article 61D TFEU.

The corresponding Article 71 TFEU introduced by the Treaty of Lisbon reads as follows:

> A standing committee shall be set up within the Council in order to ensure that operational cooperation on internal security is promoted and strengthened within the Union. Without prejudice to Article 240, it shall facilitate coordination of the action of Member States' competent authorities. Representatives of the Union bodies, offices and agencies concerned may be involved in the proceedings of this committee. The European Parliament and national Parliaments shall be kept informed of the proceedings.

The following section will examine the new committee's tasks and responsibilities, its functioning and its position within the Council structures.

3.1. Tasks and Responsibilities of COSI

According to Article 71 TFEU the committee's task is to promote and strengthen operational cooperation. But, this is only the objective. The first sentence does not mention the means and instruments to achieve this objective. The second sentence determines how the committee should achieve the objective, namely by facilitating coordination of Member States' action. This makes clear that it is neither responsible for operational measures nor leading them. It merely takes appropriate measures to promote operational cooperation among Member States. Also, legislative work, i.e. preparing and discussing legal acts, does not fall within the committee's responsibility. In individual cases, however,

reinforced coordination of operational collaboration at Union level. This distinction has guided the elaboration of the Working Group's final report".

39 Cf. CONV 802/03 of 12 June 2003, Art. III-157 (ex Art. 5): "A standing committee shall be set up in order to ensure that operational cooperation on internal security is promoted and strengthened within the Union. Without prejudice to Article [III-242], it shall facilitate coordination of the action of Member States' competent authorities. Representatives of the Union bodies and agencies concerned may be involved in the proceedings of this committee. The European Parliament and Member States' national parliaments shall be kept informed of the proceedings".

the committee might submit proposals to the Council within its area of responsibility.

Moreover, the scope of the committee's responsibility needs to be defined. The term "internal security" used in Article 71 TFEU is not restricted in any way. Therefore, its definition needs to be derived from the general context of this Title. The Treaty does not give a legal definition of the term.[40] With regard to the wording of Article 73 TFEU ("national security")[41] it may be described as follows: internal security covers all forms of cooperation between the responsible authorities of Member States and the European Union governed by national police law (prevention) or criminal law (punishment) including customs. This does not include authorities responsible for national security (intelligence services). In this field, only Member States may determine the appropriate form of cooperation (Article 73 TFEU). Thus, cooperation within COSI encompasses all law enforcement authorities except intelligence services.[42]

3.2. Composition of COSI

Article 71 TFEU does not include provisions on the composition of COSI. Whereas for the Article 36 Committee the relevant provision mentions "senior officials" no such specification is made in this article. However, given that the Treaty refers to it as a "standing committee",[43] its coordinating and advisory role as well as related statements in the Convention's final report[44] it may be assumed that the committee will be composed of senior (police) experts from the Member States. Previous discussions focused on the question whether these experts should be permanently present in Brussels or only be sent to Brussels by the Member States for the meetings. Since they need close ties to Member State authorities to fulfil COSI's tasks, it would not be useful if they

40 In addition to Art. 71 TFEU, the term "internal security" is used only in Art. 72 (exercise of the responsibilities incumbent upon Member States) and Art. 276 TFEU (restricted jurisdiction of the ECJ regarding Title V).

41 This article was not part of the Convention text and was only introduced by the Intergovernmental Conference.

42 Regarding intelligence services an exemption can be made if they are responsible in terms of law enforcement, e.g. in combating serious organised crime.

43 The term "standing committee" is not defined by the Treaty and appears only in Art. 71 TFEU. In the context of the area of freedom, security and justice and taking into account Convention work it may be assumed that COSI will meet regularly (e.g. once a month) and not *ad hoc*. Moreover, the term indicates that there will be a specific support structure in the Council.

44 Cf. CONV 614/03, p. 9, on Art. 5 referring to the final report of Working Group X, p. 16.

stayed in Brussels permanently. Continuity can be ensured by the Council Secretariat and the Member States' permanent representations.

In addition to Member States, Article 71, third sentence TFEU allows for involving responsible EU institutions and bodies such as Europol, Eurojust, Frontex, CEPOL and OLAF in the committee's work. These bodies do not have the right to permanent participation, which will depend on the agenda and the subject's relevance. The Commission will be involved in the committee's work.

According to the general rules, COSI will be chaired by the acting EU Presidency for six months assisted by the Council Secretariat.

3.3. The Position of COSI within Council Structures

Although it is mentioned in primary legislation, COSI's status is comparable to a Council working party. Article 71, second sentence TFEU states that COSI is responsible for coordination without prejudice to the responsibilities of COREPER, i.e. COSI is subordinate to COREPER and makes submissions to the Council via COREPER, if applicable. Moreover, the general Council Rules of Procedure apply.

Regarding its organisational integration, COSI's clear operational mandate has to be reconciled with the legislative and administrative activities of the other working parties responsible for the Area of Freedom, Security and Justice. Given its focus on operational issues, COSI should not be responsible for horizontal coordination of the Council working parties as is the current Article 36 Committee which is no longer mentioned in the TFEU. Therefore, COSI will have to be considered a high-level group in addition to the existing working parties. Further discussions will be necessary to determine whether a new *ad hoc* coordination group (steering group, group of coordinators) should follow the Article 36 Committee. To increase efficiency it would certainly be reasonable to consider merging and reducing existing working parties. For example, the structure (of working parties) might be based on the chapters of Title V TFEU and additionally include the necessary horizontal working parties (e.g. civil protection, Schengen, information-sharing).

At the moment, COSI's responsibilities overlap with the existing Police Chiefs Task Force (PCTF) established by the European Council in Tampere in 1999.[45] The PCTF is intended to improve the exchange

---

[45] Conclusion No. 44 of the Tampere European Council on 15-16 October 1999: "The European Council calls for the establishment of a European Police Chiefs operational Task Force to exchange, in cooperation with Europol, experience, best practices and information on current trends in cross-border crime and contribute to the planning of operative actions".

among practitioners and contribute to the planning of operational measures. From the beginning, the PCTF was able to fulfil these tasks only to a limited extent. Although a programme specifying concrete actions (COSPOL) has been adopted after some serious starting difficulties, Member States implement them only reluctantly. It should therefore be examined whether COSI could take over some of these tasks. Thus, the PCTF would be dispensable in future. If needed, Europol could coordinate operational activities in its support capacity.

4. Concluding Remarks and Outlook

The structures of police cooperation within the EU have dynamically evolved since their transposition from the intergovernmental context into the EU's legal framework in 1993.

Europol has an important role to play in the future security architecture. Regardless of further enhancements and new responsibilities, Europol is the most important operational body of crime prevention at European level. Through the new legal instrument, Europol will become an integral part of the EU's institutional framework. This creates synergies which should be used to take full advantage of the opportunities offered by Europol.

A major future challenge will also be the efficient organisation of Council structures. The 25 working parties which are subordinate to COREPER and responsible for JHA issues very specifically prepare discussions in the Council. However, reassignment of migration issues and police cooperation to the first and third pillar respectively, and the integration of the Schengen Agreement in the EU framework have also caused considerable complexity. Why, for example, do Frontex activities regarding external border controls and fighting illegal migration (police task) belong to the first pillar while combating general organised crime belongs to the third pillar? Moreover, responsibilities of Europol and Eurojust on the one hand and new institutions and agencies on the other hand partly overlap.

The process of implementing the Lisbon Treaty will provide the possibility to thoroughly review Council structures and to adjust overlapping responsibilities when revising the institutions' legal basis.

CHAPTER 7

The Role and Organisation of Eurojust

Added Value for Judicial Cooperation in Criminal Matters

Maylis LABAYLE & Hans G. NILSSON

1. Introduction

In order to fight effectively against the growing cross-border criminality resulting from globalisation, the changing nature of crime and its professionalisation, the EU has developed instruments of cooperation between its Member States in the fields of policing and criminal matters. Faced with this considerable increase of transborder crime, traditional cooperation instruments such as international conventions quickly proved to be inefficient.

A major step forward in police cooperation was made with the creation of Europol in 1992[1] (in the form of the European Drugs Unit): it was the first EU organ to offer a Joint Action against organised crime. That being said, Europol's action today is based on the exchange of information, analysis and, only to a limited extent, operational cooperation, but not on actual enforcement powers, which still belong to national police forces. In parallel, the development of judicial cooperation appeared to be insufficient and was pushed at the end of the 1990s and the beginning of the 2000s by four EU Presidencies,[2] following pressure exercised by several Member States' ministers for Justice or Home Affairs and police forces. Indeed, judicial cooperation was then ruled by Council of Europe conventional instruments from the 1950s, which were hardly appropriate to the task.

The idea of an equivalent unit to Europol, in charge of judicial cooperation and called Eurojust, was first evoked officially in 1996[3] and gained ground in the run up to the European Council held in Tampere in

1 Europol became truly operational on 1 July 1999.

2 Belgium, France, Portugal, Sweden.

3 The idea however was mooted since the early 1990s; Hans G. Nilsson, "Eurojust – the beginning or the end of the European public prosecutor?", *Europarättslig Tidskrift*, No. 4, 2000.

1999, which foresaw, although in vague terms, that such a unit should be set up by 2001 with

> the task of facilitating the proper coordination of national prosecuting authorities and of supporting criminal investigations in organised crime cases, notably based on Europol's analysis, as well as of cooperating closely with the European judicial network, in particular in order to simplify the execution of letters rogatory.[4]

Given the sensitive nature of criminal matters, eighteen months of tough negotiations ensued[5] but these were accelerated by the 9/11 terrorist attacks. In March 2001, a provisional unit with a seat inside the Council building was set up in Brussels, under the name of "Pro-Eurojust". Eurojust was finally set up in 2002[6] under the third pillar of the Treaty, and in 2003 it moved to its current location in The Hague.

Eurojust consists of prosecutors, magistrates and police officers of equivalent competence from each Member State. In some Member States such as Ireland or the United Kingdom, police officers have a prosecuting competence. However, in practice, Eurojust national members are mostly prosecutors.[7] They can be assisted by one or more persons, deputies and assistants, and in practice about half of them are.

Eurojust can act in three different capacities: as a College, through individual national members and through national authorities in relation to the sending Member State or in relation to other States by virtue of the national member having kept his statute in the national system.[8] Eurojust acting in the first two capacities have no "real" powers but "tasks", whereas individual national members have "real" powers in the third category. The extent of their powers is defined by each Member State; for instance the Swedish national member has powers of arrest or ordering house searches, whereas the UK national member may send letters rogatory by virtue of being a Crown Prosecutor and the UK Declaration under Article 24 of the 1959 Council of Europe Convention.

Eurojust combines 23 official languages and – because of three different legal systems of the UK – 29 legal systems. Initially, the enlargement of the Union was seen as a challenge from a financial and a logistical point of view. However, it is now perceived as a very positive

4 Tampere European Council, 15-16 October 1999, Presidency Conclusions, point 46.

5 In the Council Working Party alone, 32 days were devoted to the topic, thus showing the sensitivity of the matter.

6 Council Decision of 28 February 2002 setting up Eurojust with a view to reinforcing the fight against serious crime (2002/187/JHA), *O.J.*, No. L 63 of 6 March 2002.

7 Serge de Biolley, *Eurojust*, Jurisclasseur Europe Traités, Fasc. 3170, January 2008.

8 See Arts. 6, 7 and 9(3) of the 2002 Decision.

thing[9] as it allows having countries such as Bulgaria or Romania on board, as they are the starting point of many investigations.

The Eurojust organisation seeks to respect a balance between national and EU representation, as it can also act as a collective organ, the Eurojust College, composed of all the national members. It is structured in different teams dealing with various matters, from administration to all the different forms of organised crime or data protection. The College decides by unanimity in some rare cases, by qualified 2/3 majority (also in rare cases) or by simple majority. However, in practice a consensus is almost always aimed at. This can be explained by the sensitive nature of criminal law and the need for member states to see their interests and legal traditions protected in this field. The importance of the national context is also found in the unit's financing: national members are paid by their respective state of origin, while the EU finances the running costs, the staff and the whole infrastructure.[10]

The unit gathers information and coordinates prosecutions and investigations between Member States' competent authorities, in order to fasten, strengthen and improve European actions against cross-border criminality. However, it is not competent to open prosecutions or investigations in Member States. Its competence is widely defined as "serious forms of criminality" and specified in the Eurojust Decision. It covers all the forms of crime and the offences for which Europol is competent,[11] which is a very wide range of activities. It may also become competent at the request of an investigation authority of a member state. The initial Council Decision from 2002 pointed specifically to computer criminality, fraud, corruption, and criminal offences harming the EU's financial interests, laundering of the proceeds of crime, and participation to a criminal organisation[12] in Eurojust's competences but Europol's competences already encompassed these and several other offences, making the provision rather superfluous. The fact that it remained in the 2002 Decision could rather be seen as a political signal. In one respect, i.e. on the protection of the financial interests of the Community, it had a meaning since Eurojust's competence in this area could have been contested.

---

9 Interview with Michèle Coninsx, Vice-President of Eurojust.

10 Council Decision 2009/426/JHA of 16 December 2008 on the strengthening of Eurojust and amending Decision 2002/187/JHA setting up Eurojust with a view to reinforcing the fight against serious crime, *O.J.*, No. L 138 of 4 June 2009, Art. 33.

11 According to the former Art. 2 of the Europol Convention, replaced by Art. 4(1) of the July 2009 Europol Decision (reference), they are mainly: organised crime, terrorism and other serious forms of criminality enumerated in annex.

12 Council Decision 2002/187/JHA, *op. cit.*

The creation of Eurojust was a great step forward in judicial cooperation in criminal matters between EU Member States: the setting up of Eurojust is progressively transforming the traditional, horizontal and bilateral cooperation into a vertical and multilateral cooperation with focus on coordination. Eurojust is only seven years old: it is still a very young unit. Its first few years of activity could be seen as an observation and building up phase, during which it grew on the basis of the 2002 Decision without interference, despite some of its insufficiencies. In this short period of time, the unit met a considerable success.

But new steps have recently been taken in the negotiation of the draft Constitutional Treaty and the Lisbon Treaty, which both have taken into account the need for a strengthening of Eurojust. The Lisbon Treaty has not yet entered into force, but a new Eurojust Decision was adopted on 16 December 2008 to take into account some of the practical experiences that had been gained since 2002, notably by "enhancing its operational effectiveness".[13]

The aim of this chapter is to assess the added value of a unit such as Eurojust for the creation of an Area of Freedom, Security and Justice in the EU. Did Eurojust successfully allow the creation of a new form of judicial cooperation, and will it push this cooperation further in the future?

2. The Successful Development of an Unprecedented Form of Judicial Cooperation

2.1. A Complex Organisation

As has been noted, Eurojust can act both through its national members and through the College; in the latter case, the decision taken will have a stronger impact, even if the unit does not have actual coercive powers. The College will act in particularly important cases. However, the means of action at Eurojust's disposal in both cases are much the same. In addition to that, a national member can also exercise powers conferred at national level.

Eurojust's main task is to stimulate and coordinate national prosecutions and investigations. It has proven to carry this task out very efficiently in the last few years. It also improves cooperation between Member States' authorities, as it "is a multiplication of shortcuts":[14] national authorities may now communicate directly via the national members in the Eurojust College instead of using diplomatic contacts,

---

13 Council Decision 2009/426/JHA, *op. cit.*, p. 14.

14 Interview with Peter Csonka, Head of Unit Criminal Justice, Directorate-General Freedom, Security and Justice, European Commission.

Council of Europe Conventions, contacts via ministries of justice or rogatory letters. However, two thirds of the cases processed by Eurojust remain bilateral whereas it clearly has a vocation to deal with more multilateral cases. It also facilitates the implementation of "requests for, and decisions on, judicial cooperation, including regarding instruments giving effect to the principle of mutual recognition", and supports competent national authorities to strengthen the efficiency of their investigations and prosecutions.[15] Although its main objective is mainly to ensure judicial cooperation within the EU, it is also competent for cases between one or several Member States and non-EU States.

Moreover, Eurojust can request action from Member States to start investigating or prosecuting a case. This can be done by national members of concerned Member States or by a decision taken by the College with a simple majority.[16] In practice, Eurojust does not make use of it very often, but from a symbolic point of view, this is already a considerable prerogative. Eurojust can also request the creation of joint investigation teams or that a national jurisdiction gives up a case if judicial action in another Member State is more appropriate. The fact that the "power" to request action is not used very often formally, does not mean that it is devoid of meaning: just the mere possibility suggests that national authorities follow informal advice given by national members.

The new decision now foresees the creation of an On-Call Coordination procedure[17] available on a 24-hour/7-day basis in case of emergency. This new provision is justified by the current inability of national members to act on their own, without contacting their national authorities, while some situations may require an immediate response even outside working hours. If the creation of such a mechanism is logical and certainly needed, the decision is vague on this point and the way it will be implemented is still uncertain.

The clear novelty brought by Eurojust is its permanent and centralised character, as opposed to older instruments such as the European Judicial Network or liaison magistrates. There is no comparable network in the rest of the world. It cannot be qualified as a clearly supranational unit though: operational competences in criminal matters still remain in Member States' hands. Eurojust was not conceived as an organ that would hold an investigation or start a prosecution by itself. But Eurojust's existence is already a considerable integrational step in a context of globalisation of crime. New means of communication and transports

---

15 Council Decision 2009/426/JHA, *op. cit.*, Art. 3.

16 Rules of Procedure of Eurojust, 2002/C 286/01, Arts. 9 and 18 and Council Decision 2009/426/JHA, *op. cit.*, Art. 7(a).

17 Council Decision 2009/426/JHA, *op. cit.*, Art. 5.

notably blur the distinction between purely internal and transborder crimes. The Internet is a major factor of this globalisation as it is easy to access, not very regulated, and is directed to a vast audience.[18]

Each national member is a point of contact with its Member State of origin. Member States directly communicate information to their national member.[19] The national members' knowledge of their legal system allows them to contact the relevant authority if the need arises, which is a considerable gain of time. Article 9 of the new Decision defines four categories of powers: powers that are given at the discretion of a Member State, ordinary powers, powers exercised in agreement with a competent national authority and powers exercised in urgent cases. As regards the three last categories, they should be given as a minimum to each national member but Member States may go further in accordance with the first power. National members remain subject to their national law when they exercise the powers given to them.

When examining the powers granted to the national member more in detail, one may note that it is only the first and the fourth that are "real" powers in the sense that the national member may act autonomously. The first power is granted by the Member State at its discretion. This is the case for the Swedish national member. The second and the third power is either not a "real" judicial power or it is in agreement with a competent national authority, or at its request. The fourth power relates to cases when a national authority cannot be contacted or identified (for example in cases of controlled deliveries where one does not know where the car will arrive at the border). This is the only power which may be said to be autonomous. The national members also elect a President (currently the Portuguese national member José Luís Lopes da Mota) and two Vice-Presidents (currently the Belgian national member Michèle Coninsx and the Estonian national member Raivo Sepp).

In addition to the very concrete tasks of the national members, Eurojust's strength resides in its capacity to bring national members together, so that they are present in the same house, build bonds and that they are able to build official relationships with non-EU States.[20] The United States were thus associated from the beginning to meetings on terrorism. Moreover, several third States sue with each other in a fast and reliable way. Eurojust is a "house of mutual trust" first and foremost.

---

[18] Michèle Coninsx and José Luís Lopes da Mota, "The international role of Eurojust in fighting organized crime and terrorism", Guest Editorial, *European Foreign Affairs Review*, Vol. 14, No. 2, 2009, p. 168.

[19] Council Decision 2009/426/JHA, *op. cit.*, Art. 9, para. 2.

[20] Eurojust's Annual Report 2002.

2.2. An Instrument of Mutual Trust

From a more informal point of view, Eurojust is considered as a key instrument to build and promote mutual trust between national authorities regarding their criminal systems. First of all, it makes useful recommendations regarding judicial cooperation and organises meetings and seminars on various subjects. Mutual trust is the basis for an efficient judicial cooperation. Commissioner Franco Frattini stated in 2005 that "the principle of mutual recognition of judicial decisions is the cornerstone of judicial cooperation, but mutual trust between Member States is the necessary adjunct, the key to its success. Nobody can impose trust: it has to be built up bit by bit".[21]

The role of cooperation units such as Eurojust and Europol in this process is obvious to decision-makers. By bringing national actors together, Eurojust allows a better communication and a better understanding of Member States' respective legal systems. It also organises regular meetings between investigators and prosecutors from all Member States on judicial cooperation in general or on particular forms of criminality. These meetings help reducing Member States' reluctance to exchange data and best practices. They also sometimes involve representatives of third-countries that are involved in cases.[22] For that reason, Eurojust is mentioned several times in the Commission's June 2009 Communication regarding the Stockholm Programme,[23] which will replace The Hague Programme and set up the new priorities regarding Justice and Home Affairs for the next five years. This text notably promotes the involvement of Eurojust in a better implementation of EU law by practitioners in its section on mutual trust.[24]

Eurojust publishes annual reports of its activities and achievements, which are a good illustration of its success. Between 2006 and 2007, a 41% increase in cases referred by Member States was observed, with 1085 new cases referred in 2007. An even further increase was observed in 2008 as 1193 new cases were referred that year. The example is even more eloquent when compared to the mere 150 cases referred in 2002.

---

21 Press Release on the Communication from the Commission to the Council and the European Parliament on commmunication on the mutual recognition of judicial decisions in criminal matters and the strengthening of mutual trust between Member States, COM(2005) 195 final, Brussels, 19 May 2005, IP/05/581, 20 May 2005.

22 USA, Norway and Croatia have liaison prosecutors attached to Eurojust.

23 Communication from the Commission to the European Parliament and the Council on *an area of freedom, security and justice serving the citizen*, COM(2009) 262 final, Brussels, 10 June 2009.

24 *Ibid.*, p. 11.

But this positive assessment would have to be qualified if Eurojust had not established a good communication with other institutions and mechanisms acting in the same fields as it does.

3. Eurojust's Insertion in the Political Scene

3.1. Interactions with other EU Structures and Mechanisms

Eurojust's activities are not isolated; this is why it is important that it maintains close relations with EU institutions and external partners "such as third States, the European Police Office (Europol), the European Anti-Fraud Office (OLAF), the Council's Joint Situation Centre and the European Agency for the Management of Operational Cooperation at the External Borders of the Member States of the European Union (Frontex)".[25]

Even though there is no definition of the relations that should exist between Eurojust and EU institutions other than the one stated above, it keeps regular informal contacts with the Presidency Troika, the Council Secretariat and the Commission. About every three months, it organises an information and discussion meeting with these entities to examine issues of mutual interest. Eurojust is associated with important discussions regarding its activity, such as the discussions that preceded the adoption of the 2008 Decision. More generally, Eurojust's opinion can be requested by the Council or the Commission regarding any draft instrument under Title VI TEU.[26] Eurojust is also regularly asked by the Commission to give its input into Commission proposals and actions. It also participates in meetings with ministers in the Council or, for instance, at Troika meetings with the USA or Russia.

The Council of the European Union keeps a close look upon Eurojust's activities through its annual reports which are always examined by Counsellors, working groups and the Council itself. It has become standard practice that the Council adopts conclusions on the annual reports and that it asks Eurojust to report on the action it has taken on the Council conclusions. In that way, the Council keeps a political monitoring of Eurojust and its activities, while fully respecting judicial independence. The Council also has to approve some of the decisions taken by the unit, notably the designation of its President and Vice-Presidents, and agreements with third-countries having an impact on data protection. If the Council takes the view that the protection guaranteed by the agreement is not sufficient, it can ask Eurojust to renegotiate it.

---

25 Council Decision 2009/426/JHA, *op. cit.*, p. 15.

26 *Ibid.*, Art. 32, para.3.

The 2008 Decision particularly encourages close contacts with the Joint Situation Centre of the European Union, a crisis management and analysis instrument providing information and reports containing analyses to the Secretary General of the Council and the High Representative for CFSP. It is a useful link between the second and the third pillar, notably regarding terrorist threats. Eurojust can also be invited to CATS and different working groups meetings, and regularly participates as an observer in the Multidisciplinary Group on Organised Crime, the Working Party on Cooperation in Criminal Matters and the Council Working Group on Legal Data Processing.[27]

At present, Eurojust is in a way accountable to the Council of Ministers as it informs it on its activities through regular reports, but its quasi-judicial nature renders any control upon its activity very sensitive because of the independence of justice. The Parliament has no formal impact on Eurojust's activities. It is, however, informed about them by the fact that its annual reports as well as the report on the activities of the Joint Supervisory Body are forwarded by the Council Presidency. The President or any of the Vice-Presidents also give regular updates to the LIBE Committee when it so wishes. In addition, the Administrative Director of Eurojust regularly updates the Budget Control Committee on the activities of Eurojust as its budget (currently about 25 MEURO) comes from the EU budget. As one of the budgetary branches of the EU, the Parliament has shown much more understanding than the Council as regards the needs of Eurojust and has repeatedly increased the budget of Eurojust.

According to the 2008 Eurojust Decision,[28] the Commission is associated with Eurojust's work. It also has an influence on its activities as it proposes the budget (only national members' salaries fall into the Member States' competence). However, it has no say on operations and decisions. Regular meetings are organised between the Commission and Eurojust. The Commission can also consult the College on its projects regarding criminal law, such as the European Criminal Record.[29] Eurojust sometimes needs the Commission's expertise on certain points of EU law or on the administration's functioning.

The necessary association of police and judicial cooperation explain the importance for Eurojust to establish relations with Europol. This was already underlined in the Tampere Conclusions, the 2002 Decision and has been reaffirmed more precisely in the 2008 Decision. Eurojust was conceived following to some extent the model of Europol but its func-

---

[27] Eurojust Annual Report 2008, p. 41.

[28] Council Decision 2009/426/JHA, *op. cit.*, Art. 11, para. 1.

tioning is quite different. Europol is a much heavier structure, with a more important budget, an independent director and a management board meeting infrequently. The Eurojust College meets twice a week, resulting in a greater control also over management, something which is not always for the good of the organisation, for it diverts the focus of these meetings from its sole tasks.

Initially, a possible judicial control exercised by Eurojust over Europol's activities had been envisaged. However, this possibility remained hypothetical, which, considering that Europol does not have operational powers, actually makes sense.[30]

The relations between Europol and Eurojust are still only cooperative. The two bodies concluded an agreement on 9 June 2004 which regulates this collaboration by foreseeing regular meetings and consultations. However, progress was made in 2008, according to Eurojust's latest annual report and a new agreement was concluded in 2009. The two units created a secure communication link to improve their communication and developed their cooperation. Indeed, Europol was involved in 30 cases dealt with by Eurojust in 2008 and the coordinated operations that followed in the concerned Member States were successful.[31] Nonetheless, the relations between Eurojust and Europol are still deemed insufficient and remain one of the main sources of criticism regarding the two units.

OLAF (*Office de Lutte Anti-Fraude*), successor to UCLAF, was created in 1999 as an organ integrated in the Commission, although independent, to fight against fraud but has an operational independence as regards its administrative investigations. OLAF is in principle an administrative body in charge of detecting and investigating fraud cases against the Community budget and internal cases inside the institutions. By definition, it does not have any operational powers, except inside the institutions. But it conducts administrative investigations which are a preparatory work on external or internal fraud cases, which are then transferred to the competent prosecuting authority at national level. Notably OLAF has a team of magistrates to ensure the coordination of cases with judicial authorities once an administrative investigation in initiated. However, important cases of Community fraud could also be coordinated by Eurojust, as they fall under its competence. There are thus risks of overlap.

To regulate OLAF's and Eurojust's common actions, there is no formal agreement. An informal memorandum of understanding was signed in 2003, to complete the 2002 Eurojust Decision, according to

---

30 de Biolley, *op. cit.*, p. 13.

31 Eurojust Annual Report 2008, p. 42.

which "OLAF may contribute to Eurojust's work to coordinate investigations and prosecution procedures regarding the protection of the financial interests of the European Communities, either on the initiative of Eurojust or at the request of OLAF"[32] unless national authorities oppose that contribution. An informal memorandum of understanding had been concluded between the two bodies in 2003 but had a limited added value. It was followed by a practical agreement on arrangements of cooperation between Eurojust and OLAF, signed on 24 September 2008. The agreement regulates the cooperation between the two bodies on any case affecting the Community's financial interests. The two bodies will meet regularly in order to improve their communication and elaborate joint strategies, and they will exchange case summaries. A crucial point tackled in the agreement is the exchange of information, which has to be framed tightly to make sure that personal data protection is ensured. A whole chapter of the agreement is actually dedicated to data protection, and the inclusion of these rules in a formal document is one of the main reasons why the agreement was considered as a "key objective".[33] It is inevitable that Eurojust also has to process personal data to achieve its objectives. The need for a balance between efficiency and protection of fundamental rights is a core problematic of criminal law, but it is even more important when the actors are international bodies without the direct democratic legitimacy a national institution could have.

The European Judicial Network is Eurojust's main partner. It is in charge of bilateral cooperation, while Eurojust was conceived first and foremost as a multilateral instrument. The two structures work together, as illustrated by the strengthening of both of them by new Council decisions[34] adopted on the same day. Their complementarity is reinforced by the new texts.[35] The Secretariat of the EJN is also a part of the Eurojust Secretariat in The Hague.

The implementation of European Arrest Warrants is facilitated by Eurojust according to Article 3 of the Eurojust Decision, but Eurojust can also give advice in case of competing requests[36] and receive reports

---

32 Council Decision 2009/426/JHA, *op. cit.*, Art. 26, para. 4.

33 Eurojust Annual Report 2008, p. 42.

34 Council Decision 2008/976/JHA of 16 December 2008 on the European Judicial Network, *O.J.*, No. L 348 of 24 December 2008; and Council Decision 2009/426/JHA, *op. cit.*

35 Eurojust Annual Report 2008.

36 Article 16 of the Council Framework Decision of 13 June 2002 on the European arrest warrant and the surrender procedures between Member States (2002/584/JHA), *O.J.*, No. L 190 of 18 July 2002.

when there are delays in the execution of a request.[37] Eurojust notably helps to check when optional grounds for non-implementation of an EAW can be justified in order to implement a National Arrest Warrant over an EAW.

In addition to its developing interactions with other EU bodies and mechanisms, Eurojust is also in the process of building an important international network.

3.2. Eurojust as a "Central Player"[38] in EU External Relations

As stated in the introduction, organised crime is now a global phenomenon. It explains the need for a better cooperation au EU level but it is obvious that cross-border crime does not stop at EU borders. Some elements of the European construction, such as the internal market and the abolition of internal border controls, might facilitate it, but there is still a need for a world-wide judicial cooperation. The problems encountered at the European level are even stronger on wider international scale: differences between legal systems are even more important, which complicates a strong and close cooperation.

Like in Europol's case, Eurojust's external relations have been envisaged from its creation. But here stops the similarity. The Europol Convention, and now the new Europol Decision that enters into force in 2010, set very precise and complicated rules framing Europol's external relations. In comparison, the provisions of the 2002 Eurojust Decision on the question are disconcertingly simple. They are contained in Article 26 of the text, which originally vaguely dealt with "relations with partners", but were clarified in the new 2008 Decision in a more precise Article 26a specifically applicable to external relations. The text states that Eurojust "may establish and maintain cooperative relations" with third States, international organisations and Interpol.[39]

In 2002 already, the Eurojust Decision included the possibility for the unit to build official relationships with non-EU States.[40] Consequently, the United States were associated from the beginning to meetings on terrorism. Moreover, several third-countries (such as Canada, Norway, Switzerland, Liechtenstein, The Russian Federation and the USA as well as a number of Western Balkans countries) created contact points with Eurojust.

---

37 Eurojust Annual Report 2008, p. 20: in 2008, Eurojust facilitated the implementation of 237 EAW, solved 4 cases of conflicting EAW, and was reported 17 cases of breach of time limit.

38 Coninsx and Lopes da Mota, *op. cit.*, p. 167.

39 Council Decision 2009/426/JHA, *op. cit.*, Art. 26a.

40 Eurojust Annual Report 2002.

Eurojust is a unit with its own legal personality and as such, can conclude agreements with third-countries. The idea was that Eurojust could become a "one stop shop"[41] for information or evidence seizure for third-countries: it could become a central contact point for mutual legal assistance and exchange of information, although the formal cooperation has to follow bilateral agreements. Such cooperation is necessary as criminals do not stop at EU borders and the percentage of international crime is growing. The agreements can be concluded without scrutiny from the EU institutions, unless very sensitive questions like data protection are affected by the agreement. This follows the logic of the general lack of monitoring of Eurojust's activities due to its quasi-judicial nature, as already mentioned. Eurojust being in charge of judicial matters, political interferences in its activities could be seen as questionable. As a consequence, the Council does not try to influence agreements concluded by the unit, be it regarding their content or their parties. It can still request that Eurojust pays specific attention to a particular problem with a particular partner, as it was the case regarding the coordination of counter-terrorism measures with the USA after 9/11.[42] Also, the Union does not have more than one external relations' policy – it has only one and it is expected that Eurojust, like Europol, follows that policy.

Eurojust's first international agreement was concluded with Norway, an important partner in judicial cooperation as it is a member of the Schengen area. The abolition of border controls imposes a very careful attitude. Other agreements were then concluded with Iceland, Romania, Norway, the USA, the Republic of Croatia, or Switzerland. Negotiations for new cooperation agreements are currently conducted with the Russian Federation and Ukraine, and contacts have been made in that perspective with Moldova, Cape Verde, and Liechtenstein.[43]

The content of all Eurojust cooperation agreements is similar. They all aim at enhancing the cooperation between the concerned third-country and Eurojust, with a particular emphasis on the fight against terrorism in the case of the agreement with the USA. The scope of the agreements obviously is Eurojust's competences as defined in the Eurojust Decision. They all foresee the possibility for the other party to

---

41 Hans G. Nilsson, Memorandum, Minutes of evidence before the House of Lords (European Union Committee), 12 May 2004. http://www.publications.parliament.uk/pa/ld200304/ldselect/ldeucom/138/4051201.htm.

42 Hans G. Nilsson, "Organs and bodies of the third pillar as instruments of external relations of the Union?", in: Gilles de Kerchove and Anne Weyembergh (eds.), *Sécurité et justice: enjeu de la politique extérieure de l'Union européenne* (Bruxelles: Éditions de l'Université de Bruxelles, 2003), p. 207.

43 Coninsx and Lopes da Mota, *op. cit.*, p. 166.

second a liaison magistrate to Eurojust if this allows their cooperation to be improved. To that date, only the United States, Norway and Croatia have designated liaison magistrates permanently working in Eurojust in addition to the twenty-seven national members already composing the College. The current liaison prosecutors for both of these countries have been in place since 2007. Their powers and the length of their mandate are determined by their country of origin. Their main task is to share information with Eurojust and to contact relevant officials in their home country. Their presence undeniably allows a closer cooperation with the concerned countries. They are not Eurojust's only links with third-countries: the agreements also give them the possibility to nominate contact points to Eurojust within their national administration. Other provisions regard the organisation of operational meetings gathering Eurojust members and the third-country's representatives, as well as the exchange of information between them. As in the case of agreements concluded with other EU bodies, the question of data protection is specifically taken care of: conditions to use and exchange personal data are enumerated, as well as restrictions such as time limits. It is worth mentioning that one of the teams composing the College is in charge with data protection.

But Eurojust's cooperation with non-EU States is not limited to co-operation agreements. *Ad hoc* cooperation mechanisms were set up with countries of Africa, South America or Asia in order to improve judicial support by these countries' authorities regarding cases on terrorism, drug trafficking or money laundering. Eurojust has more than thirty contact points in third-countries all over the world.[44] Even though a more formal cooperation is admittedly more efficient, these relations have proved to be very useful, notably in cases involving EU Member States and third-countries. The KARI operation dismantled an organisation supposedly involved in terrorist activities that had targets in Belgium and in Iraq. Sixteen countries were involved in the case, including several non-EU States, and twenty-two requests for mutual legal assistance were issued between them. The coordination of all these requests was an enormous task and would have been quasi-impossible without Eurojust's intervention.[45]

The last seven years have allowed Eurojust to grow on the basis of the 2002 Decision. Once its functioning was successfully established and stabilised, and despite the undeniably positive assessment of its actions, its shortcomings were identified and it became time to address them, in order to improve judicial cooperation. The need to take a step

---

44 *Ibid.*, p. 167.

45 *Ibid.*

further came to the forefront and made the need for a reform of Eurojust's status and prerogatives quite obvious.

4. Eurojust's Future: Challenges and Prospects

4.1. Remaining Challenges

From the beginning of Eurojust's functioning, a number of problems were identified. The main shortcomings concerned the unit's lack of powers, the major differences between its national members' status, the need to maintain a solid link at the national level between Eurojust and national structures and the need to provide information in certain cases to Eurojust and from the need for a better cooperation with other actors of the AFSJ, notably Europol.

Eurojust guides judicial cooperation in criminal matters very efficiently but it does not have coercive powers. Although the necessity for a new cooperation unit in that field was unanimously recognised, Member States were still reluctant to transfer too many competences to Eurojust as they feared that it might affect their sovereignty. Criminal law and procedure are still perceived as national competences, which primacy cannot be affected. This explains the lack of willingness from Member States to share information on criminal cases with foreign structures, particularly when that structure comes close to a supranational entity. Eurojust is more and more accepted as a consequence of the better communication between Member States it allows, but the influence of a growing mutual trust alone would still not persuade Member States to give Eurojust supranational powers. Its acceptance is also the result of many compromises such as the complex distribution of competences between national and European authorities which were previously described.

As it is, Eurojust's functioning is subject to Member States' good will to refer cases or to accept its requests to initiate investigations or prosecutions. Of course, Member States did not decide to create such a unit not to benefit from its added value, and more and more cases are dealt with by Eurojust. But national authorities can adopt a quite schizophrenic attitude by promoting the development of Eurojust and Europol in the Council and being reluctant to use them when a concrete case arises. Moreover, the choice to resort to Eurojust's expertise belongs to judicial authorities and not to ministers negotiating in the Council. As a matter of fact, national judicial authorities are "extremely conservative":[46] they tend to consider cases as their property and they are not willing to share them with any other organ, as shown by the eloquent

[46] Nilsson, Memorandum, *op. cit.*, question 45.

example of a local judicial authority claiming its ability to handle a case of human trafficking involving thirteen Member States on its own, without referring it to Eurojust.[47]

However, Member States that refuse to refer a case to Eurojust have an obligation to motivate their decision. Member States cannot be forced to reverse their decision but the obligation to motivate their refusal still creates a pressure for them to refer transborder cases.

In December 2008, the Council structured the type of information that should be sent to Eurojust more precisely than in the previous decision. The possibility for Member States to exchange information with Eurojust was notably replaced by an obligation[48] and the relevant article is significantly longer than its previous version. This will allow Eurojust to have a more global view on international or cross-border offences than it does at present.

Eurojust thus remains a coordination instrument, albeit a sophisticated one. As a consequence, some Member States are opposed to its transformation into a "proactive" unit: they want it to remain "reactive".[49] The negotiations on the new Eurojust Decision illustrated this perfectly. Extending the unit's powers was one of the objectives of the new text, which states that "on the basis of an assessment of the experience gained by Eurojust, a further enhancement of its operational effectiveness is needed by taking account of that experience".[50] But the proposal by some Member States to increase the College's powers, as well as national members', met many constitutional concerns even from Member States which tend to be in favour of new projects to improve judicial cooperation, such as the project of European Public Prosecutor that will be looked at below. Federal Member States had particular concerns regarding the constitutional problems that could be raised by such a strengthening, as the distribution of powers in criminal matters is already problematic in their national political structure.

These observations reveal how difficult it will be to achieve a proper EU criminal system: if even the attribution of autonomous powers to their own national prosecutor, acting on their own territory but sitting in The Hague is problematic, one can only imagine how tensed the negotiations on the actual creation of an EU Public Prosecutor would be. From a Member States' perspective, Eurojust will continue to deal with

---

47 *Ibid.*

48 Council Decision 2009/426/JHA, *op. cit.*, Art. 13, para. 1: "The competent authorities of the Member States shall exchange with Eurojust any information necessary for the performance of its tasks [...]" (Emphasis added).

49 Interview with Peter Csonka, *op. cit.*

50 Council Decision 2009/426/JHA, *op. cit.*, p. 14.

national investigations and coordinate them before they are sent back to the national level. But in any case, Eurojust cannot be the origin of these investigations.

In the end, Eurojust's powers were increased in the December 2008 Decision only to a small extent. This example shows that giving actual supranational powers to Eurojust in a close future is highly unrealistic, but unfortunately, Eurojust's systematic implication in investigations is the only way to have a real expertise on transborder criminality within the EU.

The problem of Eurojust's operational powers was not the only one the new decision attempted to solve. The 2008 Decision also amended its Article 7 that now states that if a case of conflict of jurisdiction regarding responsibility for a case cannot be solved by the concerned national members or if an agreement cannot be found between the concerned national authorities, the College issues a non-binding opinion on the case. The non-binding character of that opinion obviously considerably undermines the influence that could have been given to Eurojust on conflicts of competence.

The mix between national and EU competences within Eurojust can be seen as a positive element and guarantees Member States' acceptance of the unit. Theoretically, the freedom left to Member States to organise their representation in the unit could even have allowed them to give their national members the power to initiate investigations or prosecutions upon request from the College.[51] But such a hypothesis is unrealistic. The need to take into account the diversity of national situations actually created an "asymmetry"[52] between national members. As their profile, powers and some of the financial means they are allocated are decided by national authorities alone, great disparities are observed from one national member to another, depending on their government's political will. In that mosaic of competences, some national members will be actual prosecutors with assistants remunerated by their Member State, when others are more like transmission channels. This uneven implementation by Member States, due to a clear political choice or on a simple inertia in some Member States, affects the work of less privileged national members, but also the work of the whole unit.

For that reason, the new Eurojust Decision proclaimed the need for an approximation of national members' status as one of its objectives.[53] When in the original text, the length of national members' term of office

---

[51] Jean Pradel, Geert Corstens and Gert Vermeulen, *Droit pénal européen* (Paris: Précis Dalloz, 2009, 3rd ed.), p. 490.

[52] de Biolley, *op. cit.*, p. 4.

[53] Council Decision 2009/426/JHA, *op. cit.*, p. 14.

was decided upon by its Member States,[54] the new decision now sets a minimum length of four years.[55]

The participation of national members in joint investigation teams is still not systematic as it is subject to the agreement of the competent national authority (Article 9f). It only becomes compulsory when the concerned team is granted financial support by the EU. This is only one of the illustrations of Member States' reluctance to significantly improve judicial cooperation. This is still quite hard to understand as an improvement like allowing national members to work with joint investigation teams is not the same as giving operational powers to Eurojust.

Eurojust's interrelations with other bodies, and particularly with Europol, remain a point to improve.

The cooperation with Europol, described previously in this chapter, is the most problematic. The interrelation between police and judicial cooperation is necessary: one cannot take place without the other. There is no judicial cooperation without police cooperation: one has to be arrested before being judged. In practice, at EU level, the two are still clearly separated and the two bodies that embody them continue to largely ignore each other's activity. The wording of the Eurojust and the Europol Decisions (even in their most recent forms) shows that the two bodies have been conceived separately and not as belonging to the same system. For instance, Europol is competent to ask Member States to "initiate, conduct or coordinate investigations",[56] while this task could logically be reserved to Eurojust. As a result, the creation of a real common system is hindered, while so many efforts have been put into the creation of efficient tools in police and judicial cooperation over the last twenty years. This obstacle could have been removed in 2008, as the two founding texts for Eurojust and Europol were amended at the same time, but this was a "lost opportunity", as deplored by Eurojust's 2008 Annual Report. The explanation given is that a political agreement on the two texts could not be found at the same time. The remaining solution is thus an amendment of the 2004 Cooperation Agreement between the two units, which has been signed this year.

From these observations, it is understandable that many practitioners and academics, the Commission and some Member States in favour of a more efficient judicial cooperation still raise the question of a more powerful prosecuting body.

---

[54] Council Decision 2002/187/JHA, *op. cit.*, Art. 9, para. 1.

[55] *Ibid.*

[56] Council Decision of 6 April 2009 establishing the European Police Office (Europol) (2009/371/JHA), *O.J.*, No. L 121 of 15 May 2009.

4.2. Eurojust in the Lisbon Treaty

In the Lisbon Treaty, Eurojust and Europol have been given more operational powers. The Treaty provides that Eurojust can initiate and coordinate criminal investigations, and propose to initiate prosecutions led by competent national authorities. It can also strengthen judicial cooperation by solving conflicts of jurisdiction and by cooperating tightly with the EJN.

If the Lisbon Treaty had entered into force, strengthening Eurojust would have been simpler as the new piece of legislation would have been adopted under qualified majority in the Council and co-decision with the European Parliament. However, in the present context, the new Eurojust Decision had to be unanimously adopted in December 2008. This explains why the improvements brought by this decision remain relatively limited. Therefore, the new decision only partly solves some of the shortcomings of the unit. Its negotiation was particularly difficult and lasted a whole year.[57] Their main object was the strengthening of the College's and national members' powers but in the end, the changes brought to the 2002 Decision were minimal, especially regarding the College. A lot of Member States tried to moderate these ambitions. Yet, the legitimacy of Eurojust's actions is strengthened as the Treaty foresees a parliamentary control.

The main novelty of the new Treaty – and its only substantive innovation in criminal law – is the possibility for the Council to establish a European Public Prosecutor's Office (EPP)[58] whose action would be limited to the protection of the EU's financial interests. This is strictly framed by a unanimity condition, which also applies to a potential extension of its competences. This condition was necessary to allow this controversial and quite radical provision to be inserted into the Treaty. A number of Member States are reluctant towards the EPP for various reasons, be they practical, political or constitutional. The strict wording of the provision might complicate its creation. Due to the requirement of Member States' unanimous acceptance, its creation in a short to middle term timeframe can be excluded, unless Member States choose to start an enhanced cooperation on the subject, which seems to be the only way forward.

First of all, creating a supranational EPP would entail many constitutional problems, especially for federal Member States and for those who had already raised concerns regarding the extension of Eurojust's powers. Moreover, the limitation of the EPP's competence to the protection

---

57 Interview with Peter Csonka, *op. cit.*

58 Art. 86 TFEU.

of the EU's financial interests does not persuade Member States of the need to go through a heated negotiation and a complex implementation, probably with necessary changes to their Constitutions. Drawing a clear line between criminal offences is only possible in theory. In practice, they are most of the time connected to each other. Member States do not consider the protection of the EU's financial interests as a priority, unless it is linked to another, wider issue such as fight against organised crime or terrorism. Of course, the possibility for the Council to extend the scope of the EPP's competences remains open, but it would still be subject to a unanimous acceptance. It is thus clear that this potential next step will take time before it is taken by Member States.

And yet, the idea of a European Prosecutor is not new and was even developed before the creation of Eurojust.[59] A first report from experts, the Corpus Juris, requested by the Commission to find a way to protect the EU's financial interests, was published in 1997 and amended in 2001, and was suggesting the creation of a centralised European Prosecution Service. It was completed in 2001 by a Green Paper.[60] Both texts envisaged the creation of an EPP as a "new body".[61] But the text of the Lisbon Treaty provides that the Council "may establish a European Public Prosecutor's Office *from* Eurojust".[62] From this wording, it is not clear how the new Prosecutor's Office will be positioned with existing bodies. As stated above, the allocation of new prerogatives to Eurojust in order to turn it into an EPP would certainly be opposed by Member States to protect their sovereignty, and Eurojust deals with many forms of criminality and not only the protection of the EU's financial interests. But many possibilities remain open to combine its action with the EPP's. There is a probability that the two bodies will work together: the Prosecutor could become the twenty-eighth member of Eurojust, or the College itself could endorse the role of the EPP when the protection of the financial interests of the Union are at stake.[63]

---

59 Hans G. Nilsson, "The Corpus Juris as a basis for a European criminal law", in: Barbara Huber (ed.), *Das Corpus Juris als Grundlage eines europäischen Strafrechts* (Freiburg: Edition Iuscrim, 1999).

60 European Commission, Green Paper on criminal-law protection of the financial interests of the Community and the establishment of a European Prosecutor, COM(2001) 175 final, Brussels, 11 December 2001.

61 Jiri Vlastnik, "Eurojust – A cornerstone of the federal criminal justice system in the EU?", in: Elspeth Guild and Florian Geyer (eds.), *Security versus Justice? Police and Judicial Cooperation in the European Union* (Aldershot: Ashgate Publishing, 2008), p. 35.

62 Art. 86, para. 1 TFEU (Emphasis added).

63 Nilsson, Memorandum, *op. cit.*, question 67.

5. Conclusion

The concerns raised by the EPP project are so important that it is conceived by many as a "very long-term"[64] one. As it is, Member States are not ready for such a change. For them to be ready for the long negotiations that will inevitably take place and to handle the necessary constitutional changes described above, the real need for the EPP has to be demonstrated. Some argue that the best way to achieve this is to let Eurojust grow,[65] very progressively. Indeed, the facts and figures mentioned in the first part of this chapter show the success of Eurojust and how much the added value of a judicial cooperation at EU level is widely recognised. Despite Member States' remaining reluctances regarding a more powerful unit for that purpose, it is still more likely to be progressively accepted than a drastic change like the creation of a supranational EPP acting directly on Member States' territory. Eurojust has the advantage to be perceived both as a step towards more integration by some Member States and as a less intrusive alternative to more integrationist projects by others. According to them, fight against organised crime and notably fraud against the Community's financial interests "will be achieved more efficiently through properly directed national law enforcement agencies, operating in co-operation with their international counterparts and their European counterparts, and that Eurojust, amongst other things, is a very good way of enabling that co-operation and coordination to take place".[66] It thus enjoys a quite general popularity amongst Member States, as long as it is not granted too intrusive powers. This will certainly allow it to continue to grow more than expected in the next few years. In 2002, no one would have imagined that the original vague Eurojust Decision that had been adopted would lead to the creation of the efficient unit in place today.

---

64 Interview with Peter Csonka, *op. cit.*

65 Interview with Michèle Coninsx, *op. cit.*

66 Lord Goldsmith, in House of Lords (European Union Committee), *Judicial Cooperation in the EU: the role of Eurojust*, Report with Evidence, 21 July 2004, p. 35.

CHAPTER 8

Frontex: Its Role and Organisation

Mintze BEUVING

1. The Origins and Formation of Frontex

Frontex was established as an Agency in May 2005. It originated from the "Common Unit of Border practitioners" that convened under the Presidency of EU, the agenda (for EU cooperation on the external borders) of which was often ruled by the ambition of the Member State that held the EU Presidency. Before the setting up of Frontex border management was organised in decentralised centres, with a risk analysis centre set up in Helsinki, a training centre based in Austria, two maritime centres located in Greece and Spain, a centre for land borders in Germany and an air borders centre in Italy. When Frontex was founded, all of these activities became institutionalised within the Agency, and a Management Board was created to govern the tasks of Frontex, consisting of all the EU Member States and Schengen associated countries and the Commission.

In its early days Frontex was supported by seconded national experts (SNE) from the various Members States' border guard services, who held these positions for a limited number of years. Frontex aims to convert the majority of these positions into fixed posts, or so-called Temporary Agents, who work for the Agency and no longer for a country. Over the past four years Frontex has expanded, and in 2008 alone the personnel increased from 121 to 181.[1] For 2009 the budget that is allocated to the Agency is anticipated to be around 83.25 MEURO.

Frontex is an independent body tasked to coordinate the operational cooperation between Member States in the field of border security.

Frontex was founded by a Council Regulation.[2] It was decided that Warsaw would be the seat of the Agency but at the first official meeting in May 2005, Frontex did not yet possess premises of its own. There

1 See Frontex, General Report 2008, Warsaw (Frontex) 2009, pp. 19 and 26.

2 Council Regulation (EC) No. 2007/2004 of 26 October 2004 establishing a European Agency for the Management of Operational Cooperation at the External Borders of the Member States of the European Union, *O.J.*, No. L 349 of 25 November 2004.

was great political pressure to immediately secure our external EU borders.[3]

The Management Board was installed to support the Executive Director in the running of the Agency. With its extensive operational experience, its tasks, which can be found in the Frontex Regulation, are to adopt important decisions which are crucial for the sustainable development for the Agency. In brief, the Management Board approves the work program, the budget and its various amendments (which have multiplied considerably over the past years), the structure of the Agency and cooperation with third-countries and external organisations. The Chair of the Management Board steers decisions through the board at its five yearly meetings, and so it is important that the Executive Director can rely on solid support and guidance from the Board, all of which means that discussions are be "fruitful".

2. The Role of Frontex: Border Management

Border security is simply part of the various different challenges of the EU's security. Threats originate from several issues. As Europe expands, it has become ever more urgent to increase cooperation on border security in order to share practices and technology more efficiently and to support this by EU legislation.

Border security is a constant compromise between the freedom of movement of EU citizens and third-country nationals who enter the EU. It is a daunting task for the border guards who have to check thousands of travel documents on a daily basis while dealing with the pressure of managing the flow of passengers quickly and effectively.

[3] On the background and process of the establishment of Frontex see, Damien Romestant, "La création d'une Agence européenne pour la gestion de la coopération opérationnelle aux frontières extérieures des Etats membres", *ERA-Forum*, No. 2, 2005, pp. 282-292; and Andrew W. Neal, "Securitization and risk at the EU border: the origins of Frontex", *Journal of Common Market Studies*, Vol. 47, No. 2, 2009, pp. 333-356.

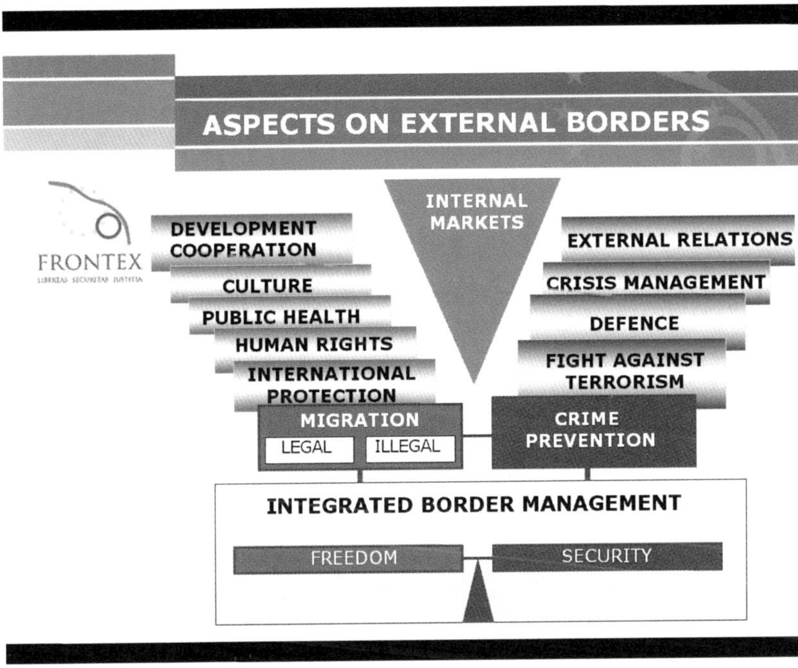

Border management however consists of more than merely checking documents. An important part of the achievements at the border stems from cooperation with other countries so that Frontex can manage (illegal) migration more efficiently in the countries of origin and in transit countries. Operational agreements therefore have to be established. Furthermore, Frontex has to deal with the international protection of people from various cultures. Public health is another aspect which needs to be safeguarded at our borders. Last but not least, human rights need to be respected in every aspect of the job. All of these elements are to be found in the latest Schengen Borders Code[4] that came into force in October 2006, which incorporates these elements into the decision if a person enters the EU legally or illegally.

Crime prevention is driven by our law enforcement task at the borders. Managing flows and checking whether a person may or may not enter a country forms only part of this: especially after 9/11 a focus has been placed on the motives people have to cross our borders illegally, with terrorist threats playing a central role. But tasks such as human

[4] Schengen Borders Code, Regulation (EC) No. 562/2006 of the European Parliament and of the Council of 15 March 2006, *O.J.*, No. L 105 of 13 April 2006.

smuggling and human trafficking are of great importance, and external relations with countries of origin have been used for capacity building.

Building on the June 2002 "Plan for the management of the external borders of the Member States of the European Union",[5] the Council agreed in November 2006 on a revised and more comprehensive concept of Integrated EU Border Management.[6]

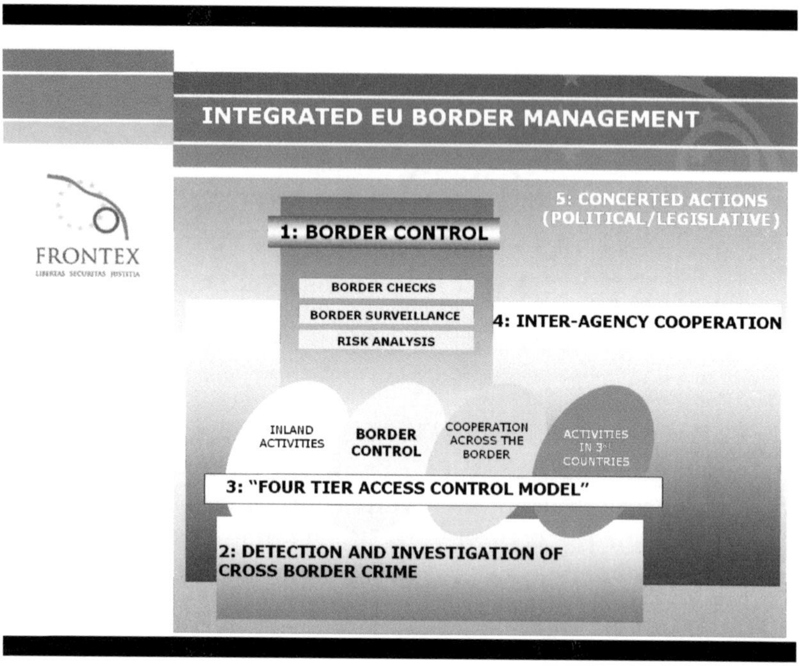

This fundamental principle underlines the function of Frontex and should be regarded as the critical success factor of how border management is executed. It incorporates five basic activities of which some have already been highlighted.

1. Firstly it deals with border control including border checks, border surveillance and risk analysis including inland activities.
2. Another aspect is the detection and investigation of cross-border crime where cooperation between law enforcement agencies is a key element between authorities of different countries.

---

5 Council Document 10019/02 of 14 June 2002.

6 Council Document 13926/3/06 of 21 November 2006.

3. The four-tier access control model, which brings important aspect together starting with activities deployed in third-countries, followed by cooperation across the border, the actual border control and finally by inland activities.
4. Security challenges have different origins and are dealt with by various organisations. Therefore close cooperation with Europol is necessary.
5. Finally, all the actions undertaken by Frontex and by fellow agencies must be regulated and audited. Frontex's focus is on operational activities but politicians need to be involved when it comes to third-country cooperation and other aspects of EU border management.

Of all the elements from Border Management, border control is central when describing the functions and legitimacy of Frontex. Border control, including checks and surveillance, ensures the safeguard of national and European interests and prevents the entry of crime from entering our countries. The primary aim of border control and surveillance is to prevent illegal border crossings regardless of the motive. However, border crossing points are important for economic interactions between countries and therefore border guards must be careful not to hinder trade. For this reason the EU's border strategy seeks to enhance cooperation with the border guard services of third-countries. Frontex stimulates operational cooperation at the external borders and joint efforts are concentrated at the various border crossings where border control is carried out.

Member States are encouraged to send their border guard officers to so-called focal point offices at all kinds of borders (land-, sea-, and air borders). Members States' officers can be trained by exchanging best practices and sharing specific knowledge, but these focal points can also be used for interagency cooperation and to work with colleagues on the other side of the EU border. At the Members States level information systems can be tested and implemented, such as the Schengen Information System whereby Member States can check whether a person has tried to enter another Members State illegally. Third-countries can benefit from the combined knowledge to fight corruption and to enhance their border check systems, enhancing border crossing flows.

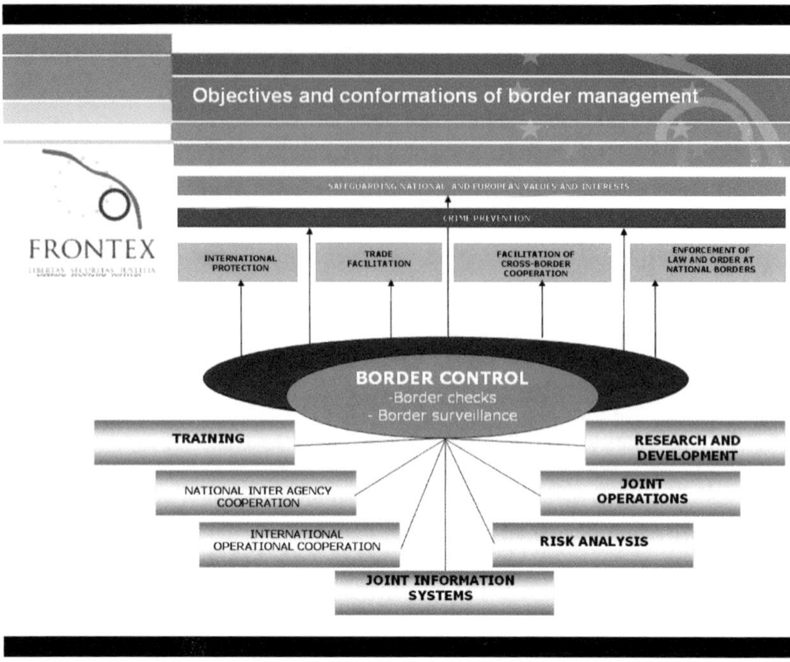

3. Risk Analysis, Coordination of Joint Operations and Training

Over the past four years Frontex has developed in line with its main functions of risk analysis and the coordination of joint operations:

Risk analysis is a key element which lies at the heart of all Frontex's activities. Member States send information to Frontex on the activities at their borders which is then assembled and translated into a comprehensive view of the main flows of illegal migration towards the EU. During 2008, Frontex collated and analysed inter alia information related to altogether some 175,000 detections of illegal border crossing at the external sea- and land borders of the EU reported by the Member States. In addition, Frontex collected and analysed in 2008 for the first time information on trafficking in human beings, with more than 10,000 victims of trafficking being reported by the Member States' authorities[7]

The analysis can be used to organise either joint operations or pilot projects, which may be initiated by both Frontex and Member States. However, for any action to be financially endorsed by the Agency, Frontex assesses the initiative of a Member State according to criteria

7 Frontex, General Report 2008, Warsaw (Frontex) 2009, pp. 12 and 14.

such as the Member States' capacity to deal with the threat, the relative efficiency of community measures, resources required and so on.

The results of threats assessments regarding illegal migration are equally factored into training activities. Frontex is able to assemble different specialised knowledge from Member States such as detection of travel document forgeries, technical systems to communicate between border guard services or surveillance systems and to deploy this expertise at the appropriate areas to maximise its overall efficiency. To secure and structure this activity, Frontex has established a training network with Member States using local expertise which has been formalised into so-called partnership academies. Research and Development is a function that focuses on technology that is not yet widely available and where no common standard has been reached. An example is automatic border crossing systems which are installed in some of the larger air borders in the EU. These systems use biometry to allow travellers which have a permit to cross the border. Based on the findings from risk analysis, main routes of illegal migration into the EU which clearly pose major challenges to the Member States can be identified. An example of a frequently used route is the West African route, with predominantly African nationals facing an ordeal to reach the Canary Island from which they hope to reach mainland Spain. This has received a lot of public interest over the past four years. Interestingly, the greatest flows of illegal migrants still use large hubs or main airports in Europe to enter illegally.

In order to enhance its intelligence gathering capabilities Frontex launched in September 2008 a pilot project on "Frontex Intelligence Support Officers" (FISO). The aim was to set up a peripheral tool for intelligence gathering and dissemination in three strategic areas at the external borders of the southern Member States. Frontex established, in cooperation with those countries, FISO offices in Madrid (for the strategic area including Spain and Portugal), Rome (for the Central Mediterranean) and Athens (for Greece, Bulgaria, Cyrus and Romania). External officers were acting in the hosting Member States as a response mechanism for the preparation, implementation and evaluation of Frontex joint operations, in respect of intelligence matters and, in addition, to gather and forward information to Frontex for specific Tailored Risk Assessments. Although further adjustments were needed, the results were considered as positive.[8]

With a variety of threats and changing *modi operandi*, intelligence driven operational cooperation at the EU level to strengthen security at the external borders is the critical success factor and forms the core

---

8 *Ibid.*, pp. 29-30.

mission of Frontex. Joint operations are activities organised at EU outer borders whereby countries pool resources to deal with a certain threat. The operational process of the EU's border management is the main reason why Frontex was established. Frontex's role is to coordinate Member States' activities at the EU borders in a formalised and efficient way. Generally speaking the Frontex operational process starts with a risk analysis and assessment leading to operation recommendations. These are then transformed through intense consultations with experts and the Member States' competent authorities into an operation plan which will then be carried out by the operational units of the participating Member States.

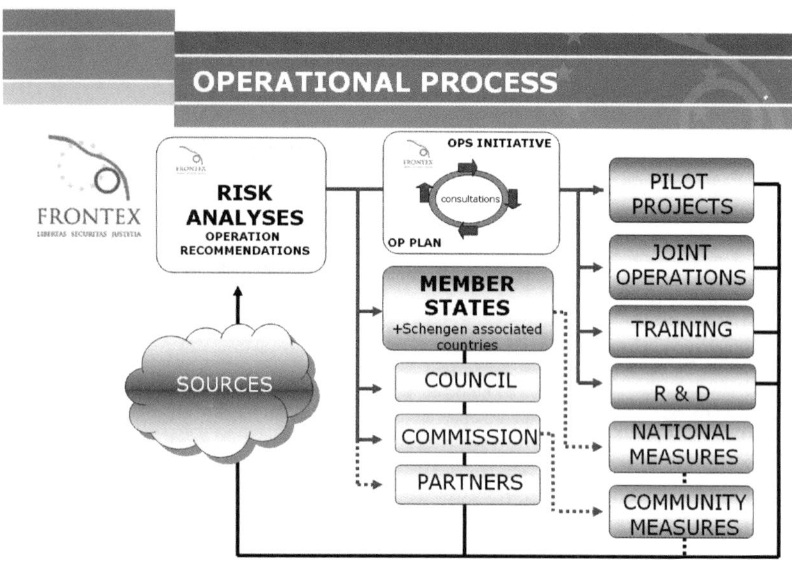

Frontex has initiated and started a number of joint operations, and often we see that illegal immigration routes evolve because of combined actions. Flows of illegal migration can be dispersed or concentrated. During the last year (2008) alone Frontex has organised 8 sea border, 10 land border and, 8 air border operations.[9] An example for such an operation was HAMMER, a joint operation designed to disrupt people

9 A complete list is provided in Frontex, General Report 2008, Warsaw (Frontex) 2009, pp. 40-41.

smugglers' criminal activities by putting a high, short-term and localised pressure on external air borders of the Member States and Schengen Associated Countries. During 2008, three operational phases were carried out, covering approximately 95-99% of non-Schengen flights per operational area. Several Frontex Joint Support Teams, guest officers and special advisors from 25 countries were deployed to 189 locations on the basis of a previous Frontex tailored risk analysis. Additionally 115 airports took part in the reporting exercise coordinated by Frontex' Situation Centre. The operation has provided a valuable insight into illegal migration at smaller European airports and the involvement of 'low cost' carriers in this field. Apart from Member States and Schengen Associated Countries, several partners such as Europol, Interpol, UNHCR and the EU Council General Secretariat took part in the operation. In the first three phases 762 illegal migrants were detected at airports in the operational areas, resulting in 695 refusals of entry. In addition, 71 forged documents were identified.[10]

When certain Member States are faced with sudden large influxes a new tool has been introduced to assist these Member States. Often large influxes are accompanied with human tragedies, especially when routes over the Atlantic or the Mediterranean are used. That is why – on the basis of a 2007 EC Regulation[11] – Rapid Border Intervention Teams or RABITs have been introduced.

---

10 *Ibid.*, pp. 28-29.

11 Regulation (EC) No. 863/2007 of the European Parliament and of the Council of 11 July 2007 establishing a mechanism for the creation of Rapid Border Intervention Teams, *O.J.*, No. L 199 of 31 July 2007, p. 30.

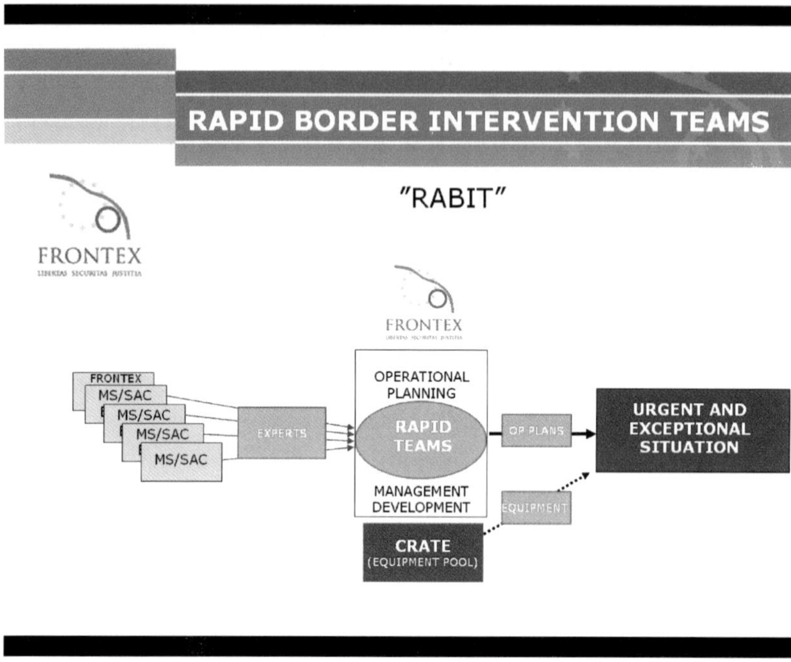

Such teams consist of highly trained and specialised border guard officers from various Member States who can be put to work in such areas within two weeks notice. They assist Member States to cope with sudden (unexpected) problems. Furthermore, Frontex has developed a catalogue of resources that can, under such circumstances and conditions, be called upon. This database is known as the Centralized Records of Available Technical Equipment (CRATE) and Member States have provided Frontex with a quantity of equipment that can be used by other Member States.

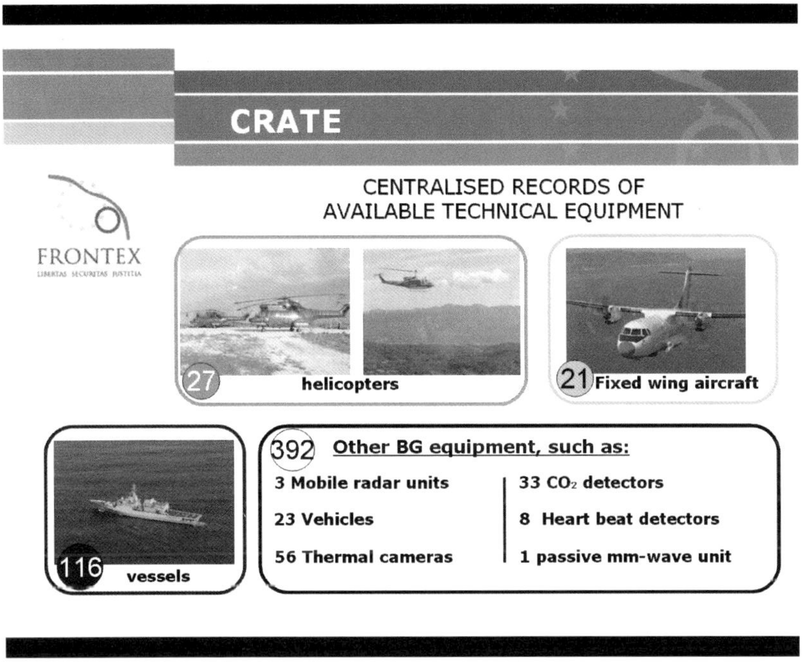

Strict conditions and reimbursement rules are in place for such equipment to be put to work. CRATE can also be called upon in regular Frontex joint operations. Such a development could make operations more effective. CRATE comprises tools or means which vary from vessels and helicopters to technical devices like document toolboxes which are useful to detect false documents.

In less urgent situations and when a situation is still relatively in control, Frontex can also deploy so-called Frontex Joint Support Teams (FJSTs). The philosophy behind these teams is not dissimilar from the RABIT teams, although the rationale behind their deployment differs. FJSTs are used for all regular functions of Frontex. The composition of teams could be the same as the RABIT teams. Frontex ensures that the RABIT teams can always be deployed. However, they can work together, train together as FJST teams in a joint operation whereby all the aspects such as best practices, the use of different technologies and the cooperation between Member States' border guards is effectuated. Teams are built on a variety of expertise and can be trained for certain types of borders. Equipment can be pooled from CRATE.

On the operational side it should as well be mentioned that Frontex can provide financial support to Joint (forced) Return Operations (JRO) of illegal immigrants which are carried out by national authorities.

During 2008 Frontex supported nine of a total of fifteen of such EU operations.[12]

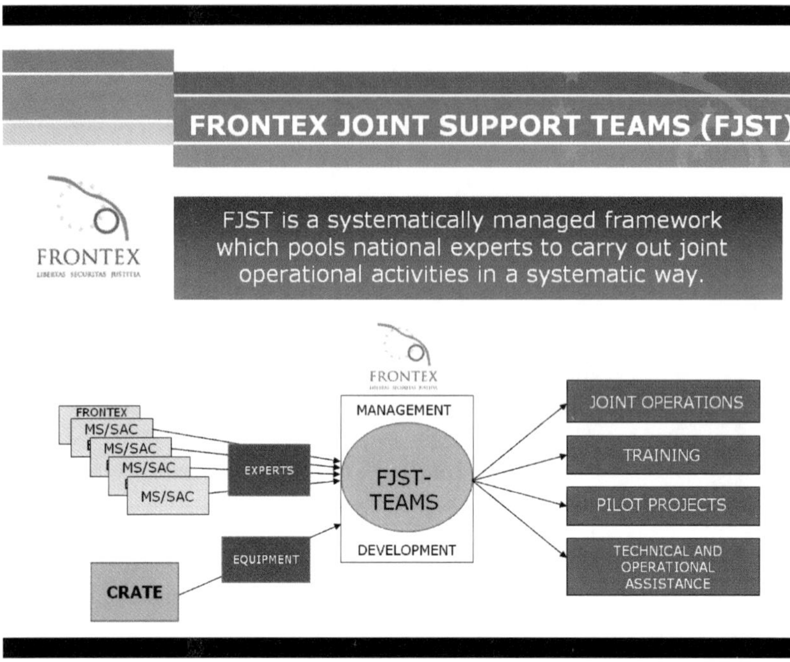

Frontex also coordinates training of border guards and has used and further developed some training tools that already existed under the former "Common Unit". The training activities – which are generally aimed at the further harmonisation of national training programmes but also include specific targeted courses for RABIT members – nearly doubled in volume in 2008 with 197 activities and 2,100 participants compared to 114 activities and 1,200 participants in 2007.[13] Frontex has introduced a research and development department whereby all sorts of border checking systems from Member States or from private companies are reviewed in order to make Member States aware that new technologies exist or even can be used for mutual benefit.

4. The Organisation of Frontex

At the top of the organisational hierarchy of Frontex is the Management Board composed of one representative of each Member State and two representatives of the European Commission. It is currently chaired

12 Frontex, General Report 2008, Warsaw (Frontex) 2009, p. 19.

13 *Ibid.*, p. 20.

by Major General Robert Strondl from the Austrian ministry of the interior. The Board members are all border police chiefs or in similar positions so to enable them to act as a competent and efficient team capable of assisting the Agency and its mainly operational tasks. The Board is responsible for appointing the Executive Director of Frontex, establishing the Agency's organisational structure and staffing policy and adopting (by a three-quarter majority) the Agency's annual work programme, the draft budget (to be approved by Council and Parliament in accordance with EU budgetary rules) as well as the Agency's annual report to all the main EU institutions.[14]

The overall management of Frontex is the responsibility of the Executive Director, currently the Finnish Border Guard Brigadier General Ilkka Laitinen. His tasks include the preparation and implementation of the decisions and programmes and activities adopted by the Management Board, the taking of all necessary steps, including the adoption of internal administrative instructions, to ensure the functioning of the Agency, the preparation of the yearly draft working programme for submission to the Management Board, the drawing up of estimates of the revenues and expenditure and the implementation of the budget.[15] The Director and his Deputy are supported by an Executive Support structure which deals, amongst others, with external relations, planning, quality management and public relations issues. Like most agencies Frontex also needs so-called back office functions to conduct daily business in a transparent manner. To this end an independent auditor monitors internal processes.

Since a major restructuration in 2008 Frontex is below the executive level divided into three divisions: one for operations, one for training and one for administration. Each of them is sub-divided into a number of specialised units. The Operations Division is responsible for both the coordination of operations (handled by the Operations Unit (OPS)) and the risk analysis functions (handled by the Risk Analysis Unit (RAU)) of Frontex, which corresponds to the close interrelationship between the two. The training and research and development units have been brought together within the Capacity Building Division.

---

14 Council Regulation (EC) No. 2007/2004 of 26 October 2004 establishing a European Agency for the Management of Operational Cooperation at the External Borders of the Member States of the European Union, *O.J.*, No. L 349 of 25 November 2004, Arts. 20, 21 and 29.

15 *Ibid.*, Art. 25.

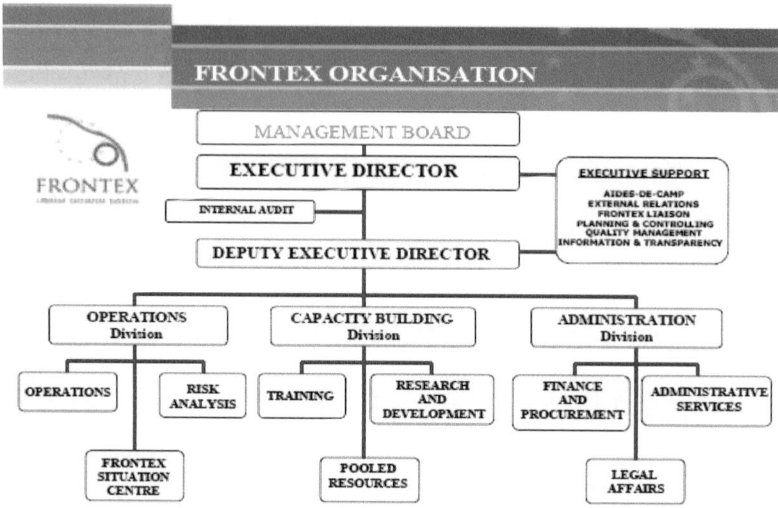

In 2008 the Frontex Situation Centre (FSC) was created as a separate unit within the Operations Division, in order to maintain and constantly update a short-term picture of the situation at the external borders of the EU. When a situation becomes critical and needs a high level of attention, a 24 hours/7 days emergency response mechanism is to be initiated with the involvement of internal and external partners. In order to take into account the Frontex legal framework, the Frontex Situation Centre needs to guarantee the availability, confidentiality and integrity of information exchange.[16] This short-term operation focus distinguishes the FSC from the RAU with its more long term and strategic tasks.

5. Conclusions on Frontex's Performance

Frontex has been well-equipped over the past four years with a number of resources not to mention the political will to increase intelligent cooperation on the external EU borders. The EU faces challenges in terms of illegal migration and the need to streamline cooperation in order to ensure that our common borders are safeguarded, and inter-Agency cooperation is necessary to paint a comprehensive picture. Progress has been made in terms of countermeasures in various situations and means that can be used to effectuate these measures.

These combined efforts have been in place for just over two years and it is therefore necessary to evaluate the effectiveness of these activities. To this end the Agency has three planned evaluations all with

[16] Frontex, General Report 2008, Warsaw (Frontex) 2009, p. 18.

different objectives. The first one is based on the Hague Programme, the second one is carried out by the Commission and focuses on Frontex managers and finally the Management Board is currently evaluating Frontex through an independent auditor. This evaluation is part of the function that is mentioned in the Council Regulation.

It is the firm belief of the author that Frontex has been developing successfully. A 2008 report of the British House of Lords on Frontex took the same view, although it also highlighted the risks of demanding too much of an institution which during its first three years of existence had seen its size, work and budget doubling every year.[17] It has indeed to be said that as a result of rapidly evolving political priorities Frontex had almost immediately after its establishment to face an ever increasing range of tasks. This tested the limits of its organisational capacity. The fact that in 2008 the utilisation of its (again substantially increased) budget reached only 51% in payment terms[18] is an indication of those limits. Political decisions which are rapidly increasing tasks and financial means can sometimes leave institutional and administrative capabilities slightly behind. There are inevitable loopholes which will need to be identified and countered with joint support over the years to come. An external evaluation of Frontex commissioned by the Management Board and carried out during 2008 indicated a number of points to be addressed, such as improvements as regards the practical planning of joint operations, a better impact assessment and a reconsideration of priorities in the research field. Yet the report also indicated that some problems are outside of Frontex' control, such as Member States often not making the most appropriate CRATE equipment or assets available as planned.[19]

Yet the figures clearly show that activities are increasing and that a sufficient budget is currently allocated. In its 2008 evaluation report on Frontex the European Commission called the quantifiable results achieved by Frontex during 2006 and 2007 (more than 53,000 persons apprehended or denied entry at the border, more than 2,900 detected false or falsified travel documents and the arrest of 58 facilitators of illegal migration) "impressive". But it also emphasised the range of

[17] House of Lords (EU Committee), 9th Report of Session 2007-2008, FRONTEX: the EU external borders agency, Report with Evidence, *HL Paper* 60 (London: The Stationary Office, 2008), p. 53.

[18] See the Analysis and Assessment of Frontex' Annual Activity Report 2008, adopted by Frontex' Management Board on 25 June 2009, Council Document 12359/09 of 28 July 2009, p. 2.

[19] Frontex, COWI: External evaluation of the European Agency for the Management of Operational Cooperation at the External Borders of the Member States of the European Union Final Report, January 2009 (available at: http://www.frontex.europa.eu/specific_documents/other/).

other non-quantifiable benefits Frontex provides such as the facilitation of the exchange of best practices and information between Member States, the stimulation of day-to-day cooperation between national border guard authorities and the support Frontex' tailor-made risk assessments provides to Member States in reacting to new and the planning of individual joint operations and training activities.[20]

The next challenges for Frontex will be to complete its adaptation to the rapid growth of its tasks and budget and to prepare for the pivotal role it is expected to play in the integrated European Border Surveillance System (EUROSUR) – to be set up until 2013 – with its enhanced technological means (including satellite surveillance) and increased networking between national and European institutions. The 2009 Frontex work programme[21] contains already many elements in response to these challenges.

---

20 European Commission, Communication from the Commission to the European Parliament, the Council, the European Economic and Social Committee and the Committee of the Regions. *Report on the evaluation and future development of the FRONTEX Agency*, COM(2008) 67 final, Brussels, 13 February 2008, pp. 2-5.

21 Frontex Programme of Work 2009, Council Document 6337/09 of 11 February 2009.

CHAPTER 9

The EU Counter-Terrorism Coordinator

Gilles DE KERCHOVE & Serge DE BIOLLEY*

This chapter describes the function of the EU Counter-Terrorism Coordinator (CTC). It starts with some background information on the creation of the position and on the appointment of the first two CTCs (1) and on the 2005 EU strategy against terrorism which is the basis of the work of the CTC (2). Its tasks, which are mainly the coordination and the monitoring of the implementation of this EU strategy, are described in the following section (3). The last part explores the position of the CTC by analysing its relationship with various partners and institutions (4).

1. Introduction

The position of Counter-Terrorism Coordinator was established by the Secretary General/High Representative, Javier Solana, and endorsed by the European Council in the aftermath of the attacks in Madrid on 11 March 2004. This decision was part of a general Declaration on terrorism adopted by the European Council on 25 March 2004.[1]

When establishing this new post, the European Council emphasised "that a comprehensive and strongly coordinated approach is required in response to the threat posed by terrorism" and that the CTC should "maintain an overview of all the instruments at the Union's disposal with a view to regular reporting to the Council and effective follow-up of Council decisions". Coordination and monitoring of the implementation are therefore at the core of the CTC's tasks.

At the same meeting, the European Council welcomed the appointment of Gijs de Vries as the first CTC. Mr. de Vries is a Dutch politician who, before being appointed as the CTC, had been a Member of the European Parliament for 14 years (and Leader of the Liberal and Democratic Group for the last 4 years), Deputy Minister of Interior of the Netherlands and Representative of the Government of the Netherlands at

---

* This article reflects the views of the authors, not those of the institutions they work for.

1 European Council, Declaration on Combating Terrorism, Brussels, 25 March 2004, para. 14.

the Convention on the Future of the European Union. Gijs de Vries stepped down in March 2007 at the end of a three-year mandate.

Gilles de Kerchove was appointed as the new CTC by Javier Solana on 19 September 2007. Before being appointed as CTC, Gilles de Kerchove was Director in the Justice and Home Affairs General Directorate of the General Secretariat of the Council and had been Deputy Secretary of the Convention which drafted the Charter of Fundamental Rights of the European Union.

2. The EU Counter-Terrorism Strategy: The Basis for the Work of the CTC

The key tasks of the CTC are the coordination and monitoring of the implementation of the EU strategy against terrorism. It is not the purpose of this contribution to describe this strategy, but a brief explanation is necessary to clarify the basis of the work of the CTC.

Various strategic instruments (action plans, road maps, strategies) have been adopted since 9/11.[2] Currently, the main basis is the European Union Counter-Terrorism Strategy (CTS), which was adopted by the European Council on 15-16 December 2005.[3] The CTS demonstrates a willingness to provide a horizontal approach transcending institutional divisions between the pillars and between the formations of the Council.

The CTS is based on the following four strands:

1. prevention = to prevent people from turning to terrorism and to stop the next generation of terrorists from emerging by combating radicalisation and recruitment into terrorism;
2. protection = to improve control of external borders and strengthen the defences of key targets ("critical infrastructure") by reducing their vulnerability to attack and by reducing the impact of any attack;

[2] The first EU strategy against terrorism was the action plan adopted by the European Council on 21 September 2001 (Council Document SN 140/01), which endorsed the JHA Council Conclusions of 20 September 2001 (Council Document 12156/01). The implementation of the action plan was monitored via a "road map" (see Council Document 12800/01 for the first version of the road map) detailing all measures to be taken. The road map was updated on a regular basis until the end of 2002. After the attacks in Madrid and on the basis of the Declaration of the European Council of 25 March 2004, a new EU Action Plan on Combating Terrorism was prepared and updated (the latest version is found in Council Document 9809/1/05 REV 1).

[3] The basis for this strategy is a joint paper of the CTC and the UK Presidency of October 2005 (Council Document 13613/05). The strategy adopted by the European Council of 15-16 December 2005 can be found in Council Document 14469/4/05).

3. pursuit = to impede terrorists' planning, disrupt their networks and the activities of recruiters to terrorism, cut off terrorists' funding and access to attack materials, and bring them to justice;
4. response = to be able to deal with the consequences of attacks when they occur (including e.g. sharing resources to recover from a CBRN attack).

The CTS is supplemented by sub-strategies:

- the EU strategy for combating radicalisation and recruitment to terrorism, which was adopted by the JHA Council on 1 December 2005.[4] It is accompanied by a (classified) Action Plan, the content of which is updated every year. It is also itself implemented by means of another sub-strategy, the Media Communication Strategy;[5]
- the EU strategy on terrorist financing, which was adopted by the European Council on 16-17 December 2004.[6] It was revised in June 2008 on the basis of a proposal from the CTC.[7]

These strategies are the basis for the mandate of the CTC.

3. Tasks of the CTC

The three main tasks of the CTC are: (1) monitoring implementation of the CTS; (2) promoting coordination of EU efforts against terrorism; and (3) ensuring that combating terrorism is among the top priorities of the Common Foreign and Security Policy (CFSP).

3.1. Monitoring the Implementation of the CTS

When creating the post of CTC, the European Council indicated that the CTC should "maintain an overview of all the instruments at the Union's disposal with a view to regular reporting to the Council and effective follow-up of Council decisions".[8]

Ensuring effectiveness is a major concern for the EU in all sectors. One of the main tools is the power of the Commission to launch an infringement procedure against a Member State which does not implement Community legislation. In the current situation, this is helpful only for limited parts of the CTS. In many areas, there is a need to enact new

4 Council Document 14781/1/05 REV 1.

5 See Council Document 5469/3/07 REV 3 for the last declassified version of this strategy.

6 Council Document 16089/04.

7 Council Document 11778/1/08 REV 1.

8 European Council, Declaration on Combating Terrorism, *op. cit.*, para.14.

legislation and not only to implement the existing one. Furthermore, the infringement procedure can only be launched in respect of first pillar instruments; it does not apply to cooperation in criminal matters (the so-called third pillar) nor to the CFSP (the so-called second pillar), which are of course very relevant for counter-terrorism. And not all areas can be dealt with by legislative means.

There are various tools by which the CTC can fulfil his task of monitoring the implementation of the CTS.

The most formal tool is the use of regular reports on the implementation of the CTS, including sub-strategies. The CTC produces various reports pointing out shortcomings and achievements:

- Six-monthly report on the implementation of the CTS itself.[9] In a table annexed to these reports, the CTC monitors the implementation by the Member States of a list of EU legal acts or of relevant international conventions.[10] A distinctive feature of this table is that it clearly indicates which Member States have not yet taken the necessary measures (transposition, ratification), which is a step the Council is usually very reluctant to take, especially in the third pillar.
- Yearly report on the implementation of the EU strategy for combating radicalisation and recruitment to terrorism[11] and of the media communication strategy.[12]
- Six-monthly report on the fight against terrorist financing: the last issue was produced in May 2009.[13]

The main objectives provided by the CTS are defined in broad terms. Monitoring their implementation implies that the task of the CTC is not limited to analysis of the implementation of the most concrete and detailed goals listed in the strategy (such as pointing out that a particular piece of legislation is or is not yet finalised). On the contrary, it also requires the CTC to assess the quality of measures taken as a result of the strategy, to propose new initiatives necessary to fulfil the objectives set out by the Council or the European Council[14] and to propose priorities in the measures to be taken.

9 See for the last issue Council Document 9715/1/09 REV 1.

10 Council Document 9715/1/09 ADD 1 REV 1.

11 Council Document 15443/07 + COR 1.

12 For the last declassified version of the report, see Council Document 10388/06.

13 Council Document 8864/1/09 REV 1 + COR 1.

14 Without of course himself submitting draft legislation, which is a prerogative of the Commission and, in the third pillar, the Member States and the Commission.

Having in mind the need to go beyond a limited vision of his monitoring role, at the end of 2007 the CTC started producing short strategic notes accompanying his reports in order to propose concrete action and priorities.[15]

3.2. Promoting Coordination of EU Efforts against Terrorism

As indicated above, the approach (prevention, protection, pursuit and response) adopted by the Union in the CTS reflects the need for a horizontal approach. More particularly in the case of the Union, combating terrorism requires that five types of divisions be transcended:

- the thematic division between formations of the Council (as well as between the Members of the Commission and between the Committees of the European Parliament);
- the division between the EU institutions, in particular the Council, the Commission and the European Parliament;
- the division between the three pillars of the EU;
- the division between EU and national levels;
- the division between the EU and other international organisations.

For example:

- the fight against terrorist financing is dealt with both by the JHA and the ECOFIN formations of the Council; some measures adopted in this sector fall under the first pillar (the three money laundering directives), others under the third pillar (incriminating financial support to terrorist groups);
- measures related to the listing of persons and groups considered as terrorists have their legal basis in the three pillars; the EU implements UN Security Council Resolution 1373 by establishing its own list of terrorist organisations and individuals and UN Security Council Resolution 1267 by freezing the assets of individuals and organisations listed by the UN 1267 Committee. Some Member States have their own lists which include people and groups which appear in neither the UN nor the EU list;
- even within the third pillar (judicial cooperation in criminal matters), there is a risk, due to the growing complexity of the sector, of too much rigidity in the division between police and

[15] Council Document 15448/07. The European Council welcomed this initiative at its meetings on 14-15 December 2007 and on 19-20 June 2008. The CTC followed the same method in June 2008 (Council Document 9417/08) and in November 2008 (Council Document 15983/08).

judicial cooperation. Such rigidity is reflected in national structures as well as in the divisions within the working structure of the Council, within the General Secretariat of the Council and within the Commission's administration. The coordinating role of the CTC is therefore very important even in this limited sector.

As personal representative of the Secretary General/High Representative, legally speaking the CTC can only be tasked with coordination of the Council's work. In practice, good cooperation with the European Parliament and the Commission makes it possible for the CTC to play a coordinating role for the EU as a whole.

3.3. Ensuring that Combating Terrorism Is among the Top Priorities in the Common Foreign and Security Policy (CFSP)

Under the authority and guidance of the Secretary General/High Representative for the CFSP, the CTC assists the Presidency in the external aspects of prevention and the fight against terrorism.

In his June 2008 report to the Council/European Council the CTC suggested that the EU concentrate its efforts on two regions which pose the main threat to the EU internal security, i.e. Afghanistan/Pakistan on the one hand and Northern Africa/Sahel on the other hand.[16]

4. Position of the CTC in the Institutional Framework

The position of the CTC can be described by analysing (1) his situation within the General Secretariat of the Council and his relationship with the working structure of (2) the Council, (3) the Commission and (4) the European Parliament.

This description will be based on the present situation, in which the CTC is located in the General Secretariat of the Council. It should be noted that the entry into force of the Lisbon Treaty may affect that situation in some respects because of the evolution of the post of High Representative for the Common Foreign and Security Policy, which will be merged with that of the European Commissioner for External Relations under a new title of High Representative of the Union for Foreign Affairs and Security Policy. Currently, the High Representative for the Common Foreign and Security Policy is also the Secretary General of the Council, to whom the CTC is directly attached. It is unclear whether under the new Treaty the CTC will remain formally attached to the Council and its General Secretariat (he could be linked to the President

[16] Council Document 9417/08.

of the European Council) or will follow the new High Representative of the Union for Foreign Affairs and Security Policy. Because of the uncertainty on this issue, it will not be discussed further in the following sections.

4.1. Within the General Secretariat of the Council

The CTC works within the General Secretariat of the Council. He works directly under the authority of the Secretary General and acts as his Personal Representative. He reports to the Council/European Council and is regularly interviewed by the media, which increases the impact of his work.

The CTC is directly assisted by a small unit of four people (two secretaries and two national experts seconded by Member States) and can rely on the assistance of the whole Council administration, in particular the following Directorates-General (DG) directly involved in counter-terrorism matters:

- DG H (Justice and Home Affairs): police and judicial cooperation in criminal matters, external borders, free movement, Schengen area, civil protection;
- DG E (External Economic Relations, Politico-Military Affairs): foreign policy, defence;
- DG C (Internal Market, Competitiveness, Industry, Research, Energy, Transport, Information Security): transport security, security-related research;
- DG G (Economic and Social Affairs): terrorist financing.

The CTC also cooperates closely with other bodies which are attached to the Secretary General, especially:

– the Policy Unit;

– the Military Staff;

– the Joint Situation Centre (SitCen).

4.2. Relationship with the Working Structure of the Council

There is no formal rule on the involvement of the CTC in the working structure of the Council and, in practice, the CTC may act at all levels, on an *ad hoc* basis: working groups, committees, COREPER and Council as well as the European Council. His reports are sent to the Council and the European Council.

The following scheme identifies the most relevant components:

- JHA (Justice and Home Affairs) Council
  - COREPER II
    - CATS (Article 36 Committee)
      - WP Terrorism
      - WP Police Cooperation
      - WP Europol
      - Multidisciplinary Group on Organised Crime
      - WP Cooperation in Criminal Matters
      - Police Chiefs Task Force
    - SCIFA (Strategic Committee on Immigration, Frontiers, Asylum)
      - WP Visa
      - WP Frontiers
      - WP False documents
    - PROCIV (working party on civil protection)
- GAERC (General Affairs and External Relations Council)
  - COREPER II
    - PSC (Political and Security Committee)
    - COTER (Committee on Terrorism)
    - Geographical Working Parties (COAFR, COASI, MAGHREB, MASHREK etc.)
    - Military Committee
    - RELEX
    - CP 931 Working Party (on Common Position 931)
- ECOFIN

The members of the relevant DG keep the CTC informed of the work of these working parties and committees. The CTC may decide to participate in all meetings. He is also regularly invited by the Presidency, sometimes at his request, to take the floor.

For example, in 2007-2008, the CTC was invited by the Presidency, at his initiative, to various meetings (working groups, CATS, COREPER, Council) to express his concerns about the fact that, despite the negotiation of two parallel instruments reforming, on the one hand, Europol and, on the other hand, Eurojust, the improvement of the cooperation between these two bodies was not adequately considered. Although the competent working parties for the negotiation of these two instruments were acting under the same committee (the CATS), the CTC was of the opinion that coordination could be improved.

His proposal led the Council to invite the two agencies to amend their cooperation agreement.

The Lisbon Treaty will affect the working structure of the Council and this will also affect the CTC but the precise changes are not yet clear.

One of the main changes will be the implementation of Article 71 of the Treaty on the Functioning of the EU (TFEU) which provides for the creation of a "Standing Committee" tasked with ensuring "that operational cooperation on internal security is promoted and strengthened within the Union". The scope, tasks and composition of this committee, the so-called COSI ("Comité de sécurité intérieure"),[17] have not yet been specified but it is obvious that it will become a major player in the field of counter-terrorism and that the CTC will be closely associated with the work of the new committee.

4.3. *Relationship with the Commission*

As mentioned above, the CTC is attached to the Secretary General of the Council and there is therefore no formal link with the Commission. But the CTC cooperates closely with the Commission, especially the Commissioners responsible for Freedom, Security and Justice, External Relations, Development, Environment, Transport and Research.

Within the administration of the Commission, the most direct partners for the CTC are DG Justice, Freedom and Security[18] and DG External Relations. But the work of the following Directorates-General is also relevant: DG Energy and Transport (e.g. for security of transport), DG Development (e.g. for designing assistance programmes to countries like Mali, Niger and Mauritania), DG Economic and Financial Affairs (e.g. for terrorist financing) or DG Research (see e.g. the work of ESRIF and the forthcoming Commission communication on security-related research).

---

17 See the chapter by Michael Niemeier and Marc André Wiegand in this volume.

18 Unit D1 is in charge of the fight against terrorism and is therefore a special partner for the CTC but other units are concerned, for example in the field of immigration, visas and borders.

4.4. Relationship with the European Parliament

The CTC works also closely with the European Parliament (EP). The most relevant Committee of the EP for cooperation with the CTC is the LIBE committee (Civil Liberties, Justice and Home Affairs)[19] but the CTC also cooperates with e.g. the AFET Committee (Foreign Affairs), including its two subcommittees, DROI (Human Rights) and SEDE (Security and Defence).

The relationship between the CTC and the EP became sensitive around 2004-2006 when the EP decided to investigate "the alleged use of European countries by the CIA for the transport and illegal detention of prisoners". The mandate of the CTC made it impossible for him to speak for the Member States and this led to frustration among the MEPs. It is interesting to note that, in the final report, the EP concluded, on the one hand, that "a revision and strengthening of his competence and power" were necessary and that, on the other hand, "the increased transparency and monitoring of his activities by Parliament must be undertaken in the near future".[20]

Apart from that specific case, there is smooth cooperation between the CTC and the EP, especially through the LIBE Committee, which regularly invites the CTC to provide an overview of the current situation with regard to the threat of terrorism; to prepare the EP position on draft EU legislation requiring Member States to criminalise public provocation, recruitment to terrorism and training of terrorists; or to present his reports.

4.5. The CTC and EU/EC Agencies or Bodies

Cooperation between the CTC on the one hand and Europol and Eurojust (both located in The Hague) on the other takes place at several levels:

– the work of Europol and Eurojust is a major source of information for the CTC, including e.g. Europol's TE-SAT report (to which Eurojust contributes), which is an annual report on the situation of terrorism in the EU;

– the CTC promotes the development and strengthening of both Europol and Eurojust because they are essential players to improve European cooperation in the fight against terrorism: transmission of information to Europol and Eurojust by national authorities is among the main priorities currently identified by the CTC;[21]

---

19 See the chapter by Emilio De Capitani in this volume.

20 2006/2200(INI) – 14 February 2007.

21 See Council Document 9417/08.

– the CTC constantly insists on cooperation between Europol and Eurojust in concrete cases, especially by requiring better participation by Eurojust in Europol's analytical work files.[22]

The CTC has also regular contact with Frontex, the EDA and the Fundamental Rights Agency.

5. The CTC and National Structures

The CTC has regular contact with officials in the Member States, including ministers, ministries, prosecutors, intelligence and law enforcement agencies. These contacts vary from one Member State to another, depending mainly on the level of the terrorist threat. The CTC has no power in relation to Member States and cooperation is therefore based on mutual trust between the CTC and national authorities and on their willingness to cooperate.

With these limitations in mind, it is important for the CTC to be active at national level, especially to promote better coordination. After the 9/11 attacks, the Council set up a mechanism for mutual evaluation of national arrangements in the fight against terrorism.[23] The first round of this peer evaluation clearly demonstrated that good coordination at national level between competent authorities (police, customs, magistrates, intelligence and security services) is the first step towards better cooperation at European level. The CTC therefore actively promotes the setting up of national units tasked with the coordination of counter-terrorism activity.

Most national agencies involved in counter-terrorism have developed extensive cooperation with the structure of the Union, and EU legislation already exists to organise that cooperation. Contacts between the CTC and these national counter-terrorism agencies are therefore, generally speaking, easy and well developed.

In addition, there are already some links between the EU and the security agencies. Examples include the Joint Situation Centre (SitCen), which is composed of experts seconded by Member Statess security agencies and which produces strategic threat analysis. Furthermore, the round of mutual evaluation mentioned above made it clear that better cooperation is necessary between law enforcement agencies and security agencies.

It is therefore a major objective of the CTC, and also one of the main challenges, to develop and maintain strong cooperation with the intelligence community, based on mutual trust and the achievement of a

22 See Council Document 9417/08.

23 See Council Document 12156/01.

common objective. This cooperation is of course strategic and not operational.

The CTC needs to have an in-depth understanding of all aspects of the terrorist threat to advise the Council on the policies to follow.

6. The CTC and Third States or International Organisations

The need to work closely with third-countries leads the CTC to meet officials of those countries regularly and to assist the Presidency and the Commission political dialogues.

Because of the importance the EU attaches to multilateralism, the CTC has reinforced cooperation with the UN, both the Security Council and the General Assembly.

The CTC also has regular contact with international organisations such as the Council of Europe, the OSCE, and the FATF (OECD).

CHAPTER 10

Liaison Magistrates: A Success Story

Emmanuel BARBE*

It was in March 1993 that France and Italy decided to give substance to an idea of the Sicilian Judge, Giovanni Falcone,[1] and create "liaison magistrates".[2] Indeed, Judge Falcone had had the opportunity to assess the usefulness of the liaison officers[3] in police and customs departments and the information exchanged under bilateral agreements during the performance requests contained in the numerous letters rogatory sent by him to other countries during his investigations into Cosa Nostra. It was clear that an equivalent structure for judiciary cooperation was lacking, particularly since the criminal sphere (criminal proceedings even more than criminal law) is most certainly an environment where there are the most in-depth differences between juridical cultures and, consequently, an environment where the need for a more effective interface was felt the most acutely. There was, no doubt, just one thing common to the different countries in the area of cooperation: bureaucracy that played its role in making requests for mutual judiciary assistance rather like "bottles thrown into the sea".[4]

In Italy the position of liaison magistrate, which was initially created solely to combat the mafia, very rapidly spread to all forms of cooperation, both criminal and civil.[5] The number of liaison magistrates also

* The ideas or opinions expressed in this article are those of the author and under no circumstances are those of the administration that he serves.

1 Assassinated by the mafia in Palermo on 23 June 1991 with his wife and the 4 men in his escort.

2 The French magistrate, Michel Debacq, was moreover mentioned by Judge Falcone as his French referring magistrate for criminal judicial cooperation (Giovanni Falcone, in collaborazione con Marcelle Padovani, *Cose di Cosa Nostra*, Fabbri Editori – Corriere della Sera, 1991, p. 141 and 142).

3 These officers are posted to foreign countries and act as intermediaries between the department who sent them and the competent authorities in the foreign country.

4 Professor Michel Masse in Colloque *L'Espace judiciaire européen*, Avignon, 16 October 1998 (Paris: La Documentation Française, 1999), p. 104.

5 See on the topic Philippe Labrégère, "Les fonctions du magistrat de liaison et ses rapports avec les autres organes de coopération", in: Gilles de Kerchove & Anne Weyembergh (eds.), *Vers un espace judiciaire pénal européen* (Bruxelles: Éditions de l'Université de Bruxelles, 2000).

rapidly increased, often constituting a first response to specific bilateral issues: the nagging question of drugs for the Netherlands, the problem of bi-national divorces for Germany, the next enlargement for the Czech Republic, etc.[6] Here again, the task for which the post was created rapidly became only part of the job. France now has thirteen liaison magistrates within the European Union (Italy, Netherlands, Germany, Spain, United Kingdom and Poland) and outside it (United States, Morocco, Canada, Russia, China and Zagreb).[7] A post will soon be created in Algeria and another, at the end of 2009, in Qatar. France will become host for German, Dutch, Italian, Spanish, American, British, Moroccan, Canadian and Czech liaison magistrates, making Paris the liaison magistrate "capital". Other European countries have also exchanged liaison magistrates (Italy, Spain and the United Kingdom). We would point out that the United Kingdom has not sent a liaison magistrate to the United States, although these two countries speak the same language[8] and have very similar juridical systems.[9]

In 1997, the French ministry of justice, auditing the empirical approach of the first years, outlined in a circular[10] the main characteristics of what now constitutes true judiciary diplomacy.[11] A liaison magistrate is, in principle,[12] installed in the premises of his host country's ministry of justice. This total immersion in the juridical system of the other country ensures his privileged access to information and constitutes, with his status of magistrate, a guarantee of credibility and trust for all those with whom he is in contact in government departments and courts of law.

The duties of a liaison magistrate fall into five major categories, in proportions that vary according to the country, identified by the minister of justice circular:

---

6 See on this point the Stefano Mogini, published by the Ministry of Justice (SAEI) for the tenth anniversary of liaison magistrates.

7 This liaison magistrate, placed with the anti-crime department at the French Embassy in Zagreb covers the entire Balkan and Eastern Europe area, that is to say thirteen countries in all.

8 George Bernard Shaw was therefore right in saying "The United Kingdom and the United States are two countries separated by the same language".

9 The second French liaison magistrate in London had also held this position for five years in Washington.

10 Minister of Justice circular of 14 November 1997, SAEI-97-4-CAB No. Nor JUS-1-97-80190C.

11 French liaison magistrates are placed under the Ambassador's authority and have diplomatic protection.

12 In certain countries, for various reasons, the liaison magistrate may need to spend part of his time in the Embassy, or even have his only office there.

1. Improved Judiciary Cooperation

a) in *criminal matters*, the liaison magistrate plays a role in two major sectors: judiciary cooperation and extradition/European Arrest Warrant.

The field of judiciary cooperation covers mainly[13] the collection of evidence abroad through international letters rogatory. This poses many problems: juridical differences or misunderstandings, investigation coordination and management problems, combined often with misunderstandings due to the different languages spoken. These are accentuated by the fact that certain juridical concepts do not exist in the other country, so that they cannot really be translated. As regards the language aspect, the liaison magistrate generally has perfect knowledge of the language(s) of his host country. As regards cooperation, the liaison magistrate most certainly benefits from the fact that he has no or practically no legal existence. Magistrates will contact him all the more willingly since they do not consider him to be part of the ministry of justice (although he works for this ministry) or to be part of a European institution that is often seen as rather distant.

As regards extradition or the European Arrest Warrant, the liaison magistrate fully benefits from his installation within the host ministry of justice which gives him daily contacts, very often informal, with magistrates or civil servants in charge of the case files or with court law officers.[14] The entry into force of the European Arrest Warrant on 1 January 2004 eliminated, in the majority of countries, the role of the ministers of justice in extradition procedures,[15] and in the majority of these countries,[16] instituted direct transmission between judiciary authorities. Some countries – this is the case of France and Italy – allow a representative of the issuing State to make observations during the hearing deciding on whether a person should be surrendered. This representative is, generally, the liaison magistrate for the countries that accept them, in this way making official the role that they widely played unofficially.

[13] It should be noted that liaison magistrates may sometimes play a role in the transfer of prisoners associated with extradition or return in the case of the European Arrest Warrant, or after sentencing.

[14] It is indeed easier for a liaison magistrate to contact a Court by phoning from the Ministry of Justice than by phoning from an Embassy.

[15] Except if a European Arrest Warrant enters into competition with a third-party State's request for extradition.

[16] Art. 9 of the 2002 Framework Decision on the European Arrest Warrant enables a Member State to appoint a central authority for the administrative transmission of the case files.

b) in *civil matters*, the liaison magistrate is generally (but this depends on the country) called upon less frequently although the commitment in such cases is often stronger due to the emotional factor: divorces, child abductions, guardianships, etc.

2. Representation of the Ministry of Justice at International Meetings

The liaison magistrate is often designated to represent the ministry of justice in bilateral meetings organised in his host country. In such cases, he is always a member of his country's delegation. His knowledge of both juridical systems and his contacts in his host country are turned to good account. Over the years liaison magistrates have also become the main organisers, assisted by the Embassy, of visits by the minister of justice or his representatives to their host countries and even members of parliament on study trips.

3. Harmonisation of Positions in European or International Negotiations

The development, particularly within the European Union, of an intense activity of multilateral negotiation, has made it necessary for Member States to obtain precise information on the positions of their partners. The liaison magistrate can play an active role in this respect, in particular by helping to better understand the difficulties of his host country. Consequently, the ministry of justice often calls on his network of liaison magistrates to find out about the opinions of his partners.

4. Communication of Information on the Legislation of the State of Residence

Requests for information from governments or legislative authorities on foreign legislations or practices are, fortunately, ever more frequent. Liaison magistrates, due to their position and training, are an invaluable source of information. They are increasingly called upon to answer questions on very varied subjects by the ministry of justice that is seeking information on its own account or for other institutions (Parliament, Supreme Court, etc.). Similar information is also requested by consulates, lawyers, students and even private individuals.

5. Harmonisation of Judiciary Institutions

The liaison magistrate is well placed for encouraging the bringing together of judiciary institutions through operational or academic meetings between magistrates and court law officers, governing councils of the judiciary, professional training courses in particular for justice auditors, research seminars, and contributions to national or international publications.

As can be seen, the liaison magistrates' scope of action is vast, which has perhaps led to over-diversification. It is, however, the proof of the success of their function, particularly since some of the tasks linked to this post are not listed in the minister of justice's circular: liaison magistrates have gradually become part of Embassies, very often as heads of department[17] and contribute to the Embassy's work either by analysing developments at judiciary level in their host country or by solving certain specific situations, for instance in the framework of consular assistance for French nationals abroad.

The place of the liaison magistrate should, of course, be considered in the context of the EU's Area of Freedom, Security and Justice.

Admittedly, this function, born of the initiative of two States, was created a short time after the Maastricht Treaty[18] came into effect and outside any European framework. However, it quickly found, on the initiative of Italy, a European function through the Joint Action of 22 April 1996.[19] These joint measures were not, in fact, very binding to say the least: there are very few liaison officers whose existence has been notified to the General Secretariat of the Council, in compliance with Article 3 of the joint measures. However, from a "historical" angle, the Joint Action of 1996 introduced, for the first time in the construction of Europe a magistrate working, admittedly for his own country, but within another judiciary system as a subject of international law.

The Joint Action of 29 June 1998,[20] instituting the European Judicial Network in criminal matters, constituted the introduction of a second subject of international law, clearly embarking on a route going in the opposite direction: the creation of a network of specialists working in their own countries.[21] Admittedly, Article 2, paragraph 4 of the Joint Action specifies that liaison magistrates may be linked to the European Judicial Network by the Member States that appoint them. France, by proceeding in this way, chose to have all its liaison magistrates, who are

---

17 Many ministries are represented in the majority of French Embassies abroad.

18 1 November 1993.

19 *O.J.*, No. L 105 of 27 April 1996, p. 1, Joint Action is an instrument of the Maastricht Treaty although not very binding. Since the Treaty of Amsterdam (1997) it has been replaced by the decision or framework decision, much more binding, under certain conditions subject to the jurisdiction of the Court of Justice of the European Communities.

20 *O.J.*, No. L 191 of July 1998, p. 4.

21 The judicial networks in criminal or civil matters are, in fact, composed of national points of contact.

posted to a European Union Member State, members of the European Judicial Network.

The creation of Eurojust[22] is perhaps more directly related to the idea of liaison magistrates. There are, moreover, many who see it as a group of "super liaison magistrates" (in the sense that they can take action in relation to all Member States), which is a particularly limited, simplistic understanding of the Eurojust decision.[23] It is true, particularly for the Member States that do not have liaison magistrates, that Eurojust can also be used to settle issues falling within the competence of liaison magistrates. A glance at the large number of bilateral cases with which it is dealing with leaves no doubt of this. Moreover, Eurojust could constitute a cost-effective way of creating a good network of liaison magistrates: twenty-seven magistrates (not including their assistants) are enough to constitute Eurojust, whereas three hundred and seventy-eight (27! that is to say 27 + 26 + 25, etc.) would, in theory, be required to enable each Member State to have a liaison magistrate in each country of the European Union.

It should also be underlined that the decision instituting Eurojust specifies, under Article 26, paragraph 6 that "*Eurojust may, on a case-by-case basis, cooperate with liaison magistrates* [...]".[24] The nature of this cooperation is not necessarily easy to determine since the liaison magistrate posted to a country, in the event of this cooperation, appears to come into competition with the national member of Eurojust of this same country. It is, in any case, useful for liaison magistrates to have good knowledge of the functioning of Eurojust in order to serve it as a "facilitator" or "business contributor" in multilateral cases or when just one liaison magistrate would find it difficult to assume a particularly large amount of coordination work.

Another observation shows that the Member States, and primarily France, see Eurojust as something quite different from a group of liaison magistrates. No suppression of a post of liaison magistrate has even been contemplated since its creation. In 2003, Italy sent a liaison magistrate to the United Kingdom and another to Spain. The United King-

---

22 Council's decision of 28 February 2002 instituting Eurojust to reinforce the combat against serious crime, *O.J.*, No. L 63 of 6 March 2002, p. 1.

23 For a more detailed explanation of the functions of Eurojust, see Emmanuel Barbe, *L'espace judiciaire européen*, foreword by Valéry Giscard d'Estaing (Paris: La Documentation Française, Collection Réflexe Europe, November 2007), www.ue.espacejudiciare.net.

24 Without taking into account that the decision instituting Eurojust (Art. 26, para. 6) enables liaison magistrates of third-party countries to be part of Eurojust.

dom[25] strengthened its European network by appointing a person to Madrid. In this development of multiple tools, whose overall coherence is not always obvious, the main beneficiaries are most certainly the magistrates of European Member States. They are free to submit the case to the institution (liaison magistrate, European judiciary network or Eurojust) that they feel is the most suitable or the most reactive. It is not rare in fact, to see the most impatient submitting a case to all three at the same time!

In a few months there will be true European recognition of the development of the liaison magistrate. Indeed, the JHA Council adopted politically on 25 July a draft framework decision, modifying[26] the decision instituting Eurojust, which should become effective in the first half of 2009. It specifies, in Article 27 bis,[27] the possibility for Eurojust to appoint a liaison magistrate in a third party country, with the agreement of the latter. This is a superb recognition for an institution created fifteen years ago by France and Italy. It is also the beginning of a new era for position that has received a vote of confidence by practitioners in international judiciary cooperation.

25 That is to say the Crown Prosecution Service and not the Home Office. The British liaison magistrates, as a general rule Prosecutors, therefore have more limited functions than their French counterparts.

26 Document 11769/08 accessible on the register of Council acts.

27 The text will undergo renumbering during its examination by linguist jurists.

PART FOUR

CONCLUSIONS

CHAPTER 11

Personal Reflections on the Institutional Framework of the Area of Freedom, Security and Justice

Charles ELSEN

1. Introduction

I have participated in the work which led to what we call now the "Area of Freedom, Security and Justice" (AFSJ), since the Amsterdam Treaty first introduced this terminology. As the first Director General of the Council General Secretariat's Directorate-General for Justice and Home Affairs, I was involved in the Council's activities during the period March 1994 to April 2004. As a civil servant in the Ministry of Justice of my home country Luxembourg, I participated in all the bodies which can be considered as precursors of the AFSJ (TREVI, Pompidou Group, European Judicial Cooperation, Ad hoc Group Immigration, CELAD, the "Rhodos" Coordinators' Group and, last but not least, Schengen).

I would like to put on paper some personal reflections on the institutional questions and especially the cooperation between Council, Commission and European Parliament in the efforts leading to the AFSJ as we now know it. In so doing, I will use a historical approach, distinguishing between the pre-Maastricht phase (1), the Maastricht Treaty (2) and the Amsterdam Treaty and beyond (3).

2. The pre-Maastricht Phase (1972-1993)

As we know, the Maastricht Treaty – which entered in force on 1 November 1993 – introduced the cooperation in the fields of "Justice and Home Affairs" (JHA) into the European Treaties, under a new so-called "three pillar structure". It seems nevertheless useful to consider some of the predecessor activities to understand the move from a purely intergovernmental form of cooperation to a new way of cooperation including actors like the Commission and the European Parliament.

Historically, the first "sectoral" initiative towards closer cooperation and harmonisation was taken in 1972 by President Georges Pompidou in the field of combating drugs traffic and dealing with drug addiction. This work was later transferred into the Council of Europe framework but started between the then six Member States of the European Communities plus UK. Later in the 1980s, in 1988 in fact, the CELAD Group (*Comité Européen de Lutte Anti Drogue*) took over the fight against drugs, regrouping the Member States of the European Communities with – from then onwards – the participation of the Commission.

The TREVI activities, dealing mainly with operational aspects of fighting terrorism, started in 1976 and developed through regular meetings at expert, senior official and ministerial level. Later it comprised the fight against organised crime, police cooperation and preparatory work on Europol. The Commission attended these meetings as an observer but was excluded from participating in the anti-terrorism work.

The Schengen agreements must also be mentioned in the context of the pre-Maastricht phase. Although they entered into force only in March 1995, i.e. only after the Maastricht Treaty, they had already been signed in 1985 and 1990. The Schengen system was a purely intergovernmental one, based on unanimity rule. The added value of Schengen, as compared to the other sectoral initiatives as described above, was that it had a clear objective – the suppression of border controls at internal borders – and a comprehensive range of compensatory measures to achieve this objective, that is, common rules on external border security and visas, improved police and judicial cooperation and some achievements in terms of approximation of legislation (*inter alia* on data protection, firearms, partially on drugs). As Schengen was negotiated among only five Member States (France, Germany, and the Benelux countries) there was sufficient scope for some far-reaching solutions: new Member States did not have the option to renegotiate the substance of the agreement (with the exception of UK and Ireland, who were granted an opt-in solution to all or only parts of the Schengen Acquis).

The Commission had showed interest in the Schengen work from the beginning, and participated with observer status. The European Parliament, on the other hand, was very critical about the Schengen achievements, arguing that this Treaty suffered from the absence of both parliamentary and judicial control.

Similar criticism was also voiced by several national parliaments, and notably the Dutch parliament. This was certainly one of the strong arguments which later pushed the Dutch Presidency in 1997, in the final negotiations of the Amsterdam Treaty, to suggest the integration of the Schengen Acquis into the European Union.

It follows from the above that cooperation in the field of Justice and Home Affairs prior to the Maastricht Treaty was limited to specific areas and was developed in different fora: only the Schengen cooperation was coherent and comprehensive in nature. Schengen developed with the assistance of its own secretariat structure, but it was limited to only some Member States of the European Community and was not yet operational when the Maastricht Treaty came into force.

Neither the European Parliament nor any other parliamentary assembly was involved in the work. As observer, the European Commission played a limited role in the Schengen activities.

3. The Maastricht Treaty (1993-1999)

With the entry into force of the Maastricht Treaty on 1 November 1993, cooperation in the field of Justice and Home Affairs was introduced into the institutional framework of the European Union. Article K.1 of the new Treaty on European Union (TEU) defined nine areas of common interest in the fields of asylum and immigration as well as in police cooperation and in judicial cooperation in civil and criminal matters. It described the instruments to be used (Conventions, Joint Actions, Joint Positions), as well as the institutional framework, including the role of the Commission and the European Parliament. A coordinating committee was also set up under the Treaty, which became known as the "K.4 Committee", after the Treaty provision concerned.

Then we started our work – especially at the level of the K.4 Committee – by drafting an Action Plan of urgent work to be done. Many of my colleagues had been, as I was, members of the "Rhodos" Coordinators' Group on the free movement of persons which had been created by the December 1988 Rhodos European Council. This facilitated cooperation and mutual comprehension. Nevertheless, there were a lot of problems to be solved, among which I would just like to mention the following:

– how to set priorities, bearing in mind that there should be a fair balance between asylum, immigration, police matters and judicial cooperation?

– how to select the appropriate legal instruments, bearing in mind that the new instruments "Joint Action" and "Joint Position" were nowhere defined and it was not clear whether they were intended to be legally binding (they were considered to be typical "second pillar" (CFSP) instruments);

– how to organise the action of Member States and the Commission (both were given a right of initiative in the areas referred to in Article K.1(1) to (6) TEU?

– how to make progress, bearing in mind that all instruments have to be adopted by unanimity (subject to some exceptions in the area of visas)?

– how to establish a working structure which could take into account the specificities of Third Pillar matters.

It has to be borne in mind that at national level the areas covered by Article K.1 TEU were in the hands of at least two ministers (of justice and of the interior) and sometimes a third (a minister of immigration or for public order). It is only in very few Member States that competence for the whole range of JHA matters is in the hands of a single minister (the Home Secretary in the UK, for example, though very recently a separate UK ministry of justice has also been created).

This situation led to difficulties as regards the head of delegations in the K.4 Committee in some Member States. It led further to the creation, between the working group level and the K4 Committee, of so-called "*Groupes directeurs*" (one on asylum and immigration, a second on police and customs cooperation, and a third on judicial cooperation).

Ministers with responsibility for Justice and Home Affairs matters were newcomers to the European fora, and the matters covered by the new Title VI TEU were often matters touching on national sovereignty. This might explain to a certain extent why the Coordinators' Committee was created under Article K.4 TEU and enshrined in the Maastricht Treaty itself.

But Article K.4 took care to maintain a single institutional framework with a reference to Article 151 TEC. This means that the Permanent Representatives Committee (COREPER) remains involved in the institutional framework and plays a major role in preparing JHA Council meetings as it does it for other Council meetings.

It seems clear that some or even many Member States had expected that K.4 coordinators would, as regards substantive negotiations, replace the ambassadors and that COREPER would play a minor role on more technical or formal questions. Yet this was not the intention of the legislator and did not happen in practice. On the contrary, COREPER involved itself more and more in the solution of unresolved questions. The K.4 Committee was, on some matters, unable to solve questions, considered to be either too technical (and thus sent them back to the working group) or too political (and thus left to COREPER to resolve).

After a period of some years it became clear that the "*Groupes directeurs*" did not add much value to the discussions. This additional layer proved rather to be time consuming, especially as the meetings at ministerial level increased to two or three for each Presidency. By tacit agreement the Member States decided that these groups should no longer meet.

Part of the institutional change was that the Permanent Representations in Brussels added to their staff counselors in the different areas covered by the third pillar. JHA counselor meetings evolved into an important tool in negotiating compromise solutions between delegations.

Having analysed the institutional aspects surrounding the work of the Council, I would like to turn next to the relations between Council, Commission and the European Parliament.

First, with regard to the role of the Commission, Article K.3 TEU was very clear. The Commission was granted a right of initiative in six out of the nine "matters of common interest" listed in Article K.1 TEU. On these matters, the right of initiative was shared with the Member States. Yet with regard to the three other remaining matters (judicial cooperation in criminal matters, customs cooperation and police cooperation) the Commission enjoyed no right of initiative.

As regards the European Parliament, Article K.6 TEU provided as follows:

– a right for the European Parliament to be informed regularly (by the Presidency and the Commission) of discussions in the areas covered by Title VI;

-a right to be consulted on the principal aspects of activities by the Presidency which was to ensure that the views of the European Parliament were duly taken into consideration;

– a possibility for the European Parliament to ask questions or make recommendations to the Council;

– a yearly debate (in the plenary session) on the progress made in implementation of the areas of Title VI.

The Maastricht language appeared unclear and certainly left room for interpretation. This might have been one of the reasons why relations between the Council and the European Parliament were not easy.

In my view, the difficulties between the European Parliament and the Commission, on one side, and the Council, on the other side, can be explained to a large extent by the fact that the two former institutions did not understand (or did not want to understand) the specificities of the third pillar. It has to be noted that the "pillar construction" was not just some invention of treaty-makers to single out cooperation in JHA and in security and defence matters: this construction was the only way to introduce – under new rules, with new instruments and with limited competence for the Commission and the European Parliament – new sensitive areas of cooperation into the Treaties. It appears from the analysis of the Maastricht negotiations that a number of delegations were opposed to the idea of having JHA introduced into the Treaties with Community type rules: the only solution they could accept was the intergovernmental method in a more structured framework. In other words, in the negotiations which led to the Maastricht Treaty, the choice was not to introduce the JHA matters either into the first (Community) pillar or the third pillar; the choice was to have them in a new third pillar or not to have them at all. It appears to me that this was not understood by some European actors.

Wenceslas de Lobkowicz was, from the beginning, the closest collaborator of the late Sir Adrian Fortescue, first Director General for Justice and Home Affairs in the Commission. His analyses of the institutional situation, in his work "*L'Europe et la Sécurité intérieure*"[1] is accurate. He considers that under the Maastricht Treaty the Community institutions were kept under control and that the Member States remained the most powerful players ("*les maîtres du jeu*"). The Commission is described as a "tolerated partner" with a right of initiative limited to certain domains and there shared with the Member States. The European Parliament is referred to as a "bridled partner" ("*un partenaire bridé*"). To a certain extent, the powers of the European Parliament were however enhanced as compared to the situation before Maastricht, where the European Parliament was totally absent in the decision-making process in all the fora referred to above.

The powers of the European Parliament laid down in Article K.6 TEU were clearly limited, as we have seen above. Among these I would now like to focus on how Article K.6(3) TEU was used. The final sentence of that provision stated that "each year it [i.e. the European Parliament] shall hold a debate on the progress made in implementation of areas referred to in this title".

The annual debate took place in the plenary session in Strasbourg towards the end of each year. The acting Presidency of the Council, represented by its competent ministers (normally justice and interior) presented factual reports on the progress made during the previous twelve months. This was a unique opportunity, foreseen nowhere else in the Treaties, for an in-depth discussion. Instead of this, the exercise was mainly used by parliamentarians to complain about the fact that they were – under the Treaties – widely excluded from participating in the decision-making process. The Commission, from time to time, joined the European Parliament in its criticism of the Council's activities.

I remember the first use which was made of this provision in December 1994, by a German Presidency which presented in detail the achievements since the entry into force of the Maastricht Treaty. The European Parliament, joined to a large extent by Commissioner Pádraig

1 Wenceslas de Lobkwicz, *L'Europe de la sécurité intérieure – Une élaboration par étapes* (Paris: La Documentation Française, 2002).

Flynn, voiced only criticism of the work of the Council, which it considered to be too slow and insufficiently transparent.

In the course of the years, Presidencies of the Council made serious efforts to establish sound relations with the different Committees of the European Parliament (especially with the LIBE Committee). As a rule, at the beginning of each Presidency ministers would explain their work programme to parliamentarians and present a briefing on the results of each Council meeting in the days following such a meeting. Later on, a delegation of the LIBE Committee attended informal ministerial meetings. However, other requests by the European Parliament, for instance to discuss every Council meeting agenda prior to the meeting or to allow parliamentarians to participate in some Council meetings, could not be met.

I attended all of those meetings and I think that I did not often hear a word of appreciation by the Members of the European Parliament of the Council's work. I remember also the sovereign contempt of the European Parliament for the work undertaken in the Schengen framework. As no parliamentary control was foreseen in the Schengen agreements and as the European Parliament had no influence on this work until the integration of Schengen into the Treaties by the Amsterdam Treaty, it was in no way entitled to act in this manner.

Looking back to the Maastricht years, I consider that the opportunities for a dialogue as they were laid down in Article K.6 TEU were not best used by the European Parliament. The Council for its part also perhaps failed to use to the fullest extent the possibilities of Article K.6. This applies particularly to paragraph 2, which calls on the Presidency to consult the European Parliament on the principal aspects of activities and to ensure that the views of the European Parliament are duly taken into account. Especially with regard to Member States' activities, the consultation of the Parliament was neither regular nor did it take place at the beginning of the procedure; amendments proposed by the European Parliament were looked at but not often taken into consideration. Thus, while the contacts between European Parliament and the Council may have been mostly regular and correct, they were neither profound nor trustful.

4. The Amsterdam Treaty and Beyond

The year 1999 – the year in which the Amsterdam Treaty entered into force – was so far the best year in the history of European cooperation in Justice and Home Affairs. The Amsterdam Treaty brought significant changes:

– new, effective instruments like the third pillar (Title VI TEU) Framework Decision and the Decision;

– transfer of important parts of JHA into the first pillar (Title IV TEC);

– the creation of an Area of Freedom, Security and Justice designed to improve the situation of the European citizen;

– the integration of Schengen cooperation into the first and third pillar frameworks. This proved to be a substantial added value to the existing European Union *acquis*, especially in the field of external borders and police cooperation ("hot pursuit" by police forces across borders, Schengen Information System, etc.).

A few months after the entry into force of the Amsterdam Treaty, the Tampere Summit set the framework for cooperation for the years to come. This was not just an action plan like those we had before, like the Vienna Action Plan of 1998. The later Hague Action Plan of 2004 was also to prove less ambitious. Tampere was a clear, precise and solemn commitment by the Heads of State and Government, who engaged themselves to put the building of an Area of Freedom, Security and Justice on top of their agenda and to keep it there. In addition, the Tampere "milestones" defined the action to be taken in a more precise way: the creation of Eurojust for instance was enshrined in the Tampere European Council Conclusions.[2] The Tampere Summit had been well prepared in advance thanks to good cooperation between the Finnish Presidency, the Commission and the Council Secretariat. The idea of having a "scoreboard", for follow-up of proposed measures, which proved to be very useful in the years following Tampere, had been adopted on a proposal made by Commission representatives.

Finally, two more events made 1999 a very successful year for the development of an Area of Freedom, Security and Justice. On the one hand, there was the entry into force of the Europol Convention, suggested eight years earlier at the Luxembourg Summit of 1991 by Chancellor Helmut Kohl. On the other hand, two major events occurred in the Commission: the Prodi Commission appointed a commissioner to deal exclusively with the AFSJ; in the person of Antonio Vitorino, a very experienced and dynamic person was tasked with making progress towards achievement of this new area. One month later, in October 1999, i.e. parallel to the Tampere Summit, a new Directorate-General ("DG JAI") was created inside the Commission. This replaced the rather weak structure attached to the Secretary General's Office, thus paving

---

2 Tampere European Council of 15 and 16 October 1999, Presidency Conclusions, paragraph 46.

the way for a solid team which developed quickly under the wise guidance of Director General the late Sir Adrian Fortescue.

The Commission, which so far had been rather reluctant to take initiatives in matters where it had a shared right of initiative with the Member States, intensified its activities greatly, introducing initiatives in particular in the fields of asylum and immigration, as well as in civil matters where adopted conventions were "Amsterdamised". In fact, the coordination with the Member States, especially the successive Presidencies, was quite correct and coherent: there were no major difficulties. Commission and Member State initiatives did not collide or lead to a confrontation.

The story of the 2003 Framework Decision on the protection of the environment through criminal law[3] can be seen as an exception to this rather good cooperation. It is no secret that, as a rule, the Commission preferred first pillar instruments to third pillar instruments. The Council took an opposite view and adopted third pillar legislation first on environmental penalties in general and then on ship source pollution. In both cases, the Commission challenged the Council Decision before the Court of Justice, which decided in favour of the Commission thesis in the environment sanctions case (Case C-176/03, judgement of 13 September 2005) but fine-tuned its position later in the ship source pollution case (Case C-440/05, judgement of 23 October 2005).

The question should be permitted whether it was worth challenging the Council on a solution which would have allowed severe sentences to be imposed on persons who commit the most serious environmental crimes. After the Court Decision, the Council is still trying to define a new position, and environmental crimes are not being prosecuted and punished on the basis of common rules.

The European Parliament can be considered as having improved its position in the institutional game inside the AFSJ. As a result of the Amsterdam Treaty, it has a right to be consulted on instruments adopted both under Title IV TEC and Title VI TEU. The Council respected carefully the new rules, without however managing to improve its relations with the Parliament. Criticism was regularly voiced due to the fact that the Council did not consult the Parliament at the appropriate time, or did not re-consult it after changing some parts (considered to be substantial) of the instrument concerned. The lack of transparency was criticised on matters where, in the view of the Council, the substance of the information cannot be made public, for example with regard to terrorist activities. National parliaments have a role in relation to third

3 Council Framework Decision 2003/80/JHA of 27 January 2003, *O.J.*, No. L 29 of 5 February 2003.

pillar initiatives which can help to overcome some of this "democratic deficit", but not all parliaments seem equipped to perform an effective controlling function. In some Member States, however, *ex ante* scrutiny by a national parliamentary committee works perfectly.

Even if the Amsterdam Treaty offered new perspectives to the European Parliament, this did not seem to satisfy most of the actors in that parliament. The incoming Lisbon Treaty, by scrapping the pillar structure and establishing qualified majority voting and the co-decision procedure as a general rule, is by contrast surely considered by the European Parliament as a decisive step in its fight to gain influence in the decision-making process. It remains however to be seen what position the Parliament will adopt with regard to Commission proposals, once it will enjoy co-decision rights on most AFSJ matters. The position which the European Parliament adopted during the legislative process on the 2008 "Return Directive"[4] gives an interesting view on how the new responsibilities of the European Parliament might be exercised.

Quite unsurprisingly given the fact that the European Parliament is interested in the rapid entry into force of the Lisbon Treaty, the European Parliament decided, after the annual debate on progress in the AFSJ in 2007 which took place on 31 January 2008, to table a resolution trying to "preempt" the Lisbon Treaty. It sought to associate the European Parliament in an *ad hoc* form of co-decision before the entry into force of the new rules.

We now know that the Lisbon Treaty entered finally into force on 1 December 2009. This major event paves the way for the Council to continue the work of the building-up, step by step, in line with the Stockholm Programme, an Area of Freedom, Security and Justice, in the interests of the citizens living in the European Union.

In concluding, I think that the progress achieved over a period of about thirty years, fifteen of which have been in organised structures (Schengen, Maastricht, Amsterdam) is quite substantial. Many elements have contributed to this evolution:

– the "laboratory" function of Schengen, which permitted the suppression of all forms of control at internal borders;

– the growing interest of the European Council in JHA questions, leading to the definition of action to be undertaken through regular action plans and in-depth discussions (Tampere, Laeken);

4 Directive 2008/115/EC of the European Parliament and the Council of 16 December 2008 on common standards and procedures in Member States for returning illegally staying third-country nationals, *O.J.*, No. L 348 of 24 December 2008.

– the development of new, more effective instruments, such as Framework Decisions, which replaced the more cumbersome Conventions;

– the growing influence of the Commission, especially since Tampere, and the creation of a separate Directorate-General JLS;

– the attempts by the Council to evaluate the new instruments put in place and to monitor transposition in the Member States.

The shared right of initiative between the Commission and the Member States did not lead to major conflicts; it can be considered that all the actors contributed to produce substantial work.

The action of the European Parliament, as I see it, was however not always constructive. The Parliament took great interest in the work on JHA matters, but it took too often an (exclusively) critical standpoint. The powers of the Members of the European Parliament were very limited, at least in the Maastricht version of the Treaties. On the other hand, the Council was not always ready to take sufficient time to examine the Parliament's positions.

The results of fifteen years of cooperation under the TEU and TEC may appear disappointing to some analysts. The major reason for this situation does not however lie in the organisation of the work, nor in insufficient or poor cooperation between the institutional players, but is mainly the result of the unanimity rule which allows Member States to block situations and which does not allow proper negotiation nor ambitious results.

To move matters from third to first pillar is not a major step *per se* if the unanimity rule is kept alive. The Lisbon Treaty could contribute, to a large extent, to overcoming this difficulty and allow further progress to be made in the creation of an Area of Freedom, Security and Justice.

About the authors

BEATRICE ASK is Swedish Minister of Justice and President-in-Office of Justice and Home Affairs Council.

EMMANUEL BARBE is Deputy Secretary General of the Secrétariat général des affaires européennes (SGAE) of the Prime Minister's Office (France).

MINTZE BEUVING is Lieutenant-General and Former Frontex Management Board Chairman.

SERGE DE BIOLLEY is JHA (Justice and Home Affairs) Adviser at the Permanent Representation of Belgium to the European Union and Assistant at the Institute for European Studies (Free University of Brussels, ULB).

EMILIO DE CAPITANI is Head of the Secretariat of the Committee of Civil Liberties, Justice and Home Affairs of the European Parliament.

GILLES DE KERCHOVE is the EU Counter-Terrorism Coordinator and teaches European law at the Catholic University of Louvain (UCL) and at the Free University of Brussels (ULB).

CHARLES ELSEN is a former Director General of DG H (Justice and Home Affairs) of the Council Secretariat.

VASSILIS HATZOPOULOS is Associate Professor at the Democritus University of Thrace (Greece); Visiting Professor at the College of Europe, Bruges (Belgium).

MAYLIS LABAYLE is an alumna of the College of Europe, in Bruges (Belgium); and currently a trainee in the office of Ms. Michèle Coninsx, Vice-President and national member for Belgium in Eurojust.

RICHARD LEWIS is a former Acting Head of Unit, Immigration and Asylum at the European Commission; and Senior Research Fellow at the Institute for European Studies (Free University of Brussels, ULB).

JÖRG MONAR is Director of the Department of European Political and Administrative Studies at the College of Europe, Bruges (Belgium); and Professor of Contemporary European Studies at the Sussex European Institute, University of Sussex, Brighton (UK).

MICHAEL NIEMEIER is the Director of the Department for international cooperation at the German Federal Criminal Police Office (Bundeskriminalamt, Berlin, Germany).

HANS G. NILSSON is Head of Division in the Council Secretariat since 1996 and has been Minister and Head of the Justice and Home Affairs department at the Swedish Permanent Representation in Brussels during the 2009 Swedish Presidency; Visiting Professor at the College of Europe, Bruges (Belgium).

JULIAN SIEGL is a graduate in political science from the University of Tübingen (Germany) and the College of Europe Bruges (Belgium); and currently a trainee in DG JLS of the European Commission.

DAVID SPENCE is First Counsellor of the Delegation of the European Commission to the United Nations in Geneva (Switzerland).

MARC ANDRÉ WIEGAND is in charge of Europol affairs at the Directorate-General for public security of the German Ministry of the Interior, Berlin (Germany).

College of Europe Studies

Europe is in a constant state of flux. European politics, economics, law and indeed European societies are changing rapidly. The European Union itself is in a continuous situation of adaptation. New challenges and new requirements arise continually, both internally and externally. The College of Europe Studies series exists to publish research on these issues done at the College of Europe, both at its Bruges and its Warsaw campus. Focused on the European Union and the European integration process, this research may be specialised in the areas of political science, law or economics, but much of it is of an interdisciplinary nature. The objective is to promote understanding of the issues concerned and to make a contribution to ongoing discussions.

Series Editors
Professors D. Hanf, D. Mahncke, I. Govaere and J. Pelkmans
for the College of Europe (Bruges and Warsaw)

Series Titles

No. 10 – Jing MEN & Giuseppe BALDUCCI (eds.), *Prospects and Challenges for EU-China Relations in the 21st Century. The Partnership and Cooperation Agreement*, 2010, 262 p., ISBN 978-90-5201-641-2

No. 11 – Jörg MONAR (ed.), *The Institutional Dimension of the European Union's Area of Freedom, Security and Justice*, 2010, 268 p., ISBN 978-90-5201-615-3

N° 10 – Dominik HANF, Klaus MALACEK & Elise MUIR (dir.), *Langues et construction européenne*, 2010, 286 p., ISBN 978-90-5201-594-1

No. 9 – Jacques PELKMANS, Dominik HANF & Michele CHANG (eds.), *The EU Internal Market in Comparative Perspective Economic. Political and Legal Analysis*, 2008, 314 p., ISBN 978-90-5201-424-1

No. 8 – Inge GOVAERE & Hanns ULLRICH (eds.), *Intellectual Property, Market Power and the Public Interest*, 2008, 315 p., ISBN 978-90-5201-422-7

No. 7 – András INOTAI, *The European Union and Southeastern Europe. Troubled Waters Ahead?*, 2007, 414 p., ISBN 978-90-5201-071-7

No. 6 – Inge GOVAERE & Hanns ULLRICH (eds.), *Intellectual Property, Public Policy and International Trade*, 2007, 234 p., ISBN 978-90-5201-064-9

No. 5 – Dominik HANF & Rodolphe MUÑOZ (dir.), *La libre circulation des personnes. États des lieux et perspectives*, 2007, 329 p., ISBN 978-90-5201-061-8

No. 4 – Dieter MAHNCKE & Sieglinde GSTÖHL (eds.), *Europe's Near Abroad. Promises and Prospects of the EU's Neighbourhood Policy*, 2008, 318 p., ISBN 978-90-5201-047-2

No. 3 – Dieter MAHNCKE & Jörg MONAR (eds.), *International Terrorism. A European Response to a Global Threat?*, 2006, 191 p., ISBN 978-90-5201-046-5

No. 2 – Paul DEMARET, Inge GOVAERE & Dominik HANF (eds.), *European Legal Dynamics – Revised and updated edition of* 30 Years of European Legal Studies at the College of Europe / *Dynamiques juridiques européennes – Édition revue et mise à jour de* 30 ans d'études juridiques européennes au Collège d'Europe, 2007, 571 p., ISBN 978-90-5201-067-0

No. 1 – Dieter MAHNCKE, Alicia AMBOS & Christopher REYNOLDS (eds.), *European Foreign Policy. From Rhetoric to Reality?*, 2004, 2nd printing/ 2e tirage 2006, 381 p., ISBN 978-90-5201-247-6